Deeper Than Suspected

Deeper Than Suspected

Thomas Daniel Nehrer

BOOKS

Winchester, UK
Washington, USA

JOHN HUNT PUBLISHING

First published by O-Books, 2020
O-Books is an imprint of John Hunt Publishing Ltd., 3 East St., Alresford,
Hampshire SO24 9EE, UK
office@jhpbooks.com
www.johnhuntpublishing.com
www.o-books.com

For distributor details and how to order please visit the 'Ordering' section on our website.

ISBN: 978 1 78535 727 5
978 1 78535 728 2 (ebook)
Library of Congress Control Number: 2018932806

A CIP catalogue record for this book is available from the British Library.

Design: Stuart Davies

UK: Printed and bound by CPI Group (UK) Ltd, Croydon, CR0 4YY
Printed in North America by CPI GPS partners

Contents

Initiation: What to Suspect	1
Engaging: An Initial Look into CONSCIOUSNESS	7
Consideration: A First Look at RELIGION	46
Attentive: Undertaking One's PERSONAL JOURNEY	62
Responsive: A Glance at PHILOSOPHY	81
Contemplating: Focus on ATHEISM	95
Outsourcing: My Standpoint	115
Introspective: Looking Deeper into CONSCIOUSNESS	120
Beyond Belief: Exposing CHRISTIANITY	150
Empiricising: Quick Look at SCIENCE	190
Progression: Continuing on That INNER JOURNEY	200
Regressing: ISLAM and its Declarations	222
Insourcing: MYSTICISM – Grasping Intangibles	230
Onwards: Resuming the INNER TREK	240
Reconsidering: A Further Look at RELIGION	255
Eastwards: A Fleeting Look at EASTERN Thinking (Or Attempts to Not)	267
Reflective: About MY PERSPECTIVES	275
Indicative: About ME Personally	291
Ummmm... : Concerning THIS and NOT THIS (i.e., THAT)	325

Also by this author

The Essence of Reality
The Illusion of "Truth"
The Psyche Exposed

Initiation: What to Suspect

It's all about Consciousness. Understanding life – the Reality you face daily in a swirl of events and relationships: *truly understanding it* is all about grasping the nature of your own personal Consciousness.

It's not about gods and spirits, determining their whims and requirements, discerning their beneficent or evil intent. It isn't about particles and waves, measuring their mass or movement and constructing complex formulae to determine such physical characteristics. It is neither about procedures to observe or predict reality nor about accepting vaunted beliefs and declarations from grand, elevated masters.

Indeed, it isn't about ideas and philosophies, religious declarations and paradigms of explanation. All of these only serve to *inhibit* awareness...

It's just simply about Consciousness: perceiving the nature of your own being – how your inner nature, your perceived Self, relates to the flow of real things encountered, its quality, its impact...

This book, like all of my distributed communication – website, books, video production and live presentations – illustrates and clarifies aspects of life to help the reader perceive it more clearly. The real benefits to your personal life are profuse: health, success, satisfaction, love. The common negative traits you shed along the way make the journey toward clarity that much more attractive: worry, fear, self-deprecation and self-doubt, conflict and self-punishment...

If you sincerely seek to understand the nature of your existence – and to improve your life markedly in the process, you have found a tool that will help in unique and profound ways...

However...

Intimately grasping the core nature of Reality itself will not come from reading alone – nor from exploring religions or philosophies, meditating or bowing to popular notions. The first three of those will doubtless form part of your or any pathway toward Awareness – that is, they can help, so long as you keep your mind open.

The last of them, however – conceding to popular ideas and rote religious dictates – will totally and unequivocally *deter* the journey.

Becoming fully aware of the nature of your own existence requires three primary quality-adjusting gestures:

1. That open mind.
2. Techniques that provide for exploration of the inner nature of your total mindset – including the functionality and content of your subconscious, focused access to it and to the connection to the unconscious, that vast scope of information and meaning that surrounds the complexity of the Self.
3. Patience and dedication...

No, that isn't four items: #3 is a fusion of attributes, tied together in their qualities.

Purpose

The primary purpose of life, its core value – indeed, the reason you incarnate at all – is to expand your awareness of your base nature. Yes, of course, a wide range of life values presents potential of creativity and reward, of enjoyment and accomplishment, of interest and encounter: child-bearing and rearing, travel, engagement of nature, art and music – both creating and experiencing – relationship exploration, athletics, entertainment, competition, philosophy and exchange of ideas…

These and many other aspects of life provide rich and fulfilling experience of creativity and love – in a distinct way, these are part of life's purpose, too. But behind them all is a quest to explore in depth the nature of the Self – the individual point of consciousness which you are: to ultimately understand **what you are** and ***how life works***.

I spent much of my life gaining what I call "Clear Awareness" of the nature of personal Consciousness. Later, I will fill you in on that, my own journey towards a clarity of perception of the Oneness of things. When you regard the message of any visionary, it is vital to recognize where that person came from and how he or she got to the standpoint they voice, the level that person claims to occupy.

Many pseudo-visionaries will promote their advanced titles, esoteric-sounding labels, academic degrees or declared status within a movement or organization. *These are devoid of meaning.* The *only* important status to any person who would explain to you the nature of Consciousness, the functionality of life, is *the degree to which that person is aware of the functional **Oneness*** of all things…

My point here is that accrual of **knowledge**, however specialized, however mystical-sounding and convincing, isn't a path that will get you to full awareness of the Oneness of things. Rather, awareness is gained by *elimination of beliefs and prior programming*. Thus, claimed levels of some esoteric scale or advanced degrees in an academic pursuit, great book sales or massive groups of followers – none of these things indicates the level of the message being offered.

That awareness, an intimate grasp of how the inner realm of psychic content relates to the outer flow of event and relationship – the degree of clarity of that personal consciousness of the

Oneness of the inner with the outer *is the only element of bearing and value...*

This situation, of course, makes it difficult for anyone, not yet aware of life's interconnected nature, to discern the value of *any* message offered by a wide range of New-Age teachers, exotic gurus and yogis, self-help experts, spirituality consultants, psychologists, hypno-therapy experts and big-name, best-seller authors on consciousness. My suggestion is, *avail yourself fully of my perspectives*: not only do I provide you all the techniques you need to explore your own inner psyche, but I add illustrations to help you navigate within, expose fallacy in other messages and promote your own experience, your own development of confidence and trust in your own capability *to attain Clear Awareness on your own*. All this empowers you to be your own guru, your own guide. And most of my message costs you nothing.

This book enhances my first three works, my longstanding, free website, The Essence of Reality, at www.nehrer.net and a long series of videos made readily available, also for free, i.e., noncommercialized, and easy public regard via YouTube. All of these and hundreds of talks I've given across the English-speaking realm serve to communicate and illustrate my personal awareness, my Clear Awareness, of how Consciousness manifests the Reality it encounters – and how you can become aware of that Oneness, with you at the center of its being.

Specifically, this work answers questions from readers and seekers of understanding. Over the 20 years of my EoR website, I have received many queries and thoughts from readers, seeking further clarification of various points. Here I recoup the most insightful of those questions, adding points of clarification from my current perspective, if that is helpful. These questions will have a prefix "E" before the number.

And for many years now, I've ventured to address many basic questions voiced on Quora.com, a website where readers can pose questions for others to regard and answer. Many of those have centered on Consciousness, Religion, Spirituality, Philosophy, etc. Here, again, I will collect the best of these, noted with a Q prefix, fitting them into a thematically-arranged flow to best illustrate the points raised.

Gaining Clear Awareness of the personal connection to *Reality* empowers you to create a life of your choice and orientation, with health and fulfillment as a base quality…

In this book, then, as in all of my public expression, I do my utmost to provide clear illustrations to help readers on their own journey. As you will notice when Consciousness and its interface to all that it encounters are explored, the requisite examination of critical elements delves very deeply into inner dimensions of the mind.

First, in order to satisfy your inner need for an Index and some anticipated order, here is what you might suspect…

Section Flavor	**Number of Questions**	**Focus**	**Page Number**
Engaging	**10**	**An Initial Look into CONSCIOUSNESS**	**7**
Consideration	**7**	**A First Look at RELIGION**	**46**
Attentive	**4**	**Undertaking One's PERSONAL JOURNEY**	**62**
Responsive	**6**	**A Glance at PHILOSOPHY**	**81**
Contemplating	**12**	**Focus on ATHEISM**	**95**
Outsourcing		**My Standpoint**	**115**
Introspective	**10**	**Looking Deeper into CONSCIOUSNESS**	**120**

Beyond Belief	**14**	**Exposing CHRISTIANITY**	**150**
Empiricising	**3**	**Quick Look at SCIENCE**	**190**
Progression	**9**	**Continuing on That INNER JOURNEY**	**200**
Regressing	**3**	**ISLAM and its Declarations**	**222**
Insourcing	**2**	**MYSTICISM – Grasping Intangibles**	**230**
Onwards	**5**	**Resuming the INNER TREK**	**240**
Reconsidering	**5**	**A Further Look at RELIGION**	**255**
Eastwards	**2**	**A Fleeting Look at EASTERN Thinking**	**267**
Reflective	**6**	**About MY PERSPECTIVES**	**275**
Indicative	**11**	**About ME Personally**	**291**
Ummmm...	**11**	**Concerning THIS and NOT THIS**	**325**

And here, as you might also suspect, is what you get...

Engaging: An Initial Look into CONSCIOUSNESS

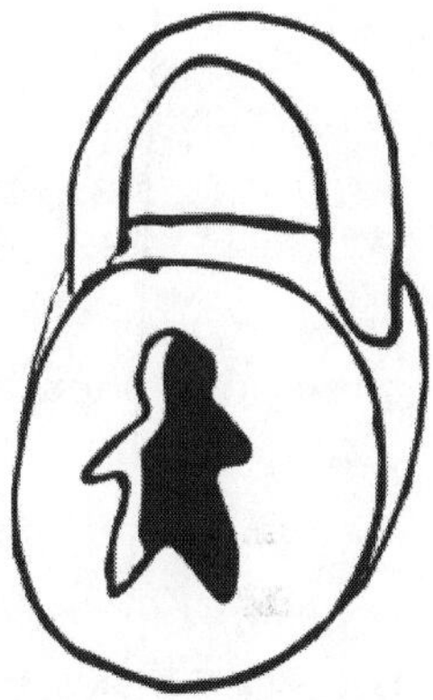

You aren't a mere physical creature at the core, riding a thought-generating, machine-like brain as controller of a six-trillion cell body. You aren't a measly collection of organically-inclined molecules, consisting of interlocked atoms coming and going, cranking onward in a dull-witted, mechanical fashion. Nor is it the case that your body-based Self blindly cavorts its way through a physical space populated by a collection of mindless, senseless, isolated material objects.

Lots of things you were told that you are, you really *aren't* – even though you've been so informed by people of considerable renown, speaking for time-honored institutions.

Don't believe them…

They don't know any more what they're talking about than the people *they* learned from – and duly, with unquestioning dedication, believed it.

You are, rather, this: **a timeless conscious entity** whose basis consists of values and meaning. You wend your way through incarnations wherein you manifest a physical realm that is imbued with meaning.

And that meaning your life entails derives from the exceedingly complex inner mix held within the psyche of your own total Self. Seemingly separate objects you encounter are all interconnected: people playing roles and objects functioning as props in the drama/comedy that comprises *your life*.

That, with primitive ideas, superstition, phony beliefs and glitz scoured away is precisely *what you are*. As noted from the outset, I spend a lot of time just trying to get people to see what's happening in front of their noses – just describing reality without gods, spirits, exotic healing techniques, subatomic structures, esoteric terms or any other nonsense, tangible or intangible, that only interferes with awareness...

And, of course, providing other prongs, techniques and such, to pierce the illusions. Oh, and answering questions that arise...

So, this first section will dive right into the primary topic of my whole message, Consciousness. Again, answers I'd proffered on Quora, featuring a Q prefix, are principally straightforward questions, although they may elicit rather complex answers.

Intermingled with those Q&A points from Quora are questions received through my website. These queries, submitted over two decades of my web presence, often present a multi-part dialog. All points carry a sequential number, but those submitted via EoR online are preceded by an E. Frequently, I've updated the original answer if needed. Occasionally, I'll comment (in parentheses) with a current point that augments the original answer.

Be advised that *there will be some redundancy* as various questions may elicit similar and – when collected as they are here – somewhat repetitive points. The reiteration, though, *will prove helpful*.

Q1 – What is consciousness?

Most answers to this basic question, you will find, *if and when* you get the real point, rely on rational conclusions: conceptualizations based on accepted scientific proofs and/or popular Eastern depictions. Western religions pay precious little attention to consciousness, which is actually the most important realization.

None of those sources will adequately illustrate the nature of Consciousness for you.

Conversely and without relying on others' complex definitions, I can explain to you the nature of Consciousness from my rather unique standpoint, but you will have difficulty receiving the message I offer with clarity. That is because the very nature of personal consciousness is distorted by beliefs and definitions you hold and accept as true. And many of the core definitions through which you, as most in our society, interpret experiential reality – religion, science, luck, fate, etc. – are inherently flawed.

Core fallacies innate to those commonly-held ideas invariably create an appearance of *duality* in your existence – that you are one thing and everything you encounter is something else. Additionally, in general, those commonly held cultural notions project causality to imagined forces and sources "out there" – gods, bacteria, the government, bad or rich people, parents, the weather, economic conditions, your mother-in-law, etc.

So, let me caution you: if you question my depiction of the nature of Consciousness, it is because you are comparing my accounts to many notions you've absorbed since childhood, elements of explanation and conclusion you hold to be true. Only those readers open-minded enough to question their own current world view will – perhaps – adequately see beyond their own fixed notions to grasp the bigger picture presented here.

Consciousness is the core nature of your existence. It isn't a capacity of a biological unit or the result of complex brain/neuron/synapse function. It isn't a quality endowed by a creator god. And it isn't a personal attribute held in the face of a dangerous environment. In essence, Consciousness can only be fully understood as an integral aspect of the Consciousness/Reality Oneness that stands as the fundamental nature of your existence.

Embedded in this functional Oneness, you engage a reality not caused by external forces and sources, but rather *you attract* daily life occurrences. You'll see this most clearly in your life when you recognize that you attract, qualitatively and unconsciously, recurring patterns in your life. People come and go in the course of your life, but the nature of your relationships unfolds in patterns: you attract similar types of people in repetition. Health issues arise and abate, but the impact on your life also repeats in patterns. Likewise, you tend to succeed or fail at achieving desired goals – again, in characteristic patterns.

The overall governing mechanism that drives the specific manifestation of your life is the total content of your mindset. Positive and negative events and relationships both spring from your will: the positive as fulfillment of your intent, the negative as fulfillment of inner conflict, fear, notions of powerlessness, etc.

You can, using meditation and self-hypnosis, querying your subconscious via ideomotor responses and dream analysis, find and change inner roots to negative life effects. As you engage life in this fashion, your real quality of life improves at each step – and you become ever more aware of the innate inner-outer connection that drives the life experience.

One difficulty to grasping the Consciousness/Reality Oneness is the nature of language in communication – it breaks a Now-moment continuum of interrelated elements into separate, defined pieces and independent actions. Consciousness seems to be merely an attribute of the body, or to lesser degrees, of any life form. Reality seems to be a universe of particles interacting through blind momentum driven by electromagnetic forces and gravity.

In essence, though, you are a unique frame of individualized being, integrated into a Now-moment flow of event and relationship that reflects your own being. You are explicitly and unavoidably personalized in the meaningful flow of your life.

So, consciousness can be defined and explained in many ways – gods making things happen, external sources causing events, hidden forces driving particles, luck or fate driving happenings, etc. But all such conceptualized causes fall within the confines of their own specified and philosophized description of life. And all are false – illusions created by the mere act of believing in them, of accepting explanations you were handed while growing up.

You will grasp your own overarching nature as causal in all aspects of your life only by dispelling those definitions and their paradigms – as embodied in religion, science and a host of holdover pagan notions as to life's driving forces. Such inner scouring is no trivial task, but doable. When you do, you will see clearly that the core nature of your being is this: a Self, encountering and engaging an unfolding Reality that contains meaningful patterns reflecting your own nature.

Thus, Consciousness can only be fully perceived as one side of the undivided, functionally indivisible Consciousness/Reality Singularity – like a magnet, where a north pole only exists in conjunction with its real extension of the south pole, or a coin where heads exists only in apparent opposition to tails, but indeed implies and requires its opposite to exist.

In that regard, all things in this vast physical realm function interactively as a stage hosting the meaningful experience of life. You are Consciousness and are connected to the Reality you encounter. *Consciousness is the core nature of your existence.*

E2 – Is it possible that an objective reality can exist? The Neanderthals did not have the knowledge... we have today, but still they did exist during that period of time...

Consciousness doesn't end at the tip of your nose. It permeates Reality, underlying all of the material universe such that it binds all things, however independently existent they might appear, as an integrated Oneness.

Neanderthals were conscious individuals, but so is your dog and so are the fleas on him and the bacteria on the fleas. Each of those life forms simply experiences its reality within the scope of its own realm, from its own perspective, in its own way. Each encounters reality with exactly the right set of corporeal equipment to sense its environment and interact with it as needed to survive.

You, as an incarnated conscious entity currently engaged in the material universe, are similarly equipped.

When does food you eat become "you"? When does the hair you cut off your head cease to be "you"? You are not an object surrounded by a collection of external items, but rather you are the Total Essence of all you encounter, experienced through your perspective. *There is no objective reality.* There never could be – where would it be? How could it be without consciousness to experience it?

Consciousness and Reality, in other words, are two aspects of the same singular essence. You can't have one without the other. Awareness of that is one cornerstone of all I wish to communicate in EoR.

Q3 – Is everyone's experience of consciousness the same?

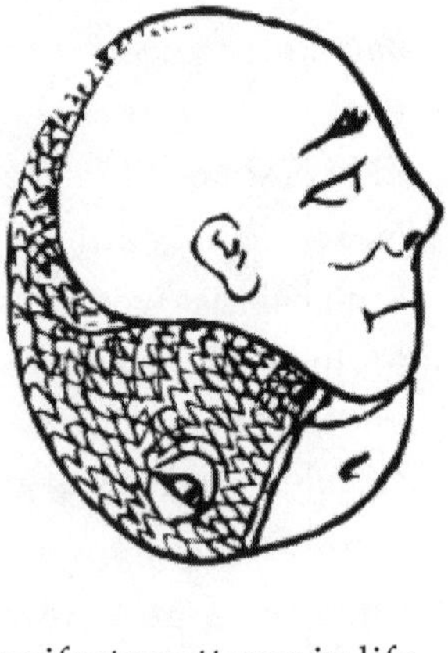

Yes, the "experience" of consciousness is functionally the same for each human – embedded in a ***now*** moment, each of us experiences through a set of senses an ongoing flow of events and relationships that contain meaning. That meaning, indeed, is derived from and reflective of the Self, as each individual manifests patterns in life resonating with his/her own core nature.

However, the *interpretation* of that experience, what is made of life situations by each individual – and thus the personal impact and response – varies considerably. The variations depend on one's belief structure and accepted definitions. And those complex elements of the subconscious differ greatly between cultures and personal upbringing. Indeed, even in the same culture, there is a wide discrepancy of held notions through which to interpret life.

Consider three different people holding three different sets of beliefs: a fundamentalist believer in religion, a follower of Eastern practices and a staunch atheist relying on science for understanding. Each of these, experiencing a similar event, would construe the happening differently. Each would derive divergent meaning, react differently in emotional terms and take contrasting action accordingly.

So, there are two considerations in play here:

1. What actually happens as life unfolds, and
2. What the experiencing individual makes of it – which directly influences his/her response.

Subsequent reaction thus depends on elements of the personal belief structure. Given a negative encounter, the Christian believer may well pray to his/her imagined god for guidance or intervention. The Eastern practitioner may retreat and meditate on its meaning, looking for greater perspective and relaxation. The scientist would likely analyze apparent contributing factors – what caused the negative situation and what action that person might take to counter it.

Thus, the *experience* of consciousness was the same for each: all three individuals, as conscious entities, engaged a meaningful experience. While each would arrive at different conclusions as to meaning and respond to the situation based on held belief, each *did* experience his/her own consciousness in the same reflexive manner.

Of course, beliefs and accepted definitions are only mental constructs – they serve to distort perception of the immediacy of reality. But the experience at its core – consciousness engaging a meaningful flow of events and relationships – is the same for each individual.

E4a – A ten-part exchange with a reader...

You write that whatever we hold in mind – beliefs, assumptions, fears, emotions, etc. – will be projected outward and flow into our reality. Is there a reality that exists regardless of what we believe, some kind of common ground on which to play – or is our reality completely of our making?

First, no "Reality" can exist without Consciousness to perceive it. If there were such a "common ground" sort of a stage to act out our lives, or a background on which our events could be displayed, in what environment would it exist? Where would it have come from?

The illusion of this life is that earth and the Solar System and our Galaxy – among billions of others – are somehow the valid elements here, while we, each as an individual focus of conscious awareness of that universe, are temporary, shallow, passing observers of it. What must be perceived to dispel that illusion is the lack of physical dimension to consciousness itself. That is to say, the physical realm exists, but *only* within the context of experiencing consciousness.

Consider the dream state. In a dream, there is an environment that seems real from that perspective. If you move in some direction, the dream state provides some apparent wall or sky or whatever – credible backdrop of some sort. But those things aren't "really" there, as you realize upon awakening. As real as all this magnificent earth and universe appear, from another perspective they are projections as well, *an illusion*. Of course, the realness is vital to provide the forum for experiencing the values you entail, and engaging elements of your Self with enough vividness to make the pain hurt and the pleasure feel good.

So, Reality is completely of our making, each individual – though this particular format is a rather consistent "operating system", with hills, trees, oceans and all. But, remember, the value of those hills, trees and all other stuff is different as interpreted by any individual. And it is always the meaning that formulates the essence – not the objects themselves.

E4b – You suggest that in order to change aspects of our reality we don't like, we have to delve into our mind content, look where our problems (mostly due to circumstances in our childhood – or even in past or parallel lives?) are rooted, release the energy involved and then change our beliefs with the help of auto-hypnosis one for one. Isn't there a more positive way of doing this, like focusing on love, light, "truth" – so that the direct awareness of *what is* will free us of all misconceptions? Like one yogi said, where there is light, darkness cannot exist. My point is, instead of trying to remove darkness bring in the light.

Suppose you walk down the main street of your town with a dozen eggs in a basket, and three of them are rotten. You can buy ten apples, all tasty and wonderful and add them to the basket, plus some meat and milk – whatever you want. But no matter what good stuff you throw on top, you still have the rotten eggs. And you will have them until you get rid of them.

You personally – your conscious Self – consist of values, not material. Those values constitute *WHAT YOU ARE*. If you hold a deep fear, you can meditate all you want, chant, accept all the symbolic, positive messages from whomever you find, visualize, grin with positive vibes, but you will still have that deep fear. And it will remain registered in your timeless subconscious until you come to see it and consciously, pointedly eliminate it.

If you don't root out that fear and its basis – likely a complex of childhood learning, perhaps of punishment and negative suggestion – the best you can do is cover it over. Like with the rotten eggs, until you jettison them, they're still in your basket. Thinking positive things, following Eastern suggestions, hoping or praying – you are only fooling yourself. The subconscious will simply layer the positive stuff on the old fears – and incorporate both into experienced reality.

Running from the fear to hide behind the guru and his imagined power – that sort of rationalization only energizes the fear. Indeed, such an act is a symptom of the fear in itself.

The negative must be culled from your mindset or it will remain there. That is how the mind works – an aspect of consciousness beyond the ken of your yogi…

E4c – Most Eastern spiritual paths lay out a complete map of the inner landscape. They speak of atman and Brahman, mind, spirit, higher self, etc.

If I understand you right, what you are saying is, there is only a oneness of being and these distinctions are created by ourselves through believing in them. Could you expand on that topic a little bit?

It doesn't matter what the paradigm, the described model, might be; it is only a model. Atman, heaven, astral planes, the Tao – these are only words that lead to further illusions. In my comprehensive message, I'm saying what I can, providing tools to delve inward, illustrating specific mechanisms within your mindset – everything I can to get you to see your own conscious nature yourself. Any description of what is consists only of words, ideas – you will distort, invariably, the meaning contained in any explanation.

Elaborate descriptions of atman, anica, dharma, dukkha, Karma, moksha – these all sound esoteric and convincing. But just like the Holy Spirit and a creator god named "God", like formulae for gravitational and electromagnetic forces, speed of light and valence shells of atoms, like creation myth or a complex layout of epistemology – these are only ideas. When you accept them and the paradigm they stem from, they appear valid and real…

You exist, consisting of a vast array of values, understandings, self-image, world-image, self-esteem, fears, beliefs, assumptions, etc. That value-Self, held within the vast, complex subconscious of your mind, is projected out onto the daily events and relationships you encounter in life. That is the Oneness of Consciousness/Reality. You ***are*** the mindset; you ***are*** the real.

You need to see that, feel it, grow comfortable with it, your own essence…

Fear is real. You experience it, you perceive it, you can come to deal with it, eliminate it when you find the source. Atman, by comparison, is a concept. It is meant to indicate the overall essence of things, but by naming it that esoteric-sounding term, when it's passed along to you as an idea, it becomes a thing unto itself.

Self-esteem is real. You can perceive its elements, see how they fit into your mind image, how they affect your life. You can change them, and see your life change as well. Brahman is an ancient term that carries mind images which can only be received by you and stacked onto many other notions within your subconscious. Resting there, it is only an idea; it inhibits clear awareness of what is by distorting awareness to conform to its layered ideas.

My point is this: if you come to deal with the fear and the self-esteem, you will be experiencing the Oneness of Reality, because you will see how Self, what is held in the mind, relates to the outer world of experiences and things. By doing so, you will come to perceive the Oneness directly. If you try to deal with Brahman or heaven or Wave Theory or Five Pillars of Definitions – or any other verbal depiction of Reality's Essence, your quest will degrade to a gesture of philosophy or of grandiose generalization.

Of course, our cultural heritage includes accounts of many individuals who were somewhat aware of that Oneness, and who tried to describe it in their way. But virtually all of it is distorted by language and time. The ancient Hindi had a glimpse of the Oneness in their Atman, karma, reincarnation concepts, and this was enhanced by Gautama. But distortions remain. And they will endure so long as ideas are presented as though they are unquestionably true – rather than direct perception of life's functional Oneness is gained, beyond mere ideas…

That's why I emphasize how vital it is for *you* to come to see "clearly" yourself. Any account you read, even from me, cannot be clear. The most deeply perceiving mystic becomes only another philosopher when he tries to communicate his perceptions.

E4d – Thanks a lot for responding to my questions. It is great to have someone like you answer questions that have been in my mind for a long time.

I have a whole lot more questions I'd like to ask. So, as long as you are willing to bear up with them, I will go on asking them.

Your questions are certainly similar to those that would come to mind for other readers, so it is helpful and constructive to ask. I'll answer as I can – but as concluded in the last response, the onus is still on you or any reader who sincerely seeks to understand life to come to see clearly – and not just take my answer as definitive.

E4e... (Reader begins by quoting my website:) You wrote, "So, reality is completely of our making, each individual – though this particular format is a rather consistent 'operating system', with hills, trees, oceans and all. But, remember, the value of those hills, trees and all other stuff is different as interpreted by any individual..."

You know, this really puzzles me. I have been thinking quite a lot about this question. Long time ago I read in a book by Paul Brunton that our world is not as solid as we usually perceive it, pointing out that solid matter consists – according to science – of molecules and atoms, and thus the solidity and objectivity of our world is only an interpretation by our mind. So far I can accept your explanation.

But what about the people I encounter? What about you, then? If my reality is completely of my own making, am I making up the people in my life (and you) too? Am I talking to myself?

I am as real as anything else you encounter, but again, as you so aptly echo, the reality is in the interpretation, not the thing. Each person you encounter fulfills certain values in the relationship you form with him/her. In other words that person fits into your life to function in a certain role. (And you in theirs!)

Suppose you have a need to be dominated, to be controlled. Your parents would have controlled you firmly, authoritatively. When you grew up, you would be attracted to a partner who was also authoritative. But suppose you couldn't stand that anymore, so you left that person. You would find that your life would adjust – now your boss would take on a more controlling attitude, or your new landlord would be domineering, or your sister would start telling you what to do.

All people in your life fit into such value-roles. The same goes for objects, your financial status, your home, your car, everything. Yes, I am my own person, complete with my own values, but how I fit into your life is unique to your perspective, just as how you fit into mine is unique to me.

So you don't "make them up" so much as *attract them*, unconsciously, to fill certain needs, certain potential relationships. It's not that they aren't "real", it's that the nature of "realness" is not hard, quantitative, and objective, but pliant, responsive, reflective, and qualitative.

E4f – What I wanted to ask was how to go about to attain a state of Clear Awareness. If I understand you right, what you are saying is basically, remove all fallacies and misconceptions and what will remain is clear awareness then.

This sounds like a very arduous task. I'd rather have a more positive way to do this. The Yogi Vivekananda says in his book *Jnana Yoga* in the German translation, "Liebe ist das Gesetz des Lebens. Wer das erkannt hat, ist vollkommen."

(My translation: "Love is the law of life. Whoever recognizes that is complete.")

It takes about two seconds to intellectually acknowledge that love is the basis of all this reality. But if you had an authoritative wife before you understand that, you will still have her afterwards.

Love, as a positive, attractive, accepting force, is the conceptual foundation, the core of what you are.

But built on top of that foundation are many things. There is a self-image, there are extensive defense mechanisms, there are fears, assumptions, volumes of "facts", many beliefs and assumptions – some obvious, some subtle. There are prejudices, worries, acquired tastes, artificial mental constructs. There is anger, sexual desire, pride, self-denial, cultural doctrine, evaluatory standards, etc., etc.

The yogi would give you a quick fix technique meant to bypass all that by shutting off the intellectual voicing of those inner effects. He would tell you to meditate, and substitute a mantra when the mind begins to fill in the silence with thoughts. This technique goes far back beyond Gautama the Buddha into the distant roots of Hinduism. It appeals to our Western culture, because we like that *quick fix* idea.

What I'm communicating is a larger picture than that technique can address. If you have a bottle full of sour, acidic, rotten organic residue, the yogi would have you put a cork on it and declare it to be OK. I'm telling you how to thoroughly clean out the bottle so you can use it for your desired purposes.

That yogi, like your local priest, or a tribal shaman, or a rabbi, knows basically what he was taught by his guru. A lot of that might be quite valuable, of course; it might help you move along your own personal path some distance. But I understand how life works because I delved into it very deeply, very intimately, and never believed any of the standardized theological or philosophical or Eastern mystical packages I was handed. I'm providing perspectives plus techniques, all meant to get you to see clearly – but you can't do that while hosting a plethora of definitions, cultural "truths", religious tenets, scientific principles, residual pagan notions, etc.

And you can be 100% sure they all populate your subconscious – and will continue to do so until you remove them…

Yes, delving deeply into the self is an arduous task. Extremely so! That is because the depth of the mind is extensive, multidimensional, multicolored, multi-everything. The question is what you want to accomplish, and on what scale. What you are now, as realized in the complex set of values which you maintain inwardly, and build into your outward life as well, is *WHAT YOU ARE*. If you don't change that accumulation of subconscious elements, you will carry those same values with you through death. Because that is what you are, you will still have those same core values – along with resultant fears and powerlessness – in other lives you create, because consciousness is always creating a reality around it.

So, my conclusion long ago, as I realized how arduous the journey might be, was and still is: I need to clean out ***all*** the debris of negativity, of powerlessness, of archaic belief, of fallacy, of illusion. And I don't care how long that journey is. It sure beats watching television or simple-minded good guy/bad guy movies. And every step brings improvement in life.

Of course, you can go try the yogi's technique. There is nothing to be lost by traveling down that path. Five or ten years from now, when you tire of incense and candles and white robes, and come to see the role the yogi is playing – along with his limitations – EoR will still be available. And I will actually have gotten around to finishing some of the material I'm slowly progressing on!!

(Note: this book is being assembled at least 15 years after my original answer, which has been slightly updated. Indeed, at this point I've added a great deal of "material" to my message! Not finished yet, though…)

E4g – I wonder what it is like, to live in a state of Clear Awareness. Do/can you always maintain this higher consciousness, or are there times when you fall back into a more or less "normal" consciousness?

Awareness is not a fancy, glittery, euphoric state that takes you *out* of life. There again, the yogi who sits in a cave meditating on higher states, living off donations from adherents, thinking he has attained some lofty status has fallen for his own illusion. The reality is he's a guy sitting in a cave living off other people, thinking he has attained a lofty status.

Life is to be lived. The most wonderful aspects of life are found in the full experience of them, living, interacting with others, creating, being involved. Awareness is seeing all those aspects clearly, as extensions of the Self, parts of the Self, not substituting other illusions, grandiose mind images, seeking "higher planes" meant to be an escape from this one.

So, no, I don't drop back to "normal" consciousness. ("Clear Awareness" actually ***is***, in fact, normal consciousness!) Once you clean your inner windshield of all the dead flies, dust, road grease and bird poop that inhibit your view, it remains clean. Once at peace, you don't drive around anymore – rationally, that is, as no further movement is necessary anymore, which would accumulate added debris of flawed notions...

I well recall how the world looked, though, when the window was dirty. Let me compare the two – maybe the illustration will be helpful: Let's say person AA is your typical 20th century human with self-consciousness. He perceives himself to be an individual entity, surrounded in daily life by objects that seem external and distant from him and people who have their own separate lives.

Person ZZ has "Clear Awareness"; he perceives that all events and relationships in his life emanate from his own inner state.

AA is always a little on edge, because he doesn't know what will happen to him – will he lose his job? Will his wife cheat on him? Will he have a traffic accident or his car break down the next time he goes somewhere? Will the economy collapse? AA always has to plan everything out, take care of all details. When AA gets sick, he worries a lot and needs medicine to heal him from the "attack" of germs or virus.

By comparison, ZZ, living nearby, is relaxed and at peace. His job is creative and interesting. If his job should suddenly end, he knows he will find something even better. He carries car insurance because it is legally required, but he never needs to make a claim. Still, the outlay of premiums doesn't bother him because he understands – and is at peace. ZZ sets goals, then follows through with his impulses to complete them, fearing no resistance or difficulty. ZZ rarely gets sick, but clearly understands why when he does, learns from the experience – then lets his body heal itself naturally.

AA struggles through the day, arguing with his boss, fighting with his neighbor. AA worries that his neighbor's mean dog will attack him one day, so he keeps some stick handy to protect himself. He keeps a gun handy if someone breaks into his house. He has tried to stop smoking, but it seems to be an outlet for his stress.

ZZ enjoys his work, contributing to a team effort and company success. His neighbors are his friends, and he chats with them often. He doesn't lock his doors. He occasionally walks by the house with the mean dog, but the dog is never out at that time.

AA fears a collapse in the stock market, and constantly checks the listings, often buying and selling stocks to avoid loss of money. ZZ owns some mutual funds, but doesn't pay much attention to them, but they grow in value at a good rate.

I know how the world looks from both viewpoints. I prefer the clean windshield.

E4h – When you feel the need for some "material" possession like say a new car, will your ways to get one be different from that of ordinary people like me (work hard, bear up with your boss to earn money, etc.), or do you have some "magical" way about that? (I'm serious about that question...)

When I want something, I either get it or do it, or, if it is out of my financial range at the moment, I set my mind to it. Either things will change that allow me to get it, or I will realize shortly that I didn't really want that object, but rather had a greater need that I wasn't paying attention to. It always works out, but mostly somewhat slower than I would like!

There is nothing "magic" about Reality. Magic is staged illusion. Reality is only an apparent illusion so long as you don't see it clearly.

And, by the way, there is nothing wrong with desiring something – despite Gautama's and many Eastern mystics' efforts to squelch desire. Consciousness always seeks the new, the different. It is only fear or misguided fervor that would seek to curtail desire. Without it remain only stagnation and blandness.

Overall, I'm not very materialistic, so I don't hold a great need for material things. I have decent, reliable, but not ostentatious vehicles. I always have goals to move towards. But I enjoy the journey, valuing accomplishment and interaction along the way. And I enjoy good music, travel, adventure, sports, exercise and lots of other things as I proceed…

E4i – I have one more question. You write that all beliefs are faulty and should be cleaned out rather than cultivated. I agree with you insofar as religious or dogmatic beliefs are concerned like changing one's beliefs from Christian beliefs to some sort of Eastern religion or belief system. But what about those other, more personal beliefs?

For instance, if in my youth I had acquired a belief that I am a worthless person with a very limited capacity to ever attain something like a fulfilling life, wouldn't it be better to change my belief to "I am a worthy person and I live a fulfilling life"? If I just clean out that "unworthiness" belief, without replacing that belief with a more rewarding belief, what rests? How can someone "not believe"?

The self-image including "worthlessness" is a belief, one that will fulfill itself by limiting the holder and his personal accomplishment. The "worthy-fulfilling" concept is not a belief, but a true potential in everybody. The act you describe is one of ridding oneself of the limiting, artificial mind image and replacing it with a positive, real mindset.

Beliefs are artificial constructs. If you are homely in appearance, you can't just artificially, suddenly believe that you are handsome or beautiful. But you can come to realize that physical characteristics are not the most important qualities. As you focus on all your real and positive attributes, your self-image builds and your self-esteem grows as well. Then you do realize that you aren't really so homely after all – only unique in appearance.

In effect, you bring all the qualities into a lifetime that you need. When you eliminate the inner, personal negatives, you'll find yourself with just exactly the characteristics that your propensities need in order to succeed.

I have no beliefs – I've culled out all the synthetic definitions I'd held, insofar as they impact my view. I still call a tree a tree and a table a table – but I recognize their place in the overall scheme of things.

I can say that there is no value to hosting artificial beliefs, as in gods or in a self-deprecating sense. Some people have trouble understanding that – or, perhaps, believing it.

E4j – Again I would like to thank you for making your knowledge available on the net and putting up with my questions.

Of course, you are quite welcome. But, it's not really "knowledge". Of greatest value in the scheme of things is what I have *UNlearned* in my lifetime. I "know" a lot of historical, scientific, musical, technical, archeological, programming, automotive, sports-oriented, philosophical, and other things. But they only form a background capacity for explaining meaningful things.

Awareness is not promoted by knowledge. It can be, in fact – but doesn't have to be – very hindered by it! Awareness is clarified in bypassing registered beliefs and definitions to see life's flow directly.

Q5 – If consciousness is an emergent property of the brain, what and how is this accomplished?

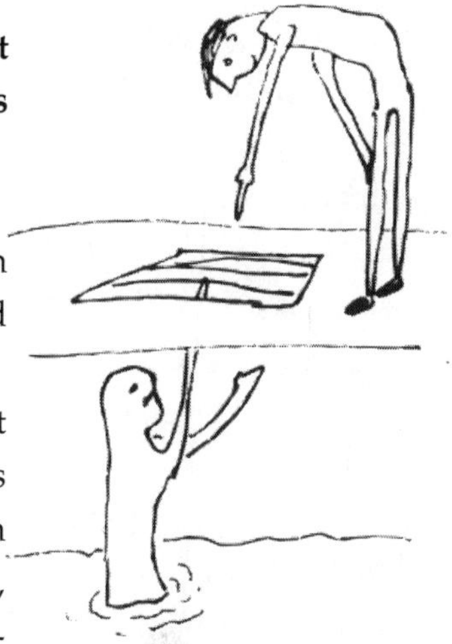

To begin with, I find numerous twists in the formulation of the query part, based on the inaccuracy of the premise.

Consciousness is not "an emergent property" of the brain. Consciousness is the basis of being. The brain is an organ that basically interfaces the individual, conscious Self with the meaningful reality it manifests. I can only really answer the question by exposing its invalid premise…

Attributing consciousness to the complex operation of the brain's 100+ trillion synapses is an outgrowth of the scientific paradigm. In the world view of science, the only thing regarded as valid are objects, movement and associated consequences of the material universe. Physical objects ranging from huge stars and massive black holes down to subatomic particles – their movement and interaction – are required for empirical testing in the real universe or in a lab to prove or disprove a theory. That's the scientific process: if a theory passes a test and can be reproduced, it's considered valid. If it doesn't pass or can't be redone by others, it isn't seen as valid.

However, consistent with reliance on empiricism as a basis of validity, what is not really scientifically testable *is generally regarded as invalid, too!* To the individual who buys into the scientific paradigm, the term *scientifically proven* equates to the term, "true" – with everything else regarded by default as false.

In the view of science, consciousness *per se* – with its human qualities of creativity, empathy, love, imagination, relative intelligence, pain, emotion, hope, etc. – has no basis of testing, therefore doesn't really exist outside the scope of the real universe.

Only the objective realm is allotted recognition; so the mind, as the conscious Self is experienced, must be a functional resultant of the brain – the only complex organ of the body that seems to deal directly with information.

Thus, the scientific paradigm would relegate all of those quite human characteristics – along with a vast array of visual impressions and other extremely complex idea storage – into the scope of brain complexity. Science imagines that *all recorded* memory, all sensory encounter, is somehow stored in the brain for future recall. It doesn't matter that there has never been a mechanism for that discovered: science only regards the real world as valid, so *somehow* memory, etc. – including all human personality attributes – *must be* stored in the brain.

Since the only complex, computer-like mechanism present in the brain is the inter-neuron connection grid, the vast network of synapses, science assumes that the brain is the *basis* of consciousness.

But that model is easily, *easily* seen as flawed.

When you take a picture in a digital camera, the mechanism records the visual field from the perspective of the lens into a grid of bits and bytes and stores that in the physical medium of computer memory for later display. A single HD image takes a megabyte or more of data to define its colors and shades – with each pixel of information requiring multiple bits to store its red, green and blue components.

A movie requires a lot more storage, as the frames are multiplied by 30 or so for each second of video. So, a 20-minute digital movie would require a good 5 megabytes of storage space.

Now understand that, by the time you reach 50 years old, you've lived **1 billion seconds of waking time** – and all of that optical *and other* sensory information is recorded in your memory. Visual memories, smells, sounds, music you've heard or memorized, thoughts you've thought at the time of events, feelings you felt associated with experiences, impressions, hopes you had then, etc. – all of this vast amount of information, plus memories from dreams, would have to be stored for instant recall…

Your collective memory is *a vast field* of recorded impressions. Add to that your accumulated, expansive knowledge: facts and figures, definitions you hold in your belief structure that allow you to make sense of all that recorded experience, all the pictures and movies you've ever viewed – and lots more…

Now, according to the scientific explanation, as its paradigm attributes all phenomena to physical components, *all of that* must be stored in the brain. Thus, in some fashion, all that vast, diverse information must be codified into some sort of mathematical system – like a computer converts graphic information into bits and bytes – and then be registered for storage in…

In what? The brain? But how? Synapses in the brain flick on and off. *They don't store anything!* They simply respond in the present moment, communicating impressions through the nervous system just to coordinate information among the 6 trillion cells in your body concerning current conditions.

If you're pretty good at remembering things – and I am – you can instantly recall memories from childhood, not considered for decades. You can remember complex music passages from Beethoven sonatas – or compose your own music with phrases never played before. You can imagine things never thought of or recall poems or recite from memory extensive dialogue from plays…

How could all of these capabilities be accommodated by a physical system, where vast gobs of information and complex mental capability are sitting, immediately available for recall instantly? For that matter, where is creativity stored or located in the brain? How could synapses codify and recoup emotional upset and overriding joy, love and compassion?

A physical-based system, even with the complexity of trillions of synapses, could not possibly carry out the complicated, diverse functionality of human consciousness in all of its emotional, deductive, creative capabilities.

Consciousness is not a quantifiable function of brain mechanisms. *Consciousness is the basis of being.* Its core attributes – love, life meaning, emotional engagement, hope, fear, creative capacities, and much, much more – are qualities of the innate Self, the individual point of timeless Consciousness which each person comprises.

It is not "an emergent property of the brain", but only seems so when life is observed through the distorting lenses of the scientific paradigm. The brain is an organ, necessary for complex interaction within the life format – it interfaces Consciousness with the body and thus with reality. But consciousness is not "accomplished" by the brain.

It's actually the other way around...

E6 – Animals seem to spend their time in the quest for survival. We are animals, but is this our purpose too? I don't feel as though I have any purpose. I don't feel any attachment to any religions or philosophies that I realize...

Animals don't really have a "quest" in the fashion we might consider a mission that we plan and intend to implement. They exist, embedded in their environment, reacting to conditions and interacting with whatever weather, climatic and other conditions they encounter. They carry out their necessary urges for food, mating and perhaps migration as their inner instincts impel them to do. And that scenario is played out on a scale the whole way down to single cells.

Survival is an artificial concept which we, as reasoning, observing humans, assign to a very real Oneness with which animals exist within their surroundings. They eat and reproduce, raise their young as is necessary, make dens or roam as they have impulse to do, and flow into the next moment. But they do *feel* as well, and experience much in the fulfillment of their life functions. Even death to the antelope, a failure to survive in the eyes of many homo sapiens, is a poignant playout of intense experience in the overall scheme of things, and leads to added nourishment for the lion, the vulture, the rodents, the insects and on down to bacteria that live off the antelope's remains.

Survival presents a very limited, illusory picture, ignoring how all life, indeed ALL THINGS interact, and looking at only one portion, one animal out of context. Looking at the whole picture, that whole interaction of a myriad of creatures on many scales, the limited concept of mere *survival* pales into nonsense.

In the framework of human existence, surviving, as in a struggle to get through daily life, can easily be superimposed onto a life trek – and indeed, comprises the daily activity of many of this planet's seven billion humans. Basic existence can become an ongoing struggle. Through traditional over-reliance on the intellect, most in this time period have stepped out of the inherent oneness with the surrounding environment, into an intellectually isolated self-ness. Seeing the self as detached from the rest of nature, as an object apart from all else, it would seem necessary to subsist by any means possible, to carry on – because if you don't, you cease to exist.

Survival, then, is a conceptual outgrowth of an objective view.

In actuality, you are living out experiences in a fashion that realizes growth and evolving self-awareness. You are not just here, fumbling blindly through daily life, for the "purpose" of persisting and carrying on through tomorrow to do the same, while perhaps raising children to blindly march the same meaningless treadmill exercise.

It's not so much that *you* have a purpose, but that all the events and relationships in your life, the creativity, the anticipation, the emotional attachments and responses, the victories, the accomplishments, even the failures – all these have *purpose*. And that purpose is engaging a living, dynamic existence that consists of the values you comprise. The purpose is growth: growth of awareness of how your creative power works, growth of patience and sympathy, growth of imagination, growth of many, many facets of mind.

Often, people are so focused on daily, mundane tasks, busy activities, entertainment glitz, or endless jobs to do, that they never focus on the vast wealth of experience life offers – a brilliant natural world to be explored, multifaceted relationships with interesting people, history of many divergent cultures to read about, literally thousands of subjects to learn about, etc. You do not so much *have* a purpose. All that you encounter *is* the purpose – you are the experiencer, and the purpose is to engage all that and learn from it.

Much of your "attachment to... religions or philosophies" is subtle – hardly noticed because you share ideas with others around you. How does the world work? What are you? What are you doing here? How is your behavior determined? How do events take place? However you answer these and many other such questions will reflect whatever philosophy you have absorbed from the culture you grew up in.

That you "don't feel the layers of any religion" is not unusual. Beliefs are often very subtle, forming the framework through which you interpret all experience. Do all things go well for you? Are you healthy? Are you successful? Are you satisfied with your life, your career, your relationships, your daily experiences? Depending on the response to all those, maybe you don't need to peel away anything!!

But if you give a lot of "NO" answers to the above, you may indeed want to start looking.

Because you are tied into the meaning you manifest in life, negatives will be rooted in your belief structure. Negative responses to those posed questions would indicate a need to look into what you do indeed hold as an understanding. Survival should be straightforward in life; quality of experience, though, may not reflect your intent...

Q7 – Did consciousness create the universe?

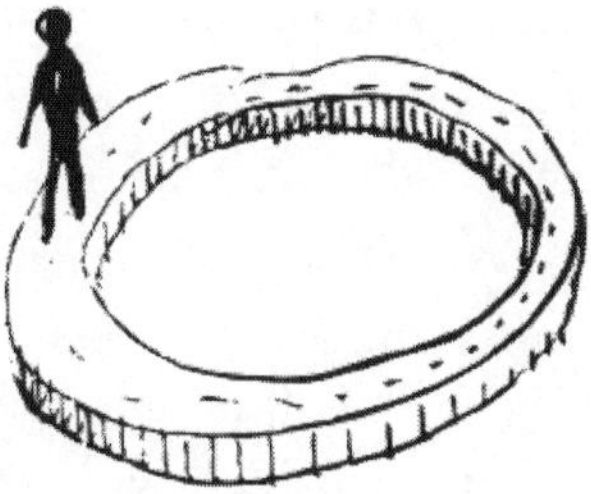

For absolute certain, Consciousness is behind the unfolding universe of matter – but referring to the process in the past tense distorts the real process.

Here are three pertinent elements requisite to fully recognizing consciousness as the driving impetus behind the manifestation of the physical universe:

1. Perceiving how life works,
2. Engaging a means to become aware of the process,
3. Personally leveraging that awareness to improve your life...

First, as to **How Life Works:** you create/attract the quality of events and relationships you encounter daily. In examining meaning as woven into the quality of experience you encounter in life, you'll find that *you create patterns* – in health issues, relationships you engage and in success/failure. These are manifested based on your total mindset, which is (worthy to note) extraordinarily complex.

It is virtually impossible to recognize this inner-outer connection in other people, as you don't have access to their total mindset. But you can see the connection clearly as it unfolds in your own life...

Second point: in expressing my perspective on that Oneness of Self with experienced reality, I illustrate techniques for delving inward to discern within the subconscious specific roots to outer problems in life.

As you become comfortable with exploring your own deep subconscious for explicit content, you become very familiar with deeper aspects of your own consciousness. And as you succeed with revising real experience by exacting change within, **you become ever more aware** of and confident in the innate inner-outer manifestation process that drives life.

An additional key aspect to gaining awareness of the Oneness with which life unfolds is elimination of flawed common notions – beliefs and definitions, paradigms and such – that hide or camouflage life's interactive nature. Principally religion and science, cornerstone elements to our common mindset, generate an illusory separation between Self and Reality. Widespread notions of luck, fate and chance – practically built into language – add to that. Holding these ideas within the subconscious as true and valid produces the impression of life as a duality – self vs. not-self…

In reality, you are connected to all things you encounter.

Third: the process of using Clear Awareness of that connection to improve real life involves discerning specific inner roots to outer issues. Using meditation, self-hypnosis, ideomotor responses and dream analysis, one can delve into the subconscious and specify which of some ten mechanisms lie at the root of real problems (suggestion, emulation, punishment, conflict, struggle, etc.). Having identified these, one can change subconscious content using Auto-Suggestion – simply revising the inner store of meaning/value by dispelling the undesirable mechanism and replacing it with a positive.

While the process appears simple, your subconscious mind will be found to be extremely complex. However, continued use of the inner-outer connection to improve life brings not only an improved quality of living, but ever greater confidence in the Self as the sole source of experience. And ever greater Awareness of the Oneness of Consciousness and Reality...

At some point, you realize, intimately and unquestioningly, that the physical realm, in its qualitative emergence into experience, is absolutely interrelated and inviolably reflective – insofar as it impacts you – of the values you yourself hold.

At that point, you realize that, yes, consciousness creates everything. But it does so *in this present, NOW moment* – just as it has in every moment you ever experience. And just as it did in all previous NOW moments, which you now consider as the "past". More accurately stated, *you are consciousness* and you manifest your life's aspects. You can become aware of that Oneness and leverage that awareness to vastly improve your life quality. Once you do that, you will recognize the integral nature of mind with the physical realm.

Until you do gain that awareness, you will be limited to speculating and philosophizing about the nature of things...

Q8 – What is super enlightenment?

The notion of "enlightenment" is difficult to grasp by anyone who doesn't have it.

And enlightenment *itself* has various levels of clarity – meaning that the pathway to greater recognition of Consciousness and its connection to Reality leaves residual impressions that distort clarity, even when the gist is understood. That is, as one grows in awareness of the Oneness of things, one's current state can only be compared to *past* levels experienced. And that means that it always seems like, as you grow in perceptivity, you've arrived at a very advanced stage of enlightenment – even though you may have considerable growth yet to experience before reaching the highest possible stages...

Let me illustrate what constitutes *enlightenment* in the first place, then we might glimpse what could be called a state even beyond that.

The great bulk of mankind exists in a state of Self-Awareness. The Self-Aware person recognizes that he/she exists and is surrounded by a reality – a physical realm in which one encounters a series of events and relationships, must eat and carry out various other actions to continue the process of physical existence. Chimpanzees and orangutans, for example, are also aware of themselves: they respond when looking in a mirror and recognize that they exist. As smart as my golden retriever was, as tuned in as he was through enhanced sense of smell and hearing, he didn't identify his own physical basis with the form he saw in a mirror – nor to most life forms.

But most people, even while recognizing themselves as existing, hold differing notions as to what they are and how life works. Some imagine gods to be directly controlling a divinely concocted universe. Others see a vast universe of galaxies and planetary systems in a purely insensitive, uncaring material realm – no god, no metaphysical connections to ethereal consciousness.

Thus Self-Awareness is *qualitatively* deeply connected to its held beliefs for the sense it makes out of existence.

Numerous people through time have become more intimately aware of the functional Oneness with which Reality actually responds to Consciousness – in addition to simply interacting with it. Whether spontaneously, as through a mystic experience or following a particular spiritual regimen over time, they gain insight into the real link between Consciousness and Reality – a connection that exists for all conscious entities whether they see it or not.

Lao-Tzu recognized a flow in life, the Tao: try to manipulate it through rational manipulation and it will only divert the flow negatively. Gautama illustrated the inner-outer connection, telling (not entirely accurately, by the way) how to change the inner to affect the outer. Jesus spoke of a "Kingdom within" – recognize it, as he pictured in his parables, and you will be blessed: life will work well for you. Plotinus, following his own mystic experiences, spoke of the "One".

I first glimpsed the functional Oneness between Self and experienced reality during my own, personal mystic experience while traveling around Europe during my twenties. Standing on a pristine beach on the Greek island of Corfu, I spontaneously recognized that I wasn't one thing surrounded by a collection of items – trees, rocks, water – but a Oneness seeing itself *from within its own being*.

As I proceeded through life, I discovered and utilized various means to delve inward. Into my early thirties, I learned that, through self-hypnosis and other techniques, I could locate specific inner elements within my mindset that were leading to problems in life – ill health, failure, bad relationships. When I changed them, real life improved as a consequence. I was clearly connected to all things – *attracting* adverse situations based on negating inner mechanisms, not simply a victim of ill-bearing external forces and sources.

For years, then, I continued to delve inward to solve real-life problems, always finding negative personal features rooted within my deeper psyche, my subconscious. When I changed those inner, underlying elements, the revision always brought improvement in real life as it subsequently unfolded.

Along the way, I also scoured my mindset of all the old beliefs and definitions that I'd picked up during childhood that projected creative power outward – to gods, forces, other people, the government, bacteria and virus, conditions, etc. These notions, every one of them, distort perception.

What resulted from that decades-long inner journey were two things: a life that worked right – health, enjoyment, adventure, success – and what I call *"Clear Awareness"*. That means a peaceful but creative and engaging point of view, rid of old, flawed beliefs and definitions – fully aware of the Oneness of things.

That, then, is *enlightenment* – but without any taint of old traditions and leftover notions influenced by Eastern notions or Christian distortion. I recognize, fully and clearly, the overarching essence of Consciousness and its continuity beyond death. And see the grand journey we all are on through many lifetimes and across limitless time and space.

From this vantage point, seeing how life looked at each step along the way and noting the perception expressed by others, I would regard my present extent of perceptivity as super enlightenment. My books (*The Essence of Reality, The Psyche Exposed, The Illusion of "Truth"* and this one), my website and my YouTube channel all share perspectives meant to help others gain this level of awareness.

It isn't a bliss-laced, continuous high, blind to mankind's conflict, brutality and pain. But it does include deep inner peace that only allows for *personal engagement* of peaceful encounter. It doesn't preclude empathy for other people's major physical or emotional maladies, but it does allow the perspective that such negatives are a process of growth for the experiencing individual. It isn't a wide-eyed, goody-goody, hugs and kisses for all New-Age idealism, but it does include an extremely positive outlook for those open-minded enough to undertake the inner journey toward enlightenment...

Now, in terms of "super enlightenment", as per the question, it is a matter of degree. I gained some extent of enlightenment suddenly, curing my mystic experience. But over years of inner cleansing, I honed that clarity of vision to a degree that few seem to reach – at least insofar as I've seen in indications of other visionaries' viewpoints.

So, I would explain that the term you question refers to an absolutely clear recognition of the Oneness of all things, of Self with Reality, of life flowing in terms of meaning from within outward...

E9a – I enjoy your perceptions... and your clarity... and sense that we have shared many similar life experiences and perceptions, but I'm somewhat confused on your perceptions about "definitions".

I sense some possible ambivalence to what you say. What I mean to say is... you seem to shun and deflect notions that you "define" and offer definitions to any of your perceptions. But is it not the case that the very use of language is the use of words that all have definitions and when together to communicate perceptions we "ipso-facto" are "defining" what we are communicating?

I understand that our definitions of similar words, concepts, and meanings may all differ to a slight or great degree, but that is the reality and limitation of using language to communicate. I find language frustrating and constantly intend to make my perceptions clearer but I accept those limitations and just go on. What do you say?

Reality is a cohesive, undivided Singularity, a Oneness. Language cuts that undivided field into portions, creating synthetic boundaries through the definitions carried by words. These boundaries artificially separate one *thing* from everything else which is supposedly not that thing.

So the words I use to communicate certainly carry their inherent definitions. And, since my understanding of a word and its use will differ somewhat from how somebody else perceives it, then yes, there is a limitation to clarity in depicting anything to others.

But my gesture to overcome that limitation is to not offer a philosophical paradigm and try to prove it. What I communicate is a view of reality meant to dispel old paradigms, old beliefs, old ways of thinking that distort the perception of the reader. My purpose is to help the sincere seeker to perceive reality for him-/herself, not to convince that person of my own ideas.

In that regard, I offer no unique definitions beyond common understanding of English usage in this period.

If I were to describe Kundalini or chakra points, for example, I would have to define those terms, probably in rather esoteric depictions. If I put forth a God of some sort, I would have to indicate in some fashion its characteristics, its power, what somebody would have to do to relate to that god, etc. All that is definition for the proposed God model.

If I tell you reality consists of particles that interact in certain ways, then I need to define them, describe them, explain the rules that govern them, lay out boundaries for what constitutes a particle and separates it from other such units.

But I don't do any of those things, because reality doesn't work like ANY of those defined schemes. Reality is a Singularity; the reality you encounter – the events and relationships of your life in terms of their experienced value – reflects the composite inner state of your mind content. That is not a model, a paradigm that requires definition – it is an observation that becomes clear when you come to perceive life *without* any paradigm to distort your view.

So there is no real ambivalence to my message. I have to use words to communicate with you. But rather than describing a system and trying to convince you of it, I provide some guidelines as to how the mind works, some pinpoint notation as to how common ideas are false, some techniques to delve inward – then I tell the reader to clear away his/her old beliefs and use the techniques to see clearly for him-/herself just how life works in reflection of the inner Self…

E9b – Response: ... you are right to admonish on your first page (although I have read your entire EoR a few times) not to blame anyone for whatever happens in our lives... but I hope you are just speaking to the "adult" in all of us. I perceive that children do not have the capacity and life experience to take on that perception. I don't blame my parents for teaching me some life debilitating lessons... but I do hold them responsible as the main givers-of-the-mind-garbage!

One essential, life enhancing discovery was the realization that they (parents) confused the heck out of me about "what is love and what is hate". What robbed me most of obtaining clear childhood awareness – and which resulted in later adult, self-sabotaging behaviors – was their use of verbal and physical abuse mixed with loving words and a good dinner. I cannot tell you how essential that realization is to my perceptions for clear awareness. Do you have any moments of realization that stand out to you?

Your parents were incapable of passing anything along to you beyond the scope of their own individual awareness – or outside the scope of your own innate values.

Effectively, you enter a life with a value set that fits into the framework of the environment. In effect, your own nature attracts the format of the incarnation: whatever your parents' nature was, you attracted that as the meaningful layout of your life. You exist as a child, as a teenager, as a young adult, on into middle age, etc., with a value set that creates and is reflected in the events and relationships you encounter. Blaming negative events on your parents – and holding a grudge or other negative feelings towards them on that account – effectively projects your own qualities *onto an external source,* along with the power to change it.

Parental treatment and training must be seen as features that reflect your own nature, be that of a painful or powerless nature.

It is of value to recognize those parental effects so that you can jettison them, dispel them, and rid yourself of the negativity. But it only promulgates the negativity to remain fixed on the painful events perpetrated in deed by parents or anybody else. I understand the abuse mixed with love and dinner; it is all too common in our culture with our heritage of conflict, power and control. But when you see it clearly, dump it – don't hang on, and don't blame somebody else.

It wasn't your parents who were the culprits, but you yourself who attracted negative treatment by your own inner conflict and struggle. Those mechanisms, held within your own mindset, are what need attention, clarification and removal…

Moments of realization? Many! I had to work through many such values. But forgiveness is the final quality that leaves painful memories in the dust of the past. You will see that the pain and abuse, when perceived and released, are valuable means of moving up the ladder. Holding on to such memories with bitterness blocks such growth. And assigning blame or holding a grudge affixes power to the parent and the memory, thus maintaining the negative within the subconscious.

Q10 – Do we control our thoughts or do our thoughts control us?

Both and Neither. We try to control our thoughts, but can't, really. Thoughts, you see, are ***results***; they are *consequences* of deeper essence, of qualitative elements held in the greater mindset: thoughts, singularly and in passing, don't determine outcomes. They influence life's flow only when applied in a certain, focused fashion, as pointed out here now and again (e.g., Q8).

To grasp the gist of how the mind works, you need to look beyond standard thinking – able to question some of our invalid, but commonly shared, notions as to what we are.

The full scope of your consciousness includes not only the rational, calculating ego-self that most people commonly think of, but a vast, comprehensive subconscious. This deeper part of mind stores *all* of your memories, learned knowledge and a broad array of impressions you've been accruing since birth. It holds a huge assortment of interrelated conclusions, beliefs and definitions, many of which are likely false, others incompatible with each other – but that doesn't matter to the subconscious.

For the Self to *think* and negotiate its way through daily encounters, it has to draw continually from the subconscious – not only for information, but for making sense of what is being encountered. Indeed, all of experienced reality is sifted through subconscious belief systems to make sense of it: two people, hosting different beliefs, will interpret the same happening with widely divergent meaning attached.

Most of the mind's dip into the subconscious is unnoticed – you simply access memory, filtering things through your belief structure *very quickly*, registering impressions and formulating thoughts into language as a natural gesture. Thoughts, then, are small particles of mentally-held meaning that rely fully on subconscious material – stores of underlying information and structured beliefs. They bubble up to conscious attention, sometimes when elicited for a purpose – but often thoughts just come to mind for no purpose connected to the present situation.

In *that* case, you might think that thoughts are "controlling" you, in that they spring to mind out of context and can interfere with what you're doing. Alternately, though, the conscious Self can control the focus, initiating thoughts simply by concentrating on a specific topic and blocking out extraneous thinking. But then thoughts can intervene, sneaking into focus as well, *seeming to* control the situation by popping into mind without being elicited.

Who, then, is in charge? You, the Self, placing focus on your preferred point of interest? Or thoughts, springing into mind, seemingly at random? In reality, the total Self – the whole of the conscious Self which you are – contains a much more complex, operative, interactive mind than you generally consider or are aware of, with great amounts of information and background understanding in play at all times.

So, neither do you have full control over thoughts (or even the thinking process), nor they over "you". That's because your beliefs and accepted definitions – which often include invalid notions (like religion, an objective reality, luck, etc.) that you accumulated since childhood – strongly influence both. In general, you learned that you are separate and apart from the reality you encounter, such that you have to manipulate it to get things to work right, to fulfill your intent. Thus, many of your spontaneous, invasive thoughts have to do with what actions you would need to take just to maintain modern living.

So, thoughts often emerge without being elicited, based on complex elements you absorbed into your belief structures since childhood.

In effect, ***YOU*** are the totality of your conscious ego-Self *AND* your exhaustive subconscious (and much more, actually). You direct some thought processes; others kick off spontaneously based on the overall content of your psyche. But the most accurate answer to your question is: **Neither!**

The mind is far more complex and interwoven than you consider if you haven't looked deeply into it. Thoughts that emerge brew out of components of your total mindset. They control you only to the extent that you fail to recognize your total conscious capacity. And you only *seem* to need to control them – but again, only to the degree of your limited awareness of the comprehensive scope of your subconscious as part of your total Self.

Once aware of your mind's depth and connection to all things as an interactive Oneness, you see your thoughts as reflective of the complex nature which you are.

We'll return to a direct regard for Consciousness; but let's first shift to a specific topic that invariably interferes with direct awareness of How Life Works. We'll consider how the mind can supplant direct perception of the reality in which it finds itself embedded with a wholly concocted, fully insubstantial set of ideas – merely because those ideas were presented early on in life, and reinforced by cultural influences...

Consideration: A First Look at RELIGION

The mind is easily – extraordinarily easily – deceived by the beliefs it holds as true. In gauging and making basic sense out of the Reality it encounters, the psyche interprets daily encounters through its complex structure of declarations and conclusions it had built up from earliest experience.

Thus – in a profound observation that will be reiterated on occasion through the various answers I put forth here – any set of beliefs will appear true to the mind closed in on its own beliefs.

A key attribute to the mind that sincerely seeks to understand its own nature and inherent ties to experienced reality is *the ability to question its own beliefs* – to examine beliefs often held since absorbed during the naïve learning stage of childhood and discard them when they are shown to be false.

Here are various questions I addressed that look at religion…

Q11 – Is one particular religion the one true religion?

The one and only "true" religion is the **one you personally hold**. At least, that's how it will appear to you. The mind wraps itself around its accepted set of beliefs and definitions, such that – *no matter what they are* – they seem to be true. Here's how it works:

From birth through toddling, childhood into teenage maturity, you absorb the prevailing beliefs and definitions common to your culture, inflicted principally by your parents, later reinforced by other like-minded relatives and neighbors. This includes pre-defined religions, but also incorporates common behavioral standards. It involves stated ideas, myth and lore, but also blends in societal roles and honored positions, rites of passage and such.

By the time you reach those teen years, unless you are particularly open-minded and questioning, you will have formed a rigid "Belief Structure". Once that's in place, you will interpret real experience *by comparison to* your solidified world view – filtering phenomena that fit your expectations for acceptance, ignoring or disbelieving things that don't. By then, to a large degree, your beliefs will have become invisible as such – they will simply be your confirmed basis of understanding the world and your role in it, background standards you hold to be true.

But that's the case regardless of your particular set of beliefs. It's the case even if your beliefs are self-contradictory or rationally absurd. The mind is simply fooled by its own held tenets, such that they always become confirmed and endorsed by experience.

That, of course, is why differing cultures have traditionally been intolerant to neighboring peoples. By far, most humans can't understand that the world looks different when viewed through the lenses of an alternate belief system. Not able to recognize this differentiation of understanding based on held beliefs, many groups throughout history have alienated neighbors, even launched wars against each other simply based on differing beliefs – principal among which are religious constructions.

All religions are concocted; most evolve, rooted in the archaic past, in times of superstition and rampant fear. As mere ideas, they alter themselves through time, becoming reinterpreted as customs evolve – and they vary regionally, based on alternate notions favored by local leaders. Indeed, all religions vary slightly from person to person. (In that regard, for example, there really is no "Christianity" per se, but rather 2 billion variations of standard conjectural themes held in believers' minds.)

In any case, they are all based on **belief**. And beliefs are nothing more than *artificial mental constructs* – no more than declarations or definitions accepted as true. Mostly, they have, at best, a vague and distorted relation to reality. At worst, they set up completely artificial notions that have *no relation to reality whatsoever*.

But they will still seem true to the believer, who unwittingly judges reality's function by comparison to held beliefs.

The only way to grow beyond this level of adherence to synthetic notions is, first, to recognize that *whatever you believe in will appear to be true* – and allow yourself to question your own convictions. Second, begin to focus on those held beliefs, sorting through them with concentration – and consciously release them, one at a time. If you can't question your own held beliefs, you'll face repeated illusory effects instigated by them throughout your life, rife with negative effects on health, relationship quality or success.

If you question them, but don't change – the result is the same: *the subconscious holds its stored definitions in a timeless structure. It won't change until you change it* – and that takes some repetition, as the subconscious was likely strongly programmed during those early, formative years.

In any case, to answer your question, the one true religion – to your current judgment – is the one you hold. The only way to see clearly the nature of the conscious Self is to jettison all beliefs and definitions you hold. When you do that, reality and your place, integrated within it, look a lot different than they did when you believed old, myth-based declarations fomented by religious adherents.

Q12 – Do you believe young students should be required to take a course on world religions?

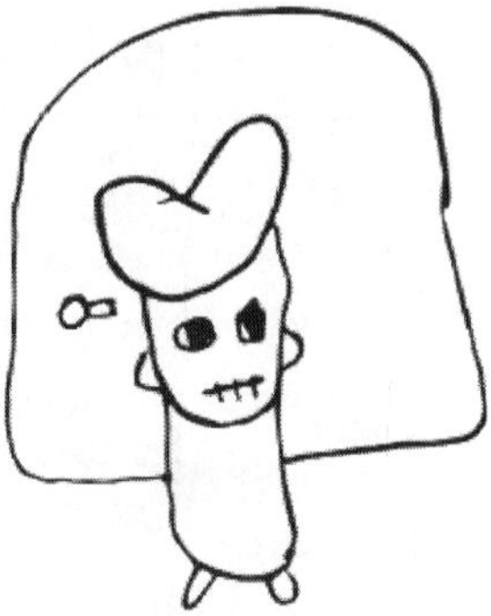

Generally, it isn't a bad thing to be well-versed in various religions. However, by "well-versed", I mean being aware of all of the shortcomings of each of the religions – not just have them reinforced by politically correct reverence to tenets that are clearly, obviously false when examined with reasoned evaluation. A course that just parrots the often silly, usually fallacious claims of each religion is worthless.

No, it's worse than worthless. It's damaging to people's psyches and lives. And the tendency in an academic environment to attribute respect and time-honored dignity to primitive, nonfunctional ideas increases that damage.

Christianity, for example, relies on a set of unfounded declarations for its orthodoxy, its basic doctrine. It views its scriptures as having been prompted – if not directly provided – by a god and are generally not to be questioned. However, the Old Testament is full of brutal treatment of ancient tribes, rape and pomp. It puts forward pure myth, accrued over centuries of oral distortion as though it is real history and was compiled accurately and recorded truthfully.

What the Old Testament consists of are archaic notions accumulated over many generations of differing conditions and political realities, revised all along the way to fit current trends and filled with exaggeration and storytelling as though it were true.

The New Testament is highly flawed as well, but in other ways: its authors (outside of eight letters by Paul) are unknown – with names attached that aren't valid to try to look credible. It is full of contradictions, absurd inventions, impossible reports (no way for the author to know what was happening in remote locations), exaggerations and aggrandized myth.

If *that* would be taught in a course – looking at the Bible for what it is (an interesting cultural icon preserving archaic thinking, man's superstitious ancestry and parables by Jesus that have some value – though not what is claimed by churches) and including an objective evaluation of how its tenets evolved from early oral traditions – it would be very helpful to really educate students.

And that would be a highly beneficial course as a requirement for a useful education – and a promotion for opening minds to sincere exploration of reality.

However, the chances of any institution including controversial criticism of Christianity would be next to zero. No higher institution would want to offend any true believing grads who might then not want to donate to their alma mater.

Conclusion: No. It is much better to simply avoid religion as an academic focus and leave it to churches to pander their ancient thinking to dupes incapable of seeing through their ancient ruse.

Q13 – Why are the Abrahamic religions of Judaism, Christianity, and Islam so stringent about monotheism?

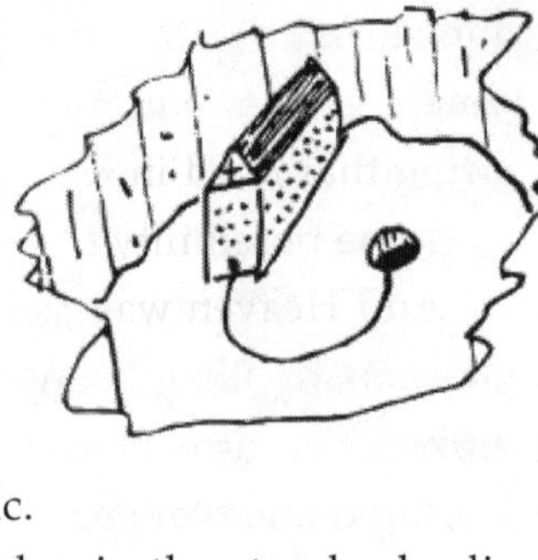

Actually, they all *talk* about being monotheism, but none of the Abrahamic traditions are really monotheistic.

The original Hebrew god was ***El***, who, in the standard religion of the Canaanites out of which the Hebrews emerged, was head of a pantheon of gods with Asherah as his consort. The names Israel (reference to tribal group, name meaning "may El persevere"), Bethel (border settlement in ancient times, name meaning "House of El"), Gabriel (imagined angel, name: "El is my strength") and Michael (archangel, name means: "Who is like El?") were all rooted in worship of El, as can be seen in their original meaning.

If you look up Deuteronomy 32:8–9, though, you'll see where El, the Most High, hands Yahweh a particular portion of people. At least you would if you were looking at pre-English versions of the Old Testament. In the Bible, scholars translate any reference to any god, be it the Canaanite El, Yahweh, Alaha (Jesus' deity reference in Aramaic) or Theou (Paul's deity as named in Greek) into the English name, "God" – even though these gods differ considerably in attributes.

Eventually the god named Yahweh became the god promoted by Moses and only much later did monotheistic notions get retrofit onto older scriptures, traditions and shared notions of gods.

In any case, originally the Israelites were not monotheists. Think of it this way. Genesis 1:27 claims God (actually, El, not the Christian notion of god with the capital "G") "created mankind in his own image." What good would a penis be for a single god – with no female consort to mate with, no need to urinate. Indeed, what good are legs and arms and such? This statement emerges from a group of people who imagined a big, physical being that lived in Heaven along with other gods, consorts and even the possibility of mating with a human.

And Heaven wasn't the other-dimension realm imagined today by Christians. In ancient times, Heaven was imagined to be above the "firmament", which was – in their primitive minds – a big dome that spanned the flat earth and held up the waters above. (Genesis 1:6 of the King James version: "And God said, let there be a firmament in the midst of the waters, and let it divide the waters from the waters…")

In recent years, more modern translations eliminate the word "firmament" because it doesn't exist and that word shows how utterly primitive the world view was three thousand years ago.

In any case, the ancient Hebrews believed in many gods – big beings that looked like people. Judaism was only transposed into a pseudo-monotheism much later in its evolution. But the human-looking, bearded image still occupies the unquestioning mind of most believers, I suspect.

Christianity's capital "G" god never really appears in the Bible. Oh, you see "God" and "Lord" all through the English version. But Biblical texts were derived from original Greek documents (New Testament) and Hebrew Old Testament roots. All of those name *other* gods (see above) – none of which are pictured in Biblical accounts or were originally imagined by ancient people as the Christian other-dimensional being of modern times.

In any case, Christianity allots creative power not only to its deity, but to God's opponent, Satan – making at least a second god they believe in. And Catholics attribute powers to Mary and other saints – adding more to the list. And add to that list Jesus and the Holy Spirit as other godlike entities, elevated to coequals in the Trinity, invented by Tertullian and others from the second through fourth centuries.

Christianity is thus *far* from monotheistic.

Islam's Allah is rooted in pre-Mohammed deities, too – "Il", principally, but that ancient god is pretty much akin to good old *"El"*. And we're back where we started. In the Koran, you find plural grammatical references to *the gods* – much like the plural forms in Biblical "Elohim" references. So much for monotheism in Islam.

The important point is, though, that none, not one, not one single solitary deity of these named gods exists – or ever did. The mind, human cognizance, is very easily deceived by its own held beliefs. Gods, any of the 2500 or so gods invented over time and concocted by various cultures, seem to be real ***because*** people believe in them.

So, to answer this question, the Abrahamic religions like to pretend they are monotheistic **because they were taught that that idea is right**. And few believers in any of these faiths have the open-minded wherewithal to question old teachings they were indoctrinated with as children – however banal and unworkable they are in reality. Ones that do, dump the religion.

E14 – Having read a bit of EoR I'm left with the impression that you are strongly opposed to religion. Although your points are well made, they come across rather strongly, perhaps a bit combative even. Is this your intent?

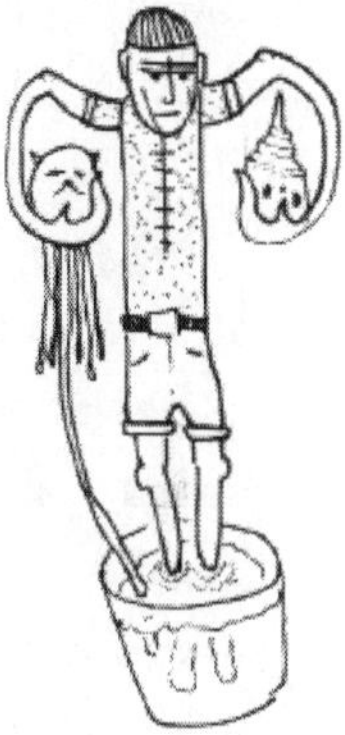

I derive my world view from extensively delving into my own inner nature and coming to relate it precisely to outer experience. This decades-long venture provides insight well beyond common ideas as to life's nature and process.

Thus, I'm not really *"opposed"* to any set of precepts. Each of the 7 billion people hereabouts hosts a unique set of beliefs and understandings. I see little value in *opposing* any of these. The intent of my message is never to debate any philosophy or religion, because each of them is an artificial, mental construct, a description, a model. The gist here is, rather, that one must become directly, immediately aware of reality to clearly perceive the nature and function of this forum – and clinging to a model only inhibits that direct, immediate awareness.

In terms of traditional religion, though, suppose I have a magnificent tree in my front yard that has provided shade and shelter for many years. But then the tree dies. That's natural, of course, as nothing lives indefinitely. Based on the value it served for so many years, sheltering my father and his before him, buffering the wind and snow – should I just leave it there as a dead monument to the past?

Of course not! I would cut it down immediately, let the

light through and new things grow. Religion is like that dead tree – it has served man for a thousand generations, but we are outgrowing those archaic impressions left from ideas conjured in myth and superstitious impression of the distant past.

One religion or another dominates the reasoning and world view of the vast majority of this time period. Lacking awareness of their innate tie to the external world, people tend to hold a default mental blame for life's issues, personal or collective, which they project outwards toward a god, luck or fate.

This projection, in itself, destroys their own personal power to create and enjoy their lives. Thus, if I seem to hit hard at the fallacies of religion, it is not because I "oppose it", but because religion – any and every single one in existence – is an invalid paradigm, and is extremely damaging to the integrity of everybody who clings to it.

You might say, I don't really oppose ideas, religious, scientific or otherwise philosophical – nor do I oppose people holding those ideas. But when the ideas are false, are rooted in superstition and myth, and are detrimental to each individual and, thus, to mankind in general, I do feel the need to expose them as false. And I've found that, when one wants to render popular, widespread ideas as less than valid, one had better do so as expressively as possible.

Q15 – Do Muslims and Christians believe in the same God?

No, certainly not. First and foremost: no god ever existed – except in the imagination of those who might believe in him, her or it. 2500 or so gods have been conjured up by humans over time. Not a single one of them ever existed – not one, not ever!

But they all were deemed real by believers.

This is because the mind is easily duped by its held beliefs, whatever they are. Taught from childhood that there's an invisible deity out there somewhere, making things happen – and with the ability to punish you now or after death – most people lack the wherewithal necessary to question those childhood-indoctrinated "truths" they were taught.

So, first you have to see both Christian and Muslim creator gods as concocted, invented mind images – which is what they are. Not only don't they exist, but couldn't possibly exist as depicted in the archaic descriptions put forth in the "holy" scriptures that depict them.

The Christian God is a full amalgamation of four earlier deities:

- **El**, Abraham's sort of personal god, fairly common in Canaan four millennia ago, mostly attached to Asherah as its consort.
- **Yahweh**, a later introduction from around the time of Moses. This was a grand (if incompetent) war god who was thought to protect the Hebrew people from other tribes and other gods (but never did or could, owing to the fact that he never really existed).
- **Alaha** or **Elaha**, the loving, forgiving deity pictured by Jesus (name in original Aramaic).
- **Theou**, the Greek name of Paul's imagined deity – the one who will arrive any day now to save believers from something or other. (He never did show up, also owing to never having existed, either.)

These are all different gods, given different names by different people in different times. They are all lumped together in Christian minds as **"God"** with the capital "G" – even though they are different in imagined nature, etc.

Allah simply means "the god", with other implications. It stems from ancient times, too, with Mohammed picking him out of a long list of gods from the pantheon of his time – and declaring him to be the omnipotent, single deity. Pictured in the Koran, sometimes referred to in the plural, with extremely vindictive, shallow characteristics, it is totally impossible that an entity of this primitive nature could create a universe of billions of galaxies, tens of billions of light years across.

That gets us back to the main point: *whatever you believe in seems to be true.* Only fully indoctrinated as a child – or being a real dupe – could you imagine any of these gods to actually exist as pictured in ancient accounts. But you only need to consider that the people who first fomented these god-notions were extremely superstitious, primitive thinkers to realize how the ideas originated.

They – the notions of deities, not the gods themselves – continue through generations principally by early indoctrination of naïve children into the fantasy world of the religions that hold these deities.

The answer to your question is, **NO**: they are different gods because they are fantasized with different characteristics. Indeed, each of them is imagined slightly differently in the deluded mind of each believer. So there are probably three and a half billion gods to question, those in the fantasies of all Christian and Muslim believers, not just two.

Q16 – Is the Middle East "doomed" to political instability?

The problem, the core to political instability in the Middle East, is ***RELIGION***. All the other issues there – artificial borders, large and disenfranchised youth population, wealth inequality, etc. – ride the core issue of *religion* like a petulant Arabian horse.

But they do so in subtle ways – not just the overt tenets of Islam that proscribe violence against nonbelievers, mistreatment of women, etc.

In general, modern man fails to grasp the innate connection between Self and experienced reality – an inner-outer connection wherein we each attract repeated patterns that reflect our own nature. Most humans are fully deluded by their held beliefs as to how life works – with religions and science being the most dominant, yet most illusory, factors in the mindset of most.

Despite widespread belief, no god hovers out there making things happen to you – nor do external forces and sources dictate your life flow, as science would indicate. Luck and fate, fortune and chance are also common but equally illusory mechanisms.

You are personally, invariably and innately tied in with the quality of reality you experience: you attract those patterns. If you hold conflict within, you'll attract conflictual relationships. If you harbor fear in your self-image, you'll experience real insecurity – financial, social or personally threatening. If you prize character, fortitude and strength as human traits, you'll build struggle into your life to realize your values.

The Middle East is rife with Islam – it dominates the population and their collective mindset. This primitive view not only infuses believers with a nonexistent deity, but promotes *submission* to that archaic god. That trait, built solidly into the mindset of people across the region, results in *powerlessness* – personal insignificance and denigration of personal worth in comparison to the grand and glorious (yet nonexistent) deity. The accompanying vigor in spreading these banal ideas to the rest of mankind has shared the negative traits widely – and deeply.

Conflict and fear, held among the populace, will infuse itself into mass events. There is no other possibility: *you can't have a healthy forest full of sick trees!*

Mix into the picture the homeland of Judaism and the birthplace of Christianity – all similarly transfixed with inner conflict, owing to belief in nonexistent deities, and vigor, based on cornerstone beliefs in the need to spread their archaic thinking to others. Add in the tendency to *blame* others for problems, as, filled with conflict, people personally and collectively attract contentious engagement – and, poof! You have conflict dominating life from a personal level, through regional to international.

So yes, indeed, the Middle East is indeed *"doomed"* to political instability, as the question poses, until it gives up Islam and its precursor superstitions, including Judaism and Christianity.

Given all indications, that will take a while! But hey, they've been at it for what, two or three millennia already? Maybe they'll eventually wise up.

Europe, by comparison, lived in widespread conflict and periodic war for centuries. Does it come as any surprise that European peace has settled in along with the waning of Christianity? Islam and the Middle East are like that. It's just tougher to shed Islam when the remedy for anybody to leave is to kill the apostate.

But that alone should indicate the depth of conflict and fear within the belief – and the guarantee of political instability among Muslims in cultures which that religion dominates.

Q17 – Christians: Are you prepared for the Great Tribulation? I am not 100% sure when the Rapture will occur. However, we must always be prepared that during the Great Tribulation we will be persecuted and must be ready to give up our lives to defend and serve God. Many Christians aren't informed about the End Times and many will sadly be unprepared.

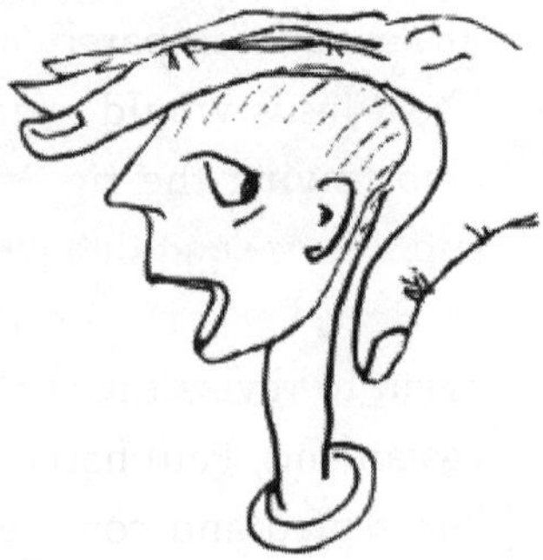

Most Christians aren't very well informed about much of anything pertaining to reality. You do understand that the notion of Jesus as the "Christ" was initiated by Paul a couple decades after Jesus' death. Based on his experience on the way to Damascus, where he heard a voice coming from the sky, he concluded that Jesus would return to institute a heavenly existence on earth.

That was core to his message and became a critical piece to Christian orthodoxy. The term "Christ" was originally a Greek translation of *Messiah* – the savior from oppressive enemies the Jews had been seeking for centuries (and still are, apparently). Paul turned the term into a superhero type, one who would return in physical form to judge or save mankind – or something like that.

In Paul's time, you should be aware, people had a different view of the earth than we do. People then, including Paul, thought the earth was a flat surface of rock and soil under which there were waters (made sense, since you could drill wells) and over which was a great dome, called the "firmament". Above that dome was water, too. Rain happened when angels or somebody opened gates and let out some of the water.

And above that was Heaven. In their minds, Heaven was a real place. And Yahweh, the god Paul and other Jews believed in then, was a real, physical entity – big, powerful and tangible.

So Paul prepared his followers for the soon-to-come time when Jesus would return with heavenly host to cull out mankind, saving the righteous and rendering evil-doers to Hell – and thus make things better.

However, that didn't happen in short order. So Paul had to begin to revise the story. In his letters (now books of the New Testament), Paul had to reassure congregations where he'd earlier visited and convinced them of his fantasy that, well, even though that "Rapture" hadn't happened, it surely would *very soon...*

Here we are, 2000 years later (give or take a few years), and *it still hasn't happened.* Somewhere along the way, the firmament disappeared when it became apparent there wasn't a large dome up there, but just an atmosphere – and infinite space beyond it. That is no "Heaven". Along the way, too, Yahweh turned into God (in English, the generic term of a deity, but equipped with a capital "G"). He stopped being a big, fearful, tangible being living above the waters above the firmament. He became an all-knowing, all-seeing creator god who exists in some other dimension, unseen, undetectable. But, be assured, he (oops, "He", as followers capitalize it) exists!

So, no longer is God actually expected to come down in physical form to weed out the bad guys – at least in most branches of Christianity. But the "Rapture" idea persists in some.

If you want to be 100% sure of when that judgment and rendering will take place, here's when: **NOW**. But not exactly as imagined by the traditional Christian believer – and only if you understand how life actually works...

Jesus, who was a visionary of high perceptiveness before Paul turned him into myth, explained that the Kingdom of Heaven isn't out there somewhere – it isn't a future event or geographical location. In Luke 17:20–21, Jesus explains: "The Kingdom of God is within you." Thomas, verse 51, reiterates: "That which you are awaiting has come, but you don't recognize it." Mark 9:1 reports that Jesus said: "Some who are standing here will not taste death before they see that the Kingdom of God has come..."

The Gospel of Thomas, too, in verse 113: Disciples ask on what day the Kingdom will come. Jesus: "It won't come by watching for it. It won't be said, 'Look, here!' or 'Look, there!' Rather the Kingdom is spread out upon the earth and people don't see it."

Jesus was clearly, unmistakably talking about a present moment – a state of mind. He illustrated that repeatedly in his parables. The meaning behind Jesus' message can only be about a Now moment – not a future, spectacular, otherworldly event. That notion was Paul's invention.

Your choice is to believe what Jesus was saying about a Kingdom ***within***, manifesting now in your experience, or what Paul was speculating on: an imagined Kingdom to come in some future time.

The disciples, Paul, dozens of popes, untold thousands of preachers and millions of subsequent followers miss Jesus' simple illustration of that *Kingdom within*. Yet, it's all right there in Jesus' direct comment.

Basically, religion – any one of them you can find on earth – is not a ticket to enlightenment, but rather, if held by the individual, a firm barrier for that person's growth in awareness of what really exists here.

We will return to points about religion later on, a look at specific doctrines, organizations, etc. But for now, let's regard one's personal pathway away from fixed, defined belief sets like religion – and toward greater awareness. Over the years I've engaged many questions about the journey towards enlightenment…

Attentive: Undertaking One's PERSONAL JOURNEY

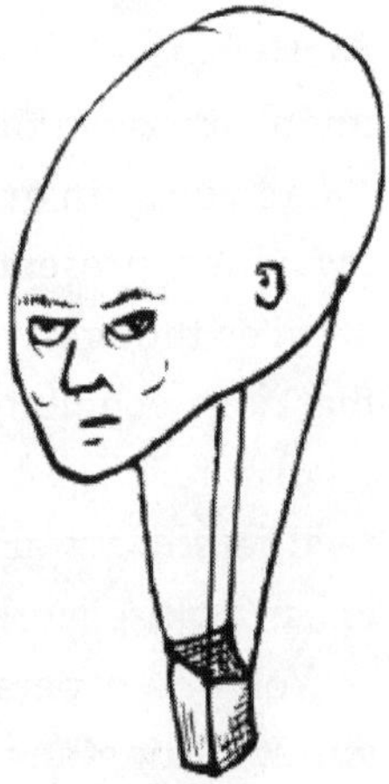

Moving from standard thinking and common, shared–but fallacious–understanding of life's function to a Clear Awareness of the Oneness of Self with experienced Reality absolutely requires change in beliefs and definitions, as well as their underlying assumptions. And that task – the basic reprogramming of the subconscious – necessitates something of a cognitive journey, an unhindered regard for other ideas, a jettison of ones now recognized as flawed.

My previous books, website and readily available videos lay out specific techniques that allow direct examination of the subconscious – and extensive perspectives on how the subconscious works and relates to the rational mind, how it can be explored and changed. Given the personal intensity of the process and my unique perspectives on the task, it isn't a surprise to see the many questions I've encountered in my public exchange…

Q18 – What is enlightenment and how it can be achieved?

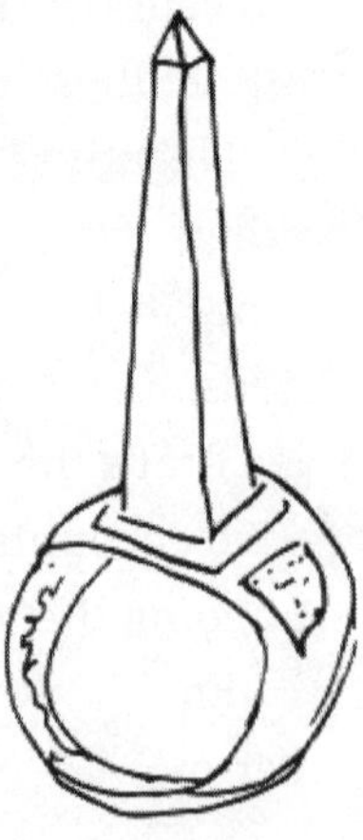

That term stands as paradoxical, given that many people who claim to be enlightened, aren't – or rather, while they may have seen through common, illusory claims, they aren't nearly as far up the mountain as they think they are.

If you've ever climbed a mountain for real, often, from a given vantage point, you see up above you what looks like the summit. But when you climb up to that level, arriving with a sense of achievement and glow of accomplishment, you see – only then – that there is yet another outcrop above that you have to surmount. Now, is that the peak – or just another step in the process? And how many more hidden bluffs might lie above that?

As you gain greater awareness, having shed some old thinking when presented with new, greater perspectives, it might seem as though you've arrived: you've attained Nirvana, gotten that elusive enlightenment that the masters of old spoke of...

But...

Life still presents mysteries, still balks at your intent, still doesn't quite work as you intend...

Your own personal life unfolds in a regular, reliable fashion. Wielding a mind clogged with traditional cultural notions, though, you are most likely not at all aware of the flow. As a conscious entity, recognize it or not, you encounter a meaningful reality that reflects your own nature: you are connected to all things, not separate and apart from ongoing events and relationships.

Stated otherwise: you attract patterns in real life. Health issues, relationship problems and failure in achieving your intent all reflect inner elements of your total mindset. There is no external causality to your unfolding life, only your own propensity to attract those repeated patterns.

Negatives you encounter – illness and injury, rejection by others, failure in undertakings large and small – always reflect inner mechanisms such as conflict, struggle, self-doubt, belief in gods, luck and illusory external forces and sources. Always...

That's the nature of your being – a Oneness of Consciousness with encountered Reality. In particular, that is the nature of your ongoing life *whether or not you are aware of it.*

Enlightenment is the process of becoming aware of that inner-outer connection. It can happen spontaneously as in mystic experience (which typically fades) or as a result of a longer process whereby you shed beliefs and definitions which mask perception. You may glimpse it as a result of a useful discipline or you may spend your life seeking it, but never get there.

Why aren't most people fully aware of their connection to all things? Most people absorb shared cultural notions while growing up – ideas woven into religion and science, into ancient folklore (luck, fortune, chance and fate) – which skew their perception. Learning that a god or bacteria, the government or parents, bad people or bad luck make negative events occur – the *very act of learning those things* as a child makes the world and life appear to function that way.

Notions you absorb growing up become registered in your timeless, deep subconscious. They remain etched there, even when you later absorb more accurate ideas – the newer perspectives simply become layered on top, bringing with them conflict insofar as they differ from your older beliefs.

Thus, a pathway toward enlightenment must include an open-minded questioning of one's favored beliefs. And moving upwards in a scale of awareness requires a significant discipline that allows the sincere seeker to approach his/her own mindset *and change it*.

There are, of course, *degrees* to which one can see clearly and traditional disciplines that lead to partial awareness. The difficulty here is that, gaining even *some* awareness of the functional (not merely ethereal or speculative) Oneness of things brings life improvement and *some* degree of inner peace. Individuals, then – indeed, many who have founded movements or specified disciplines – easily mistake a partial recognition of Oneness for the final stage.

In that regard, many stop at a lower level of awareness than they *could* attain, were they not to cease looking, having felt that they arrived at the peak.

So, enlightenment at its purest is becoming aware of the interrelated nature, the Oneness, of all things – not just accepting an idea to that effect, but clearing the mind of its plethora of beliefs and definitions that shatter the Oneness in perception.

For sure, it can be achieved through techniques like meditation, self-hypnosis, dream analysis and querying the subconscious through ideomotor responses. But it takes time, patience and dedication to scour the mind, rid it of phony beliefs and definitions – and negative programming as well.

It might be glimpsed naturally and spontaneously through a mystic experience – perhaps even through some hallucinogenic drug or other. I know about the mystic experience, but never used artificial means, i.e., substances, to simulate awareness.

The longer journey brings its own benefits: life works much better when illusory enemies and threats are dispelled and joy becomes manifest, not pain. I would only add here that whatever time you take on such an inner venture, it is well worth it. Whatever gains you achieve in this lifetime, the benefits unfold not only in this lifetime, but in other incarnations as well.

Growing in awareness is what the life format is all about…

E19a – Obviously, you have studied the perennial philosophy, Watts, Wilber, and the Gita, Vedanta, Dhammapada, probably checked out Ouspensky and Krishnamurti, Rajneesh, and all the good stuff that we have been exposed to, as have I.

Words and experience, humanity's quest for transcendence and our most basic paradoxical problem of integrating the self

into the whole and experiencing experience and all the rest never get to the ultimate truth, which is what we are, as far as I can tell, since as Watts and all of his plagiarist followers say, the eye can't see the eye...

Quoting Watts' comment, in effect, is self-defeating. Of course, you can come to perceive what you are. But accepting that reality and the self are somehow impossible to understand, and placing Watts (or any other teacher who poetically states that limitation) on a pedestal as a great authority in such matters will effectively *block your own path* toward such awareness.

I've read the teachings of some of the people you mention there, but would hasten to point out a couple things. Neither their words, nor the accounts of anybody else, were the primary vehicle that carried me to see life with clarity. That came about by coming, on my own, to delve into my mind's content and seeing how it related to the flow of events and relationships that make up my life. Reading the accounts of men such as those was helpful in a fashion, but not primary.

I had seen pictures of the Grand Canyon before I got there, seen maps of it, and read accounts about it. But these were nothing compared to being there, hiking into it, seeing, smelling, hearing it and all that. Awareness is similar in effect. It is to be attained in the encounter with life, not by accepting the descriptive accounts of individuals who may or may see with some degree of clarity.

E19b – ... and we, being it, have nowhere to go to find it. So dig the experience and don't worry be happy. OK. I am happy. I have a life. I am conscious. Cool.

So, after finding that there is nowhere to go and nothing to do and keep your mind off winter time 'cause you ain't going nowhere, we are still left with the same question that we started with when we used our equipment to find some explanation or

reason for being in the first place. Watts explained Vedanta in a cool way. God played hide and seek and forgot that he was playing. But why... why would there be a God to get bored to begin with? Oh, but, of course, there is no beginning. I know. It always was. You can't die, because you were never born, etc.

We're on this great chain of being trip back to super Atman from where we came in the first place. Right? Who knows? What's first place in a realm beyond time?

To you, as your awareness might reveal, would the best word for the whole experience be "play"? If it's "play", what's all the suffering about? To say that there is no suffering except in the minds of our race does not eradicate the actuality of it.

There isn't a "best" word; life is a very diverse experience, with each aspect containing its own inherent experiential values. In some instances, "play" might indeed apply, but you overgeneralize by lumping all of life's potential experiences into one glob and trying to categorize that glob in a single term. You would thus destroy its great complexity and thereby oversimplify the essence and destroy the innate meaning.

Of course, there is suffering, just as there is joy. Eradication of the suffering doesn't come about by ignoring it, but by finding the roots to the negative experience, each troubled individual within his/her own mindset, thus eliminating that mind-based value set – however complex it might be. Without that gesture, without that personal effort of delving inward, suffering can and will continue indefinitely within the experience of that individual – because that total mindset is what that individual consists of, in essence.

As for Atman, the Self, and ending its chain of incarnations, and all of that – I personally am not aware of what I *used to be* outside the direct vision of this lifetime. But I am intensely aware of what I am *NOW* (plus, very much cognizant of how I *got to be* intensely aware of what I am now) – and how that collection of internal values plays out in life.

If I attempt to characterize the nature of what I was many incarnations ago or what ethereal sort of consciousness I will become upon attaining some additional state of perfection, I will only recycle illusions of things outside the scope of awareness. Don't expect me to do that.

E19c – Lose to death a child or three as Verdi did by his 28th birthday and you will see that "our life is about nothing else but death", as he put it, when criticized for putting too much dying into *Il Trovatore*. In the back of all human thought is always death. We need to think to survive...

Indeed, death and loss and failure are key values to the course of one's life. But none of these, seen in the broad context of the life experience, are as critically negative as you seem to be implying. Verdi's earlier experiences, however heartrending, spurred him toward enormous, creative greatness, showing him the values implicit in life's negativity. He became in subsequent life what he couldn't have been (one might presume) without those losses.

From another angle, death is only particularly intimidating to one who holds a view of life founded on an "objective" model, a paradigm that places reality as the only framework of existence and consciousness as a chance development in that forum.

But the ocean doesn't fade away when a wave crashes on the beach; another will follow. Consciousness doesn't cease at death. Seeing that clearly nullifies the biting threat implicit in dying.

E19d – What kind of playing is this? I did not read everything you wrote... and perhaps you do get to it, but I doubt it. Isn't all philosophy nothing but a means of, hopefully, preparing us for the death of loved ones? To say don't be attached misses the human condition. How can we be human and not be attached? I know. We are not human...

You seem to anticipate my response, as though I would predictably offer some stock Eastern metaphysical conceptualization! Try not pigeonholing me as some stock, new-age, wispy-headed thinker, and you might benefit more from my words. I would also make note that, if your questions are meant to bandy about esoteric phrases without a sincere vein of trying to glean some positive growth of perspective from the queries, you are not making wise use of your time.

Of course, we are "attached" to the elements of our lives! *Of course,* we are human! But the attachment is part of the value display and the humanity is the format. I don't welcome the death of people dear to me, but such passing of them – and, one day, of me – will come as clearly and necessarily as the sun will set this evening. That is part of the unfolding of situations, the play-out of intricate values in the life display.

Trying to feign detachment as a means to buffer pain and disappointment is a fruitless gesture as well. Understanding the nature of the Self and the things and people with which that Self surrounds itself is the only means to value *attachment,* while not setting oneself up for the crush of withdrawal.

As to philosophy being nothing but a means of preparing us for the death of loved ones, some philosophies are clearly little more than that – particularly if the philosophy holds a limited view of consciousness in the first place. But philosophies are artificial, intellectual treatments that may or may not reflect some degree of clarity as to how life works.

In any case, though, recognizing the extensive scope of various philosophical disciplines, I doubt all of them or even most of them are blatantly or even subtly attempting to temper the pain of losing loved ones to death.

E19e... We just think that we are. But why? Can you put in words why intelligence puts seeds throughout the Universe to come back, after great travail, to what it was?

We live lifetimes because it places us in an immediate, intimate face-off with our own essential nature. This life format provides enormous potential for growth, but many other values as well.

Watching a thrilling movie is not nearly as invigorating as living an exciting episode in real life. That immediate engagement provides many peripheral values for a human incarnation: challenge, reward, accomplishment, victory (and even the emotional consequence of losing), creativity, child-rearing, generosity, expression, brotherhood, love, and many more.

We keep coming back, as you put it, because life is diverse, expressive, fun, challenging and intriguing. And it provides, with your life and health on the line, an engaging experience and a real opportunity to grow in awareness of your own real nature.

Q20 – Are there stages of enlightenment? Is it a process of growth? Where will it go from here?

There are indeed stages or *levels* of awareness, as you ask. But what you might consider divisions between them – some manner of boundaries you will have to "work" through to become more aware – are neither fixed nor firm, nor actually real in the sense that you are asking.

The distinguishing boundaries that basically demarcate strata of awareness (where you are, where you have been and where you might reach) consist of notions, beliefs, definitions and interconnected strands of each, such that one holds which distort perception. As each individual's psyche carries his/her own customized blend of such ideas, there aren't really *fixed* boundaries, but personal ones – each a bit different from others' mindset components.

In effect, Consciousness and Reality are *One* – two apparently separate elements of a functional Singularity. Practically all components of Western belief and world view – religion, science, notions of luck, fate and chance – sever reality by distorting perception. They conceptually set a defined self apart from the material world. Coming to see with total clarity that the Self is fully integrated with Reality: that's the ultimate of enlightenment.

On the way, though, there are many steps up the incline – such as ones of enhanced feeling, or other conceptual dispelling of former, restricted notions. Indeed, each step, each jettison of limiting idea, each accomplishment of changing inwardly to accomplish outer improvement, breaks down a personal limitation and enhances what you call enlightenment – and moves you to another stage.

But one *can't* describe "stages" one hasn't yet reached! So, answers to your initial question will vary according to the level of awareness each responding person entails.

What you describe as improvements in feeling are useful, beneficial and indicative of your own progress. But ultimately, where it will "go from here", from your current state, is *where you take "it"*.

You may bog down in fancy movements headed up by vaunted spiritual leaders. You may get enraptured by spiritual-sounding Eastern terms and fixed guru/yogic disciplines. You may reach a certain level, some distance up the mountain from where you started, and stop there – set up your own shop to attract followers and stultify your own journey by showing off your advanced level, make a bunch of money, glorify your status with a grand title, things like that.

Or you may continue until the utter, absolute connection between your own Self and the full experiential Reality you encounter is totally clear. By then your health will be full and rich – you'll never take or need medicine or vitamins, nothing artificial, nor even overtly "healthy" for the purpose of guiding bodily function. Your body will simply work right, as it reflects your inner peace/inner ease essence. You will feel great, but do so as a standard state – enjoying your accomplishments, nature, others, travel, relationships, encounters, adventures, etc. It won't be a strange high in the face of semi-pleasing encounters – but a fun, humorous, creative good feeling as your life works really well, too.

You certainly won't fear death, as you will fully, totally, without compromise recognize that your consciousness will survive death – and that you've shed, in this lifetime, a wide array of limiting notions that screwed up your mind and (consequently) your life earlier.

So, yes, there are stages to enlightenment – divisions (functional, not "real" delineation) formed by artificial notions and synthetic definitions. As you work through those mind elements – as I've laid out in my books, on my website and now in YouTube videos I'm producing – you gain awareness of your ultimate connection to all that is, the qualitative manifestation of your own nature into real events and relationships. So that, indeed, is where you can take "it" from where you are. You'll know when you get there, because, as noted, your body and life work very well without any rational intervention, manipulation or intellectual override. And you won't have to make money from others of lesser awareness by commercializing your message.

If (more likely, *when*) you can grasp my meaning, things won't be the same, as you query. But the process isn't a switch flipping. While a mystical experience can help, the real journey will require extensive introspection to discern and dispel inner limitations.

E21a – I found your words stunning, surprising, and familiar as I found myself floundering towards reconnecting with my inner self. As my perception of reality has always led me toward my requests, coming across your website was like the proverbial "seek and ye shall find". I know I will spend many hours reading and rereading your material. Thank you.

I do have a question which has always tripped me up when asked by others who find the way I perceive reality as faulty. I hold that we are all responsible for the reality we create and the choices we make in perceiving it.

Their response is "so, a baby chooses to come into the world deformed, handicapped, developmentally disabled, stillborn, etc., etc.?" "The Jews chose to be persecuted and murdered?" "A child chooses to be abused by its parents?" ... You get the gist of it. These are difficult questions to answer and I am not sure how to go about understanding these events as to make some kind of sense out of it all.

It's not unusual for people to enter into a philosophical debate on the subject. They tend to look at external evidence – hypothetical people as you list above, even real ones from a reported event – and try to argue a case based on common cultural, preconceived, and assumed values. Why would anybody want to be born developmentally disabled or handicapped?

There are actually obvious reasons why, once you come to see the interplay of Consciousness and Reality, and the vivid experience to be engaged by such a lifetime. There are many lessons to be learned by living such lives, and *no way else to learn them*.

But coming to that awareness is not possible by examining the external world. You can't look into the mind elements of those hypothetical people – or the dead ones. You can't examine the self-image of the persecuted Jew or the abused child. You can't delve into the fears and conviction of powerlessness these people hold, the projection of creative power out to "Yahweh", or the innate isolation of self held in the mindset of those individuals.

You can only examine your *own* mind content in depth. If you don't do that, or aren't willing to, you will never see the Oneness of Self with experienced Reality. You can't see it "out there", in an objective examination of the real, and you will only reinforce your old-world view by trying to cram the rich life format into a good vs. bad, black and white image, which is a pure illusion.

E21b... quoting a passage from EoR, the website, "In the greater scheme of clarity of consciousness, beliefs have no place whatsoever. So long as you harbor any beliefs, you will not perceive Reality clearly and will compromise your full being."

In grasping this above statement how can beliefs not have a purpose? I mean they must serve a purpose or how would they exist? To know the difference, one must be compared to what? Is not what you state a belief? You must believe in order not to believe? Please bear with me as I struggle with this concept.

If I hand you an advertisement for an automobile that promises great performance, shows a wonderfully polished vehicle and happy people standing around it, what do you know about that car? Actually, next to nothing. The ad is a preconceived distortion of Reality, a concocted image – not a clear depiction of *what is*.

A *belief, **any*** belief, is like that ad. It depicts and describes; but in the end, Reality is like that car. You won't know what it's like until you own and drive a real one. And you won't understand life until you see it directly and clearly – for yourself.

Beliefs are artificial depictions of some distortion of the Real.

And perception is easily fooled by such imagery, particularly when it was presented to the young, naïve mind you exposed to such explanations during your early childhood. Once you've fully accepted a belief, any belief, it will seem to be true and you will interpret subsequent perception to fit the belief's explanation. You will have bought into the advertisement.

It's not so much pondering the "purpose" beliefs serve, as to the functionality they entail and the limits they bring with them. They function by covering Reality with a screen of artificiality, a synthetic, conceptual substitute for what is real, thereby distorting its appearance in the perception of the believer.

What I present to the reader is not dependent on belief. First, I categorically state that the reader must come to see reality clearly *for himself or herself,* as it is beyond the operative realm of written text to convey. Clear Awareness is a personal experience, not a philosophical structure or theological status.

Second, my description of "what is" does not rely on belief in any conceptualized or declared external source of creative power. There is no "god", no independent consciousness making things happen in one's life, no laws governing nature. There is only a Oneness of process wherein elements of mind combine to manifest equivalent elements of experienced events and relationships. Perceiving that is a question of awareness, not a matter of accepting a new belief in it – as that mechanism is in operation at all times, regardless of the beliefs that inhibit perception of it.

E21c – Out of consciousness is self-awareness that creates reality. Do I understand this correctly? I (the Self) am an aspect of Consciousness. Somewhere along the way I (the Self) have lost the ability to be aware of this. In perceiving the world (Reality), I (the Self) externalized the essence of Consciousness into what I (the Self) see as "real", i.e., birds, trees, people; what I (the Self) feel as "real", i.e., pain, joy,

fear; so on throughout the senses.

At what point did the concept of "belief" come in to alter this reality? What happened to make us not recognize what we are? When did we lose the connection? Was "belief" introduced by Consciousness itself or was there some other mechanism that altered the "Self" in not recognizing its relationship with Consciousness and "Self's" ability to "create" Reality?

In answer to your first question, no, you apparently don't understand my words. The impression I get is that you are trying to parlay my words into a philosophy, whose conceptual pieces you are then trying to lay out verbally as a reconstruction for the purpose of eliciting my approval.

Until you come to see what you are, you will only grapple clumsily with phrases like the above – mixing time lines and looking for cause and effect, trying to lay out a philosophy that satisfies the intellect and its current world-image.

But to address your triumvirate of queries in the second paragraph, no, mankind didn't *lose* an enlightened connection to the cosmos. Our earlier ancestors of ancient to prehistoric times never had it in the first place. For certain, ages ago – two or three million years ago, maybe – our primitive Australopithecine ancestors lived within their intuitive connection to nature, as all animals do. They found food to suit their needs and thrived.

But somewhere along the way, perhaps as Homo erectus morphed into Homo sapiens, our forebears began to rely more and more on the intellect. They developed language and tools, eventually developing agriculture and smelting of metals. In all of these – the creation of religion out of myth and storytelling, settling into towns and cities, rolling conflict and competition into warfare, slavery and need to control – mankind leaned ever more on reasoned action, less and less in a personal sense on natural impulse.

Nowhere along the way, however – save for a few notably

enlightened individuals in historic times – did mankind in general or even small groups of people come to see with any degree of clarity the innate connection of Self with emerging situations in life. Practically universal was – *and is still!* – the projection of power and causality out to externalities: gods, supernatural forces, real-world sources…

So, *beliefs* slowly and subtly took over mankind's reasoning power as it developed from a pure intuitive connection to reality during early nomadic stages. And they have been passed down, ever evolving in detail and adapted fantasy as they grew from superstition to become archaic religions and later into science and philosophy into modern times.

But never did humans have "the connection", clear and common, in shared awareness. You can take my word for it that simply communicating a Clear Awareness of the Oneness of all things to even open-minded people is far from easy and straightforward.

E21d – I hope I'm not missing the point here, but it's the best rendition to what's going on in my head at this time. I expect it will change as I gain better understanding of these concepts.

The point is not in "understanding of these concepts" (and therefore, yes, you are missing it!), but in *self-perception*. In other words, don't look to my explanations for validity, but look at your own life and see how it reflects your inner realm of mind elements.

E21e – Again quoting EoR: "Clear Awareness is much more than unfettered perception. It leads to a total immersion in Reality, a state of mind and being in which events reflect the *will*, in which inner peace is always encountered in the outer experience. The individual who has grown to Clear Awareness needs no artificial rules to guide his or her life."

Does this not indicate some form of underlying structure in which the "Self" interacts with "Reality"? Does not Consciousness demand structure, form in order to perceive "Itself" through the "Self" (us)? Consciousness creates the "Self" (us) in order to experience "Reality", does it not? Are we, then, just a conduit? So, if Consciousness experiences everything through the "Self" (us), why not belief structures?

It just seems to me that it is an innate function to structure creation...

... So, how do we know unfettered perception, really? When can we say inner peace, state of mind/being that reflects "our will" is not an "illusion" of such or that we (the Self) are truly immersed in "Reality"? What truly is that "Reality"? ... Is total immersion recognition of us being an extension of Consciousness interacting with "Itself" in creating "Reality"?

How in the Hell did we get lost?

Again, with your line of questioning, you are seeking to intellectualize everything. You write of Consciousness in the third person, as though it is something else other than what you are. You deal with "us" and "we" in convoluted terms, pretty much forcing these first person, plural, terms into the third person realm.

I don't know about "we". I can only deal with "I". Again, my words aren't meant to contain a full-bodied explanation of all aspects of life, but rather convey to the reader a first-person awareness of how life works – plus providing techniques whereby the reader can see this connected nature personally. Those are two significantly different ventures.

You are trying too hard to analyze my statements. You won't find understanding or gain awareness by picking apart my explanations. You can find both, however, by coming to see how your life's events and relationships relate to your own mind content.

E21f – Again quoting EoR: "Whether labeled as New Age, Consciousness, Spiritual Development, Mystic or even Occult, the material to be found on the net can be highly beneficial to expanding your vision – if properly approached." In the sense that they are structured belief patterns?

Yes – when you are able to recognize the shortcomings as well as beneficial insights of alternative approaches, much as with religion, philosophy and science, you can grow significantly from the exposure.

E21g – How does one utilize such premises when they are based on "seeing" things a certain way in order for them to be beneficial? I must sound confused to you, but I find myself questioning everything in order to understand better this state of being that I have come more fully aware of.

If you understand from the outset that a guru is only a person with his own views and his own mindset, realizing that his words are limited to his level of perception, you can gain a lot. If you go in, dazzled by his white robes, his followers, his candles and incense, you will fall into the same conceptual trap he did, and will gain little.

There are gems of wisdom to be found in many places, but you need to be able to throw away all the surrounding shale and granite to extract the gems.

Being confused *but aware of the confusion* is a lot better state than thinking you understand everything, when you are really only firmly entrenched in an illusory philosophical world-image which you accept so fully that it seems to be absolutely true. You should question everything!

E21h – It's like touching a bubble to see if it will break. You know in your head it will, but sometimes when you do touch

it, it stays intact and mesmerizes you.

Keep touching. Most bubbles of understanding break easily. Some bubbles are tougher than others, however. But they'll break, too, eventually. At some point, you ignore the bubbles and just look beyond them...

This questioner later responded with a personal note on her subsequent experience and benefit. I responded...

I think in our search, we're always looking for something solid to grasp – some philosophy, religion, or otherwise airtight explanation that satisfies the intellect.

But in self-realization there is nothing solid to grip, because each of us is the gripper as well as grippee. Each is the totality, not the explanation, which can only cover a portion, and thus is guaranteed to be fallacious.

But the whole of *what we are*, i.e., each of us is, consists of mind elements – values, understandings, feelings, beliefs and so forth. Coming to perceive these, one begins to perceive the nature of the whole, the Self. I provide various means to delve inward in my EoR writing, but that journey, as you have noted, is up to the reader. And growth in Awareness is to be found much more in the inner journey than in my depiction of it.

Much of the Personal Journey is, of course, inward. I provide techniques to expose and explore specific content of the subconscious, allowing the individual to recognize key elements of his/her own being – and change those inner components if they lead to negative outcomes.

But a critical part of the process of growth is regarding notions commonly held or ideas put forth by others and *examining them* – revealing insight or fallacy as either is woven into the expression.

Responsive: A Glance at PHILOSOPHY

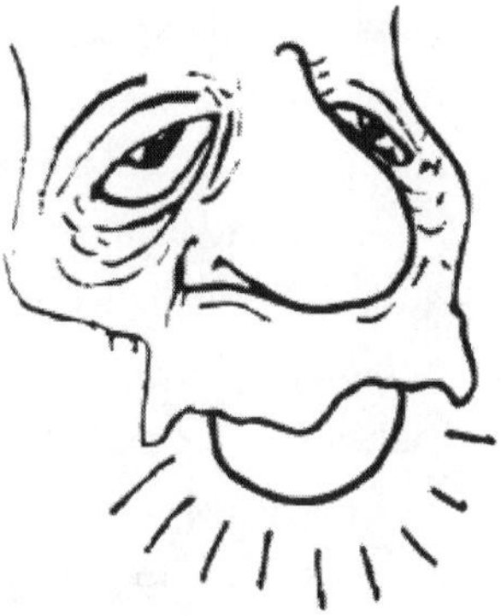

A long track of philosophical inquiry, creative thinking issued from brilliant individuals over two and a half millennia has served mankind well. Original perspectives, garnered despite rigid common thinking of the time, frequently voiced in the face of repressive opposition by religious hierarchies of contemporary cultures, have moved mankind beyond primitive notions of gods and sandbox cosmologies to an enormously more comprehensive view of reality.

However, in "modern" times, the genre of philosophy has stagnated. Entrapped and secluded in academic confines, philosophy has latched onto the scientific paradigm as undeniably valid and unquestionable.

The problem in this regard is just the same as in all common thinking: the distortion held beliefs impose on personal interpretation of reality. Where metaphysics, as a branch of philosophy that should regard the fundamental nature of reality, can look to ontology to explore and explain various categories of the real (Substance, Quantity and Quality, Relation, Place, Time, Action, etc.) it invariably gets lost in its own complex explanations.

The realm of Philosophy did, in previous centuries, spur to real advancement in mankind's very thinking. Key, innovative Philosophers literally forced a greater awareness for the nature of things from the scale of the universe's vastness down to its subatomic components. But pioneering thinking ceased a century ago. Now the realm of academic Philosophy, whether Continental or Analytic, simply bounces around the same, established ideas – principally based in objective thinking about a material universe.

But recognizing the fundamental nature of Reality – that flow of events and relationships connected in terms of meaning and value to the experiencing individual – is rendered impossible in the mind and resultant discussion of people who think they have all the answers.

Here I would regard several philosophical points, but view them from a standpoint of Clear Awareness, recognizing the personal-centric nature of Reality, unfolding in a flowing manner from within the personal mindset out into an effect, an emerging, quality-based essence that reflects the nature of the experiencing individual. I start this section with a look at my own set of significant perspectives in response to a question posed on Quora…

Q22 – What are the top 10 philosophical ideas that everyone should understand?

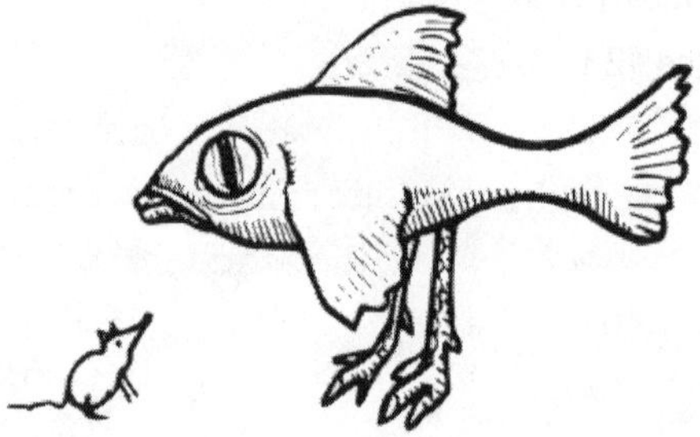

Here are *Ten Ideas* that it would behoove everybody to grasp. More than mere ideas, they are cornerstone attributes to the Reality each of us encounters daily…

1. *Whatever you believe in* ***will*** *appear to be true.* The mind interprets reality *according to* its held precepts. Thus, any set of beliefs, even ones with contradictory elements, will seem believable and even self-evident to the individual holding that belief structure.

Consequently, beliefs and definitions *do not clarify* how reality functions; they only distort perception of it.

2. *The pathway towards perceiving clearly how life works* involves deleting and dispelling old ideas and beliefs, not building up a set of fancier, more esoteric-sounding new ones. Until all shreds of definition proclaiming external causation are dispelled from the subconscious, the individual will still attribute negative events in life to outer forces and sources – and remain powerless vs. those illusory projections.

3. Consciousness and Reality are inherently connected – a *Oneness,* not a dichotomy, as implied by religion and science. In practical terms, the Self is causally connected to the flow of events and relationships it encounters, as it manifests them automatically.

4. Becoming *aware* of the Oneness of Self with experienced Reality requires #2 because of #1.

5. The conscious Self, with its highly complex subconscious storage, transcends incarnations. It engages in lifetime after lifetime for various purposes.

6. Religion – any of them in general, but absolutely the case for Christianity, Islam and Judaism – creates a set of artificial ideas and claims, projecting with self-appointed authority that they are true. The religion *seems* to be valid to believers – most of whom are indoctrinated from early childhood to believe in it, based on point #1. Religion not only doesn't describe life, *it distorts any believer's perception of reality with false precepts.*

7. Science is a synthetic paradigm, not unlike religion in many ways. It can be much more useful than religion in discerning

useful details about reality, but is also deceiving and restricting because of #1. Science only looks outward, examining reality in great detail while ignoring the inner realm. Science thus misinterprets *triggers* to events as *causes* to outcomes, blind to the inner-outer connection. (Reality, unfolding in a NOW moment, is always an effect. All causation is inner – a realization not only invisible to science, but blocked in perception by holding science as the ultimate answer.)

8. Each individual, by virtue of personal connection to experiential reality, creates patterns in life. Because standard cultural views (science, religion, luck, chance, etc.) project causation to external forces and sources, it appears in the eyes of standard Western thinking that life is driven by outside elements. However, seeing beyond common allocations of external causality, one comes to understand that life is manifested as a direct result of one's own inner nature. Because that is so, one can delve inward to find and change elements of mind that directly lead to negative events and relationships.

9. Brilliant philosophers and noted visionaries of the past added much to Western thinking, necessary to displace primitive notions of gods and spirit world being sources of real events. Some even began to perceive life's functional Oneness. But all such teachers also carried over much archaic thinking and background definitions without seeing their inherent limitations. Any serious seeker of understanding can grow to a level of much clearer awareness by not overvaluing ideas of older teachers – but rather coming to see life without the distortion of their *or any other teacher's notions*.

10. The inner mindset generates outer experience in all cases. That is, the complex subconscious, including all beliefs and definitions, hopes and fears, self-image and world view, conflict

and struggle, feelings of effectiveness and powerlessness, memories and interpretations, doubts and confidence, etc. – a highly complex mix – blends into an experienced reality whose comprehensive events and relationships comprise meaning and value fulfillment exactly reflective of the inner.

Q23 – Is logic and reason a white Christian concept?

This is a funny question, indeed, as logic predates Christianity by centuries (stemming at least from the time of Aristotle, fourth century BCE), while reason, as a tool for understanding reality, stems more from Philosophy – particularly René Descartes – around 1600. Indeed, it takes very little of either mental practice to see through the entire superficial claims of Christianity as unfounded conjecture – having nothing to do with either logic or reason.

Christianity is based on a much older form of deriving sense (or, more accurately, *nonsense*) from reality called Revelation. This practice, archaic yet common even today, implies that gods (or a single one – with no real difference outside of arithmetic) work in strange, mysterious ways. Only special people, prophets and priest-types, can see through the mystery to "reveal" truth to us dull-witted peasants and unenlightened rabble.

Religions like Christianity rely on the ignorance of masses to propagate their irrational claims and synthetic definitions. The process has gone on for millennia, as wave after wave of priesthoods, spouting different revelation, lived cushy lives passing along unfounded notions and requiring that people simply "believe" what they are told. Sometimes this requirement has been brutally enforced by the controlling priesthood. It works, though, amazingly well, principally because the mind is exceptionally gullible – it invariably confirms its own held tenets: whatever is believed in seems to be true. Thus, most people within a culture – Christianity being a prime example – grow up hearing Christian bunk and simply absorb it. Few have the open-minded bent, questioning nature and psychological wherewithal to break free of the deep-seeded religious programming. So my answer would be resoundingly: **NO**. Christianity has nothing to do with reason *or* logic except in the restricted situation that the individual doing the questioning has already bought into the core claims of orthodoxy. Then he/she can use a bastardized sort of reason and/or logic to artificially justify their foregone precepts.

Q24 – Do you need any qualifications to be a philosopher? I'm fascinated by philosophy, constantly thinking and indulging in philosophies; is this enough to make me a "philosopher" or do I need to pass some test?

If you want, seek or think you need "qualifications", you'll never be a real philosopher. You can be a philosophy *student*, a philosophy *professor* or something in that vein (or vain – or even "vane" if you can grasp my abstract meaning).

Philosophers were brilliant thinkers through the ages, people who could see beyond standard thinking and lead mankind to better understand life and the human experience. There have only been a few of them. Philosophy professors and experts, on the other hand, are well versed in *other people's* thinking – amazingly so in some instances. There are and have been thousands of them – brilliant in their own way, but incapable of formulating vision on their own. They are far too stuck in ideas initiated by other people to recognize the function of Consciousness/Reality beyond their deduced "truths".

Equate these two types (real philosopher vs. philosophy student/professor) to composers vs. performers. There are many, many wonderful pianists who can play Chopin with perfection and expression. But there was only one Chopin. Gobs of academicians argue Kant's ideas or assign meaning to Plato's Allegory of the Cave. But the originators were visionaries who could see things beyond the standard thinking of their time.

Repeating generations of philosophy students up through modern times only bandy about preset ideas, conceptualizations others initiated.

In any case, if you are fascinated with ideas, indulging in philosophy and want to explore the vast array of -isms and -ologies, set your sights on being a philosophy professor, retreating from the real world to the intellectual safety of ivy-covered walls, where you can impress people with your command of minutia concerning established (but primarily invalid and nonfunctional) ideas.

However, if you are

- Capable of seeing Reality as the flowing, fully integrated Oneness that it is, responding in the scope of each individual's life to his/her deep inner Self...
- And if you are capable of discerning the function of the subconscious in a depth beyond established theory...
- And if you have the capability of expressing your vision in understandable terms...
- And if you have the fortitude to proceed in life even though most others don't grasp your perspectives...
- And if you have added capacities or external wealth so that you needn't depend on income derived from your valuable insights...

Then you can be a ***real*** philosopher. With one, sole exception I know of, real philosophers went extinct with Wittgenstein a century ago. But in a very troubled time, there is surely an opening for such a free-thinking individual.

However, that single exception to the extinction of philosophers is, indeed, personally reluctant to look at himself as a philosopher, because the term is too limiting in scope. Indeed, he doesn't like to categorize himself at all…

Q25 – What are critiques of Kant's analysis of the mind/body problem?

Kant's shortcoming, not atypical in the realm of philosophy, was an inadequate grasp of the innate mind/body connection. Subsequently, Fichte and Hegel began to recognize the functional Oneness of things – improved upon by Schopenhauer and ultimately Nietzsche – but never quite fully perceived in the increasingly objective view of Western Philosophy. Thus, Kant's general view, fundamentally restricted by a flawed, synthetic dichotomy of existence, was doomed to flawed conclusions.

Throw in thoughts of a deity involved, over-analyzing experiential impact on the mind and primitive thoughts of a "soul" as a thing of some substance that must occupy the same space as the body, and you have a highly intellectual but inaccurate and nonfunctional description of things.

In effect, mind and body *are connected*. Real issues one faces in life, whether in health, relationships or success, always have inner components. By delving inward, one can find the explicit roots in specific mechanisms of mind and eliminate them. As life is an outer manifestation of the inner state, once inner conflict and struggle are eliminated in regards to the specific outer symptom, the problematic situation will abate. Consciousness and Reality are innately connected.

Kant not only didn't grasp this, but his otherwise convincing and influential effect on subsequent philosophers deterred rather than encouraged greater understanding of Consciousness. The issue plagues the realm of Philosophy to this day. Ideas, held as true, distort perception of Reality – and Philosophy adherents are addicted too, over-burgeoning with and fully deterred in their understanding by ideas. Indeed, in the realm of Philosophy, the more convoluted and highly argued the idea, the happier is the philosophy lover.

Awareness of Reality, of the inherent inner-outer Oneness with which Reality and Consciousness coexist, is unavoidably dimmed by one's belief structure. And Kant, as proto-typical philosopher, attempted to build understanding by developing ideas ever more logically affixed to prior notions deemed established as truth.

However, they weren't based on truth – but only on other ideas. That is, his philosophical treatise isn't reliant on and revealing of How Life Works, but only on prior statements and artificially proven "truths" that weren't.

So Kant's mind-body analyses, principally as stated in *The Critique of Pure Reason*, regardless of its vaunted place in philosophical lore, regardless of its and later argument, are mere ideas, inaccurate at that. So, the principal critique would be that Kant's view was wrong because it doesn't describe Reality.

Q26 – Epistemology: What is better, knowing or believing?

Epistemology, of course, is that focus of philosophy that explores the origin, quality and limit of human knowledge – and methods of determining that.

Knowledge, though, can be tricky, in that the senses – along with one's conclusions – can easily be and generally *are* fooled. So "knowing" is good – much better than, say, ignorance. But how can you be absolutely sure when you know something for certain, or only think you do? First-hand exposure to something doesn't guarantee foolproof knowledge about it. Hearing an explanation from someone else, even a highly regarded source, also contains no assurance of validity.

But beliefs are even worse: they *inherently* deceive because in and of themselves, they distort perception of reality.

I don't need to believe in that tree standing outside my window. I can see it, go out and touch it or measure its dimensions. It's as real as any aspect of life. Still, even sensing it reliably, there are many aspects to that tree that I may not be aware of – e.g., that it houses many species of insects, birds and squirrels, that it fits into a huge, interactive ecological system, that its leaves and seeds nourish many other life forms, that its wood may one day be used for furniture that people could continue to use for centuries, etc.

Knowledge about things is useful, then, but may not cover the whole picture – and thus set up fallacious conclusions and a resulting distorted picture of reality. Indeed, supposed knowledge can be simply wrong!

Beliefs (as I would understand the word and it is commonly used), on the other hand, are conceptualizations that have *no substantial basis* for their declaration. You can believe in God (the deity with the name beginning with a capital "G"), Allah, Vishnu, Thor, Ahura Mazda, Apollo, Quetzalcoatl or any other proclaimed god. None of them ever existed – but each seems real in the perception if you sincerely believe in any one of them.

You can, based on beliefs, attribute real-life problems to natural forces, to the government, to other people – to lots of things. But are these the real causes of difficulties? Or do they only appear to your senses and perception as initiating forces?

Beliefs are thus inherently deceiving: they distort perception to confirm their own artificial veracity.

So, both knowing and believing are deceptive and damaging to life experience.

But belief is much worse because it is principally founded on mere conjecture. Knowledge can be incorrect and invalid – but it can also be accurate and useful. As to your original question: of the two, knowing is much superior to believing – but only if what you know is true and accurate! Whether it is or not, though, is difficult to determine, as flawed knowledge will distort your perception just like phony beliefs!!

Better than either is direct perception untainted by either knowledge or belief. That's attained by ridding the mind of *both* deceptive beliefs and inaccurate knowledge.

Q27 – What are the most common ontological and metaphysical fallacies in Western-style philosophical thinking and argumentation?

You don't even need a plural in your question. There is one huge fallacy in Western Analytic Philosophy that renders other issues decidedly moot.

That fallacy is, in effect: the *default notion of science*, that we live in an objective reality – that the nature of ***things***, of objects and matter itself, must be examined in great detail to define the nature of existence. From the emergence of the empirical method in the 1600s, science, with its objective paradigm, increasingly displaced religion as the principal paradigm governing common thinking.

Through the seventeenth and eighteenth centuries, brilliant men like Descartes, Bacon, Spinoza, Locke and Kant expanded the creative thinking pioneered by Golden Age Greeks and defended by Copernicus, Galileo, Kepler and Bruno in the face of powerful religious opposition of the 15th and 16th centuries. Developing logic and ethics, reason and empirical, controlled examination and exploration of reality, utterly brilliant individuals moved mankind forward from the age of agriculture into modernity. With courage and dedication, they pulled mankind from infantile adhesion to superstition and myth toward unfettered understanding...

But at some point, philosophy stultified around the scientific paradigm it had earlier invented. In the process, subtly but rigidly, the realm of philosophy evicted any creative thinker. Philosophy now lies buried in academic institutions where doctors, grad students and undergrads bandy about the same old, foregone conclusions, resting on the scientific paradigm – engaged in endless debate on details of fundamentally flawed notions, experts in other people's ideas, convinced unwaveringly of their own.

Here is the core of the problem: the mind is fully and inescapably duped by its own held beliefs. We all, whether Christian, shaman, scientist or yogi, whether relying on revealed truth, epistemology, myth or reproduced, confirmed hypotheses – we all are subject to the mind's means of interpreting the reality it faces: it compares perceived situations to held beliefs.

Oft observed here, but never to be forgotten: whatever you believe in will seem to be confirmed by experience. Believe in a god, it seems like one is hovering there, making things happen. Accept that luck exists, so it seems. Believe that Hegel or Nietzsche, Berkeley or Sartre, Kierkegaard or Wittgenstein had the greatest insights, thus will your conclusions yield agreement or disagreement – consistent with your favored notions.

Reality is a subjective experience, engaged by a transcendent Consciousness: ***you***. Oh, and, from a personal perspective, every other sentient being...

As in the dream state, functional Reality unfolds with meaning: it consists of values and experienced successes and failures, joys and pains that reflect in precise detail the composite of your own comprehensive subconscious. You are connected to the events and relationships you encounter: you manifest them in repeated patterns...

But Western Philosophy can't – and thus, institutionally or individually – *won't* recognize that metaphysical Oneness. Analytic Philosophy may speculate about it, argue in near-incomprehensible complexity about its potential or impossibility. But holding or debating the concept is nowhere near the psychological grasp of perceiving the interactive function manifesting right in view of – but thoroughly hindered by – its pre-defined, ontological argument.

So, yes, the **Great Fallacy** is the scientific inference that reality is based on matter, collective particles moving about through mindless forces and resultant momentum – that consciousness arises from complex, interactive synapse function in the physical organ, the brain. Belief in that notion creates the illusion of its viability.

Reality is, rather, *inherently connected to the Consciousness that experiences it*. It unfolds in meaning-based events and relationships, inviolably tied to the complex mindset of the person – e.g., you – who experiences it.

The philosophical adherent, armed with advanced degrees, awards, debating prowess, self-assured vigor and funded tenure is just as caught up in his/her own illusions as the hunter-gatherer bowing to mythical gods or the Christian swooning at the thought of the almighty Trinity.

Consider this question a segue into grasping the restrictive qualities of belief and knowledge: let's shift to questions concerning *atheism*. The first step one usually takes in shedding religious indoctrination is to question the many declarations made by the clergy and, typically, parents while growing up. For me and, in my experience, many others, the shedding of religious (in my case, the Presbyterian flavor of Christianity) precepts led to an acceptance of science as explanation of all things.

Atheism, though, is a concept – not a movement or a belief

structure per se. Atheism doesn't state that empiricism, i.e., the scientific technique, is true or valid. Nor does it posit any other point or build any other paradigm – only that there isn't a god and that any religious model that believes in one is false.

But most people, not quite ready at the young age when first dumping religious jargon to personally build up a complex paradigm for the nature of things, simply accept that *other* major component of Western thinking, *science*. Given the common multiple-choice of our favored, Western societal options, science is the next and most likely step.

However…

Contemplating: Focus on ATHEISM

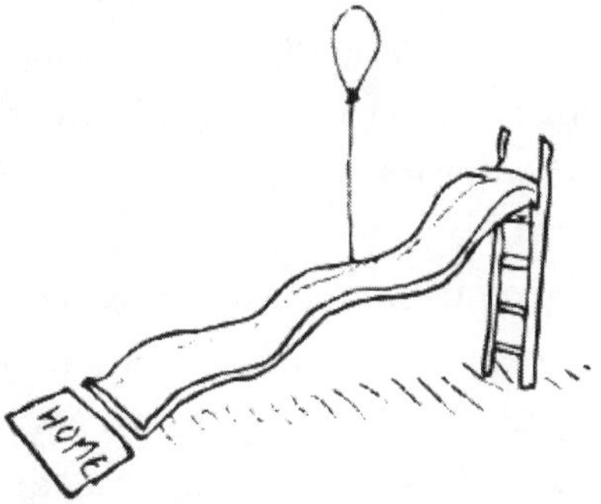

The real basis of atheism does not presuppose that science is right. And that's good, because, as noted above, it isn't. Much more is happening as Consciousness engages Reality than is apparent to the mind that only regards the apparent, material universe as real. In relegating all facets of mind – creativity, love, empathy, joy, despair, fear, hope, humor, etc. – to some complex brain function in a realm of mere particles, science misses the real essence of life itself...

Atheism simply discredits the notion of an external god. It doesn't say anything. I had become an atheist before my teenage years, but it took another decade and more before I began to see life in its depth. Most atheists, it seems, don't progress beyond the discard of religion only to attach to its cousin belief structure, science...

Let's have a look at some precepts of atheism – the study does provide some perspective on things...

Q28 – What do atheists think about death?

Nonbelievers in fantasy gods do not all have the same view of life. Most people, I suspect, who give up believing in the Christian fantasy god (named "God" with a capital "G") latch onto science as an explanation for how reality works.

Trouble is, science constitutes a structured belief system, too. And one unavoidable attribute of consciousness is this: *your beliefs invariably distort your perception.*

The mind wraps itself around its favored beliefs such that it skews interpretation of life events to confirm its tenets. That's why religions, even really absurd ones like Mormonism and ancient, obviously primitive ones like Islam, seem true to followers: they judge reality vs. learned rules and always come out confirming and thus reinforcing their core beliefs.

So, one can discard belief in a manipulative deity and buy into the objective world science depicts. Many do, as science is the only other commonly available principal belief system in our time.

But some of us have moved on from science to see a bigger picture in experienced reality. As laid out in my books, *The Essence of Reality* and *The Psyche Exposed,* I detail how consciousness is connected to reality, such that each of us attracts patterns. I show how one can delve inward to find inner roots to outer problems – health, success, relationships. By changing one's inner mindset, eliminating such elements as conflict, struggle, suggestion and emulation from the inner realm, one changes one's encountered reality qualitatively.

In effect, consciousness manifests a meaningful reality based on its composite content.

Science can't see this connection, as it never looks inward, only outward – thus ignoring many indications of life's meaningful nature.

If you consider Near Death Experiences, common accounts by people who died and were resuscitated, you'll see that, at death, consciousness exits the body and experiences a very real environment. This should be your clearest indicator of what happens when you die – accounts reported as NDEs are very consistent throughout different cultures.

However, conclusions arrived at by various atheists will vary according to their views.

Those who latch onto science as an explanation for life will doubtless imagine that their consciousness will simply dissipate into nothingness. Because science only regards the outer realm, the physical universe, it imagines the complex mind – replete with hopes, dreams, enormous creativity, complex emotional connections, love, music capability, vast memory, etc. – is simply a result of the brain's complexity of synapses.

I don't believe in any sort of external deity – and haven't since about age 9, when I could easily see that the Christianity being inflicted on me by parents didn't correspond to the reality I was experiencing. So I've been an atheist for some 60 years. But I've come to see more to the life experience and Consciousness than science does...

Consciousness survives death in a real and meaningful fashion. That's obvious when you grasp the enormously deep, complex and value-based, timeless nature of personal Consciousness. But it wouldn't be apparent to many atheists who have outgrown silly, primitive gods and goddesses, but haven't yet seen through the synthetic nature of science.

Q29 – Do most atheists start out as agnostic? Was I the only one?

Probably, most do, given that we were mostly imposed upon with religion as kids and the easiest transition out of the social cauldron of the church was to begin to question. Agnostics simply disavow knowing, so they're not making a commitment.

As a kid, already questioning Christian stuff early on, I phased through thinking of myself as an agnostic.

That rather commenced one night as I lay in bed saying my

nightly prayers. I was asking God for this or that, which my mother had taught me to do – even though he was remarkably poor at providing for my requests. Suddenly, that one night, I realized that there *wasn't anybody out there on the other end, listening!*

Anyway, I progressed to "atheist" within a few years, once I had the courage to state my feelings without fear of retribution or criticism.

But I always had trouble with the term *atheist*. I never liked to think of myself as the antithesis of something that *doesn't exist in the first place.*

In any case, like most, I latched onto science as the default explanation. As a smart kid, good student and later engineer, science seemed to answer anything and everything.

But it doesn't, as I later came to see. Science, while a really useful tool and far more advantageous paradigm than religion, is very much like religion in that, if you believe in it, it seems to be true.

As I continued through life, sincerely seeking to understand what this is all about, I learned from self-hypnosis practice that the mind and body are connected. I found I could clear up all sorts of physical ills by finding inner roots to them, clearing away those mechanisms within my subconscious – and, hey, the problems went away.

I found the same with life – relationships and career situations were also rooted within me. Life worked better when I eliminated things like suggestion, motivation, conflict and such within, all tied to real-world issues I attracted – in recurring patterns.

The point is, each of us is connected to life as it unfolds. There isn't a god out there dictating events and tempting you with sin. Nor luck, nor fate, nor chance. Life has meaning – and consciousness is fully engaged in a meaningful endeavor.

In technical terms, I'm *still* an atheist – clearly, absolutely, positively no god hovers out there calling the shots. Certainly nothing like the primitive Christian deity named "God". But life does work in perceivable, predictable ways that feature a metaphysical connection to the Self.

So, for me, recognition of that Oneness, that connected quality, moved me from gullible, naïve believer as a kid to agnostic to atheist to...

Well, there isn't a word for what I am now. And I'm happy to keep it that way...

Q30 – God doesn't exist. Why don't people understand that?

Most people grow up in their native culture simply absorbing common, popular views as to how life works. The prevailing religion or philosophy in any cultural setting is built into stories, beliefs, behavior and even language, such that each person absorbs a firm belief structure while growing up.

This belief set, however, isn't generally regarded as a set of ideas, as a malleable set of conceptualizations. It is seen and reinforced to the individual's attention by the surrounding culture as *the epitome of truth*. This is particularly the case for religions like Christianity, which disallows any questioning – labeling any free thinking as evil, even prompted by Satan himself. Most religions create a conceptual box to their paradigm – boundaries outside of which thinking is not allowed. Breaking out of that box is quite difficult.

The mind is exceptionally gullible. Whatever beliefs you hold, particularly those in place since early childhood, firmly entrenched by parental love and commonality of thinking among local society, seem true. The mind actually interprets experienced reality *through* its belief structure – judging meaning of experience according to accepted precepts.

Thus, although it is demonstrably obvious that the Christian God doesn't – and couldn't possibly – exist, most people, conned since childhood into believing in him, simply go along with their entrenched beliefs. Most people just don't have the fortitude, open-mindedness or self-confidence to buck society's favored myths. Most simply buy into their programmed thinking.

Some, however, more open-minded, compare explanations to *reality* – and prefer the latter to the fantasies put forth in myth-based religions.

So, while it is obvious to you and to me that the Christian God (the deity designated by a name with a capital "G") doesn't exist, it is far from obvious to the mind steeped in orthodox myth and miraculous silliness, ideas typically absorbed with few alternatives since early childhood.

Q31 – I don't practice any one particular religion, but I still trust in the idea of some omniscient deity. How would I identify my views?

Generally, I think the word that would most accurately apply would be "deluded".

First, what is it that you "believe"? Second, whatever it is, it likely has nothing to do with reality. And third, whatever your belief is, it will seem to be true.

Beliefs are artificial mental constructs. They never clarify what is happening in life; they only hide life's real functionality, such that anything held as true seems to be.

The path towards grasping what is happening in life involves dumping beliefs and definitions learned through childhood – they only mislead. They only *can* mislead – hiding reality behind a blur of fiction.

In effect, you live in a meaningful environment where your personal consciousness is connected with the events and relationships that constitute your life: you attract patterns. If you delve into your subconscious, you'll find that issues you face in life – health, relationship problems, failure – always have inner roots.

There are distinct mechanisms within your own mindset that lead to real problems. If you delve into your subconscious to find and eliminate the inner root, the outer, problematic pattern dissipates. *You are the cause* of all things that happen to you.

However, most components of our Western thinking project causality to things *out there* somewhere – things that are not you: gods, bacteria, wealthy sources, parents, bad guys. Or they attribute it to ancient notions of luck, fate and chance.

These elements are all hosted in the common mindset as beliefs. The point is, whatever you take on as a new or revised belief is *still* only a belief – an artificial mind construct. And it will seem true if you believe it.

Q32 – Atheists: Which religion is the most believable to you?

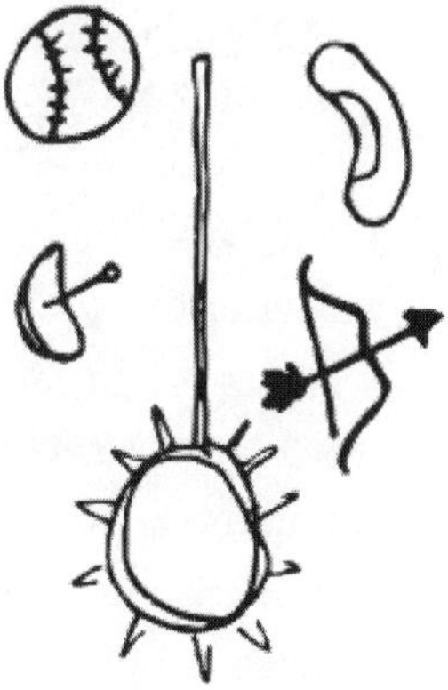

Funny question! If any explanation actually hit on the operative nature of reality, it would not have to be propounded as a religion. Religions concoct artificial story lines and put forth declarations that only seem to be true to those who accept them – mostly people who have been fully indoctrinated into the fold during childhood and who don't have the inquisitive nature to break out.

For one who sees through the artificiality of religious conjecture, judging which is slightly more believable than the others would be a silly parlor game.

Well, hold on – I'm not sure about that. Some religions, like Mormonism, Jehovah's Witnesses and Islam, are so *absurdly* impossible and divergent from reality's function that they can be considered far *less* believable! Does their fully banal world view make main-line Christianity, Shamanism, Taoism, Buddhism or anything ***more*** believable by being less unbelievable?

Q33 – Why are some people atheists?

Actually, all people are atheists. Mankind has concocted at least 2500 gods over the ages. Most people don't believe in approximately 2499 of them – making them atheists many times over.

People generally only believe in the one or many gods – specifically, the one(s) they were taught to believe in as children. And that god, only seems to exist *because* the person believes in it.

So, most in Western culture learn via Christianity that there's a creator god who made things, including you, and still interferes in life's flow. Once you believe that, it seems true. Just like it seemed true to those people's long distant ancestors when they were taught that Demeter made their crops grow or Odin watched over their battles.

Many people realized through analysis or experience that, *whoa!*, there really isn't any Big Brother out there making things happen. Shedding archaic religion, you pass into an atheist phase. Generally, those who do that buy into science. But it is also a belief structure that looks valid only as long as you believe in it.

If you keep going, though, questioning science – and exploring your own mind and its ties to reality – you'll notice that you, yourself, create your experiential reality. And that you can change it qualitatively *by changing within.*

So, people who are atheists are that because gods – none of 'em, from Thor, Zeus, Ahura Mazda, Ba'al, El, Yahweh, Allah, Lakshmi, Marduk, Apollo, you name 'em, on to God with the capital "G", none of them exist, except in the minds of believers.

But some portion of mankind, curious, open-minded and inquisitive, have the fortitude and inclination to question what they're taught. That's why those people are atheists.

Q34 – Who was the first atheist?

In Western thinking, a few Greek philosophers around 500 BCE were the first to break away from blind attribution of causality to the gods by rationally evaluating what they encountered and trying to make sense of it. Many great thinkers of that era, of course, arrived at far different conclusions, but it would be among them that the earliest atheist appeared.

Diagoras of Melos, poet and sophist, is widely regarded as the first atheist – but some schools of Greek thinking tended to explain things without the imposition of external deities as causal – the Atomists, for example.

Predating that, though, would be various schools of Hindu philosophy that didn't attribute the source of things to gods.

In ancient times, it would not have been a popular or even healthy life venture to disavow the gods of any culture. That act would open you up to blame for any ills that might befall the society. Socrates was famously accused by Athenian authorities of angering the gods with his teaching – and corrupting minors. Indeed, Diagoras, too, thought the better of sticking around when accused of impiety towards the gods.

I have to think that many a nonbeliever predated either Hindu or Greek atheists. But their chances of success or making a big name for themselves would have been slim. Ancients generally toed the line of standard thinking – and few cultures provided much by way of freedom of either thinking or expression of one's own, original ideas.

I would conclude that the first atheist either died an unnatural death at the hands of his contemporaries – or learned quickly and profoundly to keep his mouth shut. Not only are common people intolerant of those who question their favored fantasies, but priesthoods are, by long tradition, exceptionally adverse at anybody who would question their bunk and threaten their cushy livelihood as intermediaries to whatever gods they could convince their minions to believe in.

Likely, opposing most priesthoods in ancient times was just as detrimental to one's health and well-being as bucking the royalty.

The first atheist was thus, without a doubt, anonymous. And either mum about it – or short-lived.

Q35 – Why do atheists not hold agnostic views instead? Shouldn't they give themselves a little insurance in case deities do exist?

The term "atheist" is goofy to begin with. It frames a viewpoint in the context of something that doesn't exist in the first place. Like, if you're living in the middle of the Sahara Desert, would you define yourself as a principal feature of your self-image as a *non-swimmer*?

Beyond terminology and definition, the question rides the existence of, generally, the Christian god – whose assigned name is "God" with a capitalized "G". This capitalization, by the way, is traditionally intended to add some credence to the idea. But it doesn't escape the core question: does the capital G God exist?

And the answer, overwhelmingly obvious, is: ***NO***, it doesn't – indeed, it could not possibly exist with the characteristics as laid out by Christianity. But that's the case for all gods formerly held by humans. And let me just make that case.

I think most people would agree that Thor, Jupiter, Ahura Mazda, Enlil, Lakshmi, Fortuna, etc. – all archaic gods once believed in or featured in widely accepted myth – don't exist. Climb up Mt. Olympus in Greece, and you won't find Zeus and Aphrodite hanging out there.

I don't need to consider myself a Thor-atheist or a Ba'al-atheist. I don't need to argue against the existence of Marduk or Venus, against the reality of Parvati or Chalmecati, Freyja or Haukim. Nobody believes in them anymore. But I needn't consider myself an atheist in regard to 2500 gods who are long since out of work. They never did exist. But they seemed to for some people who fervently believed in them.

It only seems to be God – the imagined Christian deity with that infernal capital "G" – who elicits the need to disbelieve in. And that's *only* because some two billion humans were indoctrinated as children to imagine such an impossible entity – and they don't have the rational capability to expunge such a primitive belief from their mindset.

The question boils down to the existence of God – that specific Christian one, not any of the others. And God obviously, emphatically, clearly, not only doesn't but couldn't possibly exist.

To recognize that, first list his (oops, sorry, "His", with a capital "H") characteristics as laid out in the Bible. That's not easy to do, should you delve into the historical nature of the Christian deity. That's because "God" is never mentioned in the Bible. The Bible – in its originating manuscripts, so far as they survive – describes several deities: El, Yahweh, Alaha and Theou, principally.

El was the Canaanite god imagined in very ancient times. Generally he was head of a large pantheon, including Asherah as his cohort. He was also believed in by the Israelite tribe (Isra-EL). At some point along the time of Moses, Yahweh eclipsed El as chief god. If you read Deuteronomy 32, *both* gods are mentioned, with El referred to as Most High, with Yahweh inferior to him.

It's hard to follow that, as all of those archaic gods, believed in by the highly superstitious tribes of 3000 years ago, are conjured out of fear and ignorance of reality. People back then thought that the world consisted of a flat earth domed by a firmament, with waters below and above. El or Yahweh were regarded as real, physical beings, living up above the waters, above the dome-shaped firmament.

El was imagined as something of a personal sort of god – could take the form of a human. By the time Yahweh replaced El, he was seen as a great, fearful god – you'd die if you laid eyes on him!

Jesus tried to move his primitive peasant peers beyond that image – picturing his "Heavenly Father" as loving and caring. He would have called his deity "Alaha" or "Elaha", something like that.

But Paul invented Christianity and the New Testament was all written in Greek. Paul's god was Theou. And that deity was eventually pictured as something out of Zoroastrian lore, like Ahura Mazda – he would judge you after death, ready to send you to Hell just for being what you are (which, obviously, he would have been responsible for himself [Himself?] if he made you like that).

Those four gods are all different. They were believed in

in different time frames by different people. But they are all translated into English as "God". And that is a grand ruse – a phenomenal hoax!

No god could be judgmental and forgiving at the same time. No god could love you, yet assign you to eternal Hell for acting just like he created you in the first place. No god could create a universe so vastly huge – billions of light years across with trillions of stars and planets – yet be so petty and vindictive as is pictured in the Bible. Clearly the Christian god, named "God", is an amalgam of ancient deities, slapped together by primitive thinkers – promulgated by priesthoods who live off the donations of suckers worldwide. It (the Christian deity, with "it" a better term than "He", as God would hardly have use for a penis) only seems real if and when you believe in it.

If you look into it, the Christian deity is laced with conflicting characteristics; it couldn't possibly exist. So why believe in such a fantasy?

Q36 – Is it even worth trying to convince religious people to be atheistic?

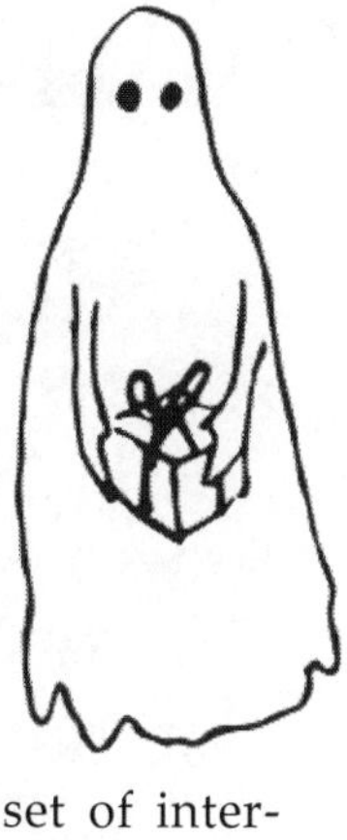

It is if you enjoy having fun with people's silly beliefs and convoluted reasoning.

In effect, the mind is extremely gullible to its own held beliefs. You learned to interpret what is happening in reality as a very small child – not only from explicit lessons and definitions, but through inferences, values woven into stories, etc.

Whatever your overall belief structure is, that set of interwoven beliefs and definitions becomes the standard by which you perceive, evaluate and ultimately make sense of the world around you. The functional consequence of that – invariably and consistently – is that good old, eternal truth: ***whatever you believe in will seem to be true!***

That's usually quite obvious when evaluating some other person's beliefs. But it's extremely tricky when considering your own: the same values and conceptualizations you are considering and judging are the ones (some very subtle and hidden behind complex, interwoven notions) you are comparing to for validation. Of course, they will align and confirm their own "Truth". It is only a very open mind that can question its own held beliefs and even consider that they might be artificial, distorted or simply fallacious.

Thus, for most religious people who fully hold beliefs as unquestionable truths, it's practically impossible to convince them of anything outside the fantasies they'd learned as kids from Mom and the friendly preacher. To them, even the act of questioning is blasphemy – the enticement of the devil, to be avoided at all costs.

Such people – and the world is full of them – are closed-minded and unreachable. You waste your and their time trying to convince a staunch Christian, for example, that a mere **idea** is *not a real thing*. To them, God is *real*, Jesus Christ is **real**, the Holy Ghost is ***REAL***. It's equally impossible to convince a scientist that the world isn't an objective realm of particles and waves. Or a Jeffersonian that all people are not created equal.

Anyway, if you enjoy the adventure into ideas and are not bothered at having rational thinking simply dismissed – or you enjoy watching Christians wallow in their own logical flaws, then go ahead, have fun! But if you really think to change somebody's mind, you'd better just talk about the weather. (Not the climate, as they are likely to deny that the earth is heating up…)

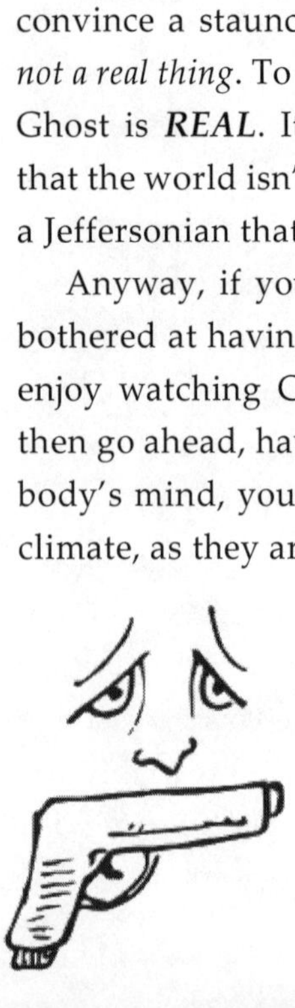

Q37 – Who owns more guns, atheists or religious people?

Don't know the statistics, but I would guess the religious folk. No, I would bet money on it! You don't need a gun unless you host within your mindset a certain amount of fear. Organized Christianity has always promoted fear – it helps greatly to keep the duped multitude coming and the cushy priesthood in business.

Fear incorporates projection of power out to someone or something else. That is purely the gist of religion. In imagining a god – especially a judgmental, tough-guy sort of deity – you automatically project creative power outwards. Within your psyche, as a consequence, you view yourself as powerless.

If you feel powerless, you very well may need weapons to protect yourself. Religion, particularly the Western ones, generally result in conflict-based societies. Psychologically, it all kind of fits together that firm religionists are highly motivated to own guns.

To me, the funny part is 99% of all guns, personally owned, never get used for anything but target practice.

Q38 – I think I am an atheist, but I have a belief that there's a reason behind everything that happens. Am I confused? Do atheists believe in that?

So far as I see, atheism simply declares that there isn't a god out there making things happen, or creating things in the first place.

Most atheists tend to latch onto science as an alternate explanation. And within the paradigm of science, there is no allowance for meaning behind the flow of events. Science postulates that the universe consists of a large batch of matter (hugely large, actually!) that is governed only by forces.

Because science allows only for the real universe, you are imagined to be a temporal being, only aware of things due to complex brain function. When you die, you will cease to exist as your neurons decay and break down.

Science can't, by virtue of its paradigm, deal with

consciousness and metaphysical connections.

However, while atheism may be populated by scientific sorts of thinkers, the name only implies that there isn't any god.

And indeed, life does have meaning, if you can get by your beliefs to see it.

Imagining a deity does require belief: there is no such big, powerful entity that made things or is doing so. There seems to be, though, if you believe in one.

However, the sterile, matter-only universe of science is also nonexistent. But it likewise seems to exist – with you as a temporary passenger – if you believe in that.

In this existence, in your real life, consciousness is an overriding quality, a driving force in manifestation of a meaningful reality. You will see that most clearly, your connection with reality, in your own life. You'll notice that you create, i.e., attract patterns.

If examined from a perspective of meaning, you'll notice that you attract certain types of people into relationships and have various health issues that impact you in specific ways. You will tend to succeed in your endeavors – or not. But always in patterns.

Consciousness and Reality are innately connected.

This Oneness has been perceived by various visionaries over time (including me, as I illustrate in my books and website, The Essence of Reality) – but it is difficult to explain to closed-minded people.

What happens is, people form belief structures through life, mostly consistent with their surrounding culture. Most are fully indoctrinated into the popular views of their time and can't see past them: in effect, whatever you believe in seems to be true. Theists are fully stuck within the box of their beliefs – it's deemed evil to even question their archaic notions.

Scientists are, too. Science, of course, has provided a great deal more benefit than religion ever did, and it nicely quantifies the reality we engage.

But it can't allow for perception of metaphysical connections, because consciousness as a quality, as an overriding feature of reality, doesn't fit into its paradigm.

So, as I see it, the only real qualification for regarding yourself as an atheist is to not believe in an external god. That is, so far as I know, the only real meaning to that word. You can thus accept a meaning-based reality without projecting causality onto some fantasy in the sky.

And you should, because that's how life works!

Q39 – Where do atheists believe the baby's soul comes from?

Answers to that question can easily exceed the bounds of what atheism really is. One can certainly recognize valid metaphysical qualities to consciousness, but not entertain the idea of an external deity who did or does exist.

True, many atheists fall back on science as an explanation for things. To them, an objective reality is what we're engaged in here – what you perceive as a material realm is what – and only what – exists, as per science. Not only is a deity out of the question for a science adherent, but so would be a soul – either in the religious sense of a low-level minion that faces judgment upon its earthly demise, or in any Self-focal point that includes consciousness outside the brain and in some fashion surviving death.

The real answer to your question is that atheists have varied impressions about the notion of a death-surviving component of Self.

I'm not sure, but would confidently speculate that most atheists do adhere to science and thus consider the brain as the generator of consciousness. The brain, though, consists of 100 billion neurons, give or take a few, giving it over 100 trillion synapses that fire off signals to communicate information. The adherent to science likely believes that this complex exchange of information, as in a computer's memory, is the basis of consciousness – given that the scientific paradigm allows only for real-world causality.

However, there are significant elements of evidence that, while they don't indicate an external deity in any way, still show that consciousness exists *primarily* and generates its physical existence in a meaningful and metaphysical way.

One is that memory consists of a huge array of information – not only the physical forms of visual memory, but meaning tied to life experience and other sensory encounters. Thoughts and conclusions themselves can be woven into memory, music and philosophy, imaginary elements, hopes and expectations, even religious beliefs and pure fantasy (sorry to be redundant) can be stored in the vast repository of memory.

Add to the comprehensive mind, in addition to its stored memories, emotional elements, fears and creative capabilities – the pure ability to concoct things that have never been imagined and then work out a way to create them. All of these deep, rich capabilities are part of consciousness – but could hardly be standard features of a system (the physical brain) that simply stores information.

Indeed, quite demonstrably, the brain doesn't even *store* information. There is no mechanism, chemical or electrical, that has been demonstrated to store specific memories somewhere in the physical brain. And by age 50, you've lived a good one and a half billion seconds, so that your memory – which is all available even if you may need self-hypnosis level concentration to access everything – is loaded with huge stores of details, visual and otherwise.

Anyway, memory and human creativity are good indications

that consciousness transcends the physical realm. The brain functions much more as an interface, a communication device between the non-dimensional conscious Self and the real universe.

Another is Near Death Experiences. Often, when a person has died and been revived, they report having left their body and continued on in a very real – not dreamlike or hallucinatory – reality. Frequently, they can describe precisely the procedures that were carried out to revive them, as observed from above the scene. This is perceived not as a hallucinatory or dreamlike experience, but as vivid and real...

Yet another such indicator is character. Clearly, when you explore the depth of the conscious mind and deeper stores, you find exacting propensities toward aspects of your personal nature that are clearly you, not just random qualities or learned elements. Music comes to mind for that. I had a love for classical music and opera the first time I heard these. My brother (similar gene structure, similar environment) didn't, but preferred big band sounds.

The point there is that you bring specific characteristics into a lifetime beyond any range of quality you could have picked up via chromosome or physical contact with parents.

I could go on, but for the purpose of answering this question, that should suffice. Atheists have differing bases for understanding life. Many would likely reject any notion of a "soul" as basis of existence, particularly those who simply accept science as an explanation of reality.

But there are those of us who see more depth to life and consciousness. I certainly don't believe in any sort of external force or source that could be called a deity. Indeed, I don't see any external force or source *at all*.

But I do recognize that life is a cohesive experience based on meaning. My books, website and YouTube videos illustrate a recognition of consciousness as the basis of existence – but have no notion whatsoever of a deity lurking out there causing anything to actually happen.

So, where does a baby's soul come from? Well, there is no physical component of consciousness, outside of that manifested once an incarnation is established. So, the answer would be: from a realm of consciousness that doesn't reside in the physical universe, but interfaces with it in a predictable manner.

Not believing in external forces and sources, then, is one key to greater awareness of the inner-outer flow of meaningful content in life. Before returning to critical thinking by regarding Christianity, Science, Islam and Eastern Thinking, let's return the focus to Consciousness – for here, there is much to illustrate by answering questions that you might have...

But first, I would provide that deeper look at my own journey to see life with Clear Awareness. Now, your journey is not my journey, your path not the same as the one I took. But certain elements of my inner cleansing are absolutely critical to clarifying perception – unavoidable, if you want to crystalize your view of what you are and how life works...

Outsourcing: My Standpoint

From the mystic experience I'd had at age 24 through a long inner journey, I jettisoned, step-by-step, all synthetic notions as to life's workings – basically all the conceptual sludge I was taught while growing up.

As I came to see once again the Oneness of things – a view first gleaned during that epiphany – I began to recognize that the inner realm of vastly complex subconscious elements directly generates outer experience. Seeing ever more clearly how that inner-outer connection directly manifested my life's qualities, I undertook an inner cleansing…

For certain, my life back then contained many aspects that sorely needed redesign.

For one, perceiving that Oneness, realizing that what I held *within* directly manifested itself qualitatively into life, I cleared away – again, element by element – each inner mechanism that led to outer problems in health, in relationship issues and failure. And I jettisoned other negatives, one at a time, as I found them rooted in childhood lessons: all the fallacies of gods, luck and other illusory forces and sources that tarnish common thinking.

By age 9 or 10, thereabouts, long before the mystic experience and inner journey, I could already see that the Christian religion inflicted on me by my mother was phony. Quite clearly, things they were telling me at church – their archaic stories of shepherds and miracles – just didn't correspond to real life. It didn't take great vision to see that nobody could walk on water or change it to wine. How could normal, rational people believe that bunk? I sure couldn't – much to the great (I'm sure) consternation of my mother.

Like most who dump religion, though, I latched onto science as the explanation for all things. Science and math came easy (a code-word phrase for me to indicate my intelligence without coming out and saying it), so, on the academic track, I earned a degree in Chemical Engineering at age 22.

But the free spirit – apparently a factory-installed option on this model – took over after a year's grind at DuPont's Industrial and Biochemical Plant in Charleston, West Virginia. If ever my adventurous nature needed a boost to erupt, the anaerobic waste pond, synthetic fertilizer facility and rigid, eggheaded work ethic of that plant's management (along with a brief and ill-advised marriage) kicked the spurs into the right place. DuPont, offering a handy draft deferment, had kept me out of the Vietnam War – the bane of my generation and one of mankind's supremely idiotic undertakings. So, free of marital and employment shackles, with a few bucks in my pocket via sale of my briefly-owned Corvette – in short order, I headed out for a year of hitchhiking all over Europe.

Details of that adventure await my autobiography, which this is decidedly not. But the pertinent resultant of that venture was the epiphany – with its impact described in the answer to Q78. Key Point: I had begun to see the Oneness of all things in that single revelation – including the limitation science posed in grasping that Unity.

My early thirties found greater awakening: I'd returned to Europe and lived in Munich for several years, learned German and dabbled in writing science fiction. But a move to San Diego followed that – and opened exposure to Holistic Health concepts and personal development through techniques of Self-Hypnosis. This period included a unique opportunity to explore intangible realms of unconscious, yet reachable, information which I could access while giving psychic readings to the public. And simultaneously, given the West Coast diversity of inquiry, I had many an opportunity to encounter alternate disciplines in healing and personal growth.

But by nature, I'm rather self-assured and critical of any explanation whose fallacy I could easily discern. My personal knack for rational thinking and logic always prompted debunking of complex ideas that claimed to be true. By maintaining an inherent personal freedom and integrity of understanding, I never could simply bow to any explanation, discipline or teacher/preacher/guru type, however vaunted and charismatic. Whatever any would-be expert said had to fit into the reality I was experiencing.

That same critical thinking which had allowed me to jettison religion kept me from latching onto Siddha Yoga, the Bahá'í faith or any other discipline – or demurring my independence by following Krishnamurti or bowing to Watts' teaching or any other…

I sensed from early on that one's personal awareness required *clarity of view* – not accumulated definitions and beliefs. Awareness is invariably distorted by blindly accepting any set of ideas or bowing to any other's expertise. By allotting superior awareness to some vaunted teacher, it seemed obvious (because it was and remains so), that one would never see the Self clearly while viewing it through somebody else's lenses…

Thus, to reiterate, because beliefs *always* distort perception, clear awareness of life's functionality is attained by jettison of common dogmas and shared cultural notions – never by simply latching onto some other set of them, exotic, esoteric, complex or widely lauded. And the extent of personal growth, while initially aided by exposure to alternative, even greater perspectives, is only ultimately limited by following any visionary or that teacher's message: *you'll never pass your guide in stature…*

So, my thirties and forties were spent disengaging myself

from my own subliminal barriers. By my fifties, I'd shed many self-limiting elements of my own mindset. I'd eliminated prior health issues, such that I maintained energetic good health without any need for artificial intervention: medicine, vitamins or any other manipulative means. And I'd progressed into shedding real-life limits: lack of authority, affixing causal power onto other sources, vaunting earlier teachers, etc.

With burgeoning freedom and confidence in my own message, I began to share my perspectives, establishing my website by 1996 as a public, noncommercial outlet of expression. Shortly thereafter, by that point in my fifties, I began to speak to groups of open-minded seekers.

Nearing age 60, I had received an unsolicited query from this British publisher, offering to publish my work, should I care to weave my perspectives into book form. That complete, by age 61, I undertook extended travel to present that first book, *The Essence of Reality* – then added more travel to introduce a second and third through 2015. By this point, now 70, I've spoken to over 250 groups across the US, Canada and UK, presenting my perspectives.

Within the last couple years, I've established and self-funded production of an ongoing series of videos to personally present my perspectives. Meant to communicate my unique viewpoint to a wider audience, I created a YouTube channel (www.youtube.com/7nehrer7) – again, without ads or other commercialization.

Worthy to emphasize is, that, while many others get a hint of enlightenment and rush off to make money from their low-level illumination, I don't commercialize my message. Outside of book sales (which only partially cover expenses), I never charge to speak and never seek remuneration for other elements of my public expression.

If you really understand how life works, *you needn't extract fees or donations from those who don't*. Consider *that* the Nehrer

Rule for Unshackled Expression. Chalk up all religions, science, healing disciplines, new-age practices, vaunted philosophies and big-name spiritual experts as violators of the Nehrer Rule: neither do they understand life, nor can they function without demanding money from their ostensible inferiors.

My standpoint, then, culminates from a very neutral mindset: untainted by classic beliefs, cleared over time of culturally shared notions common to modern Western thinking and totally free of need or desire to profit from the gesture. Gone from my view are all shreds of ideas featuring gods, luck, chance, destiny, fate or external, real-world forces and sources as causal in the trek of my life.

And *totally* absent is an interest in attracting followers or starting a movement – other violations of the Nehrer Rule. If you live off your supposed grand perspectives, you'll bend whatever shred of enlightenment you do have to maximize revenue. And if you have to live off revenue, tithes, donations or any other income stream from commercializing your message, then you – as your guru, self-help expert, academic mentor or priest before you – don't know what the Hell you are talking about.

As a direct result of that and long-term jettison of inner, negating mechanisms of mind, a very pragmatic benefit has been realized that I share with readers, embodied in my message: excellent health without need for artificial intervention and a life as ongoing adventure, freedom and success. This book joins three predecessors, extensive web writing, videos and many talks as a means to communicate my useful and highly beneficial insights.

And most of those insights put focus, subtly or blatantly, on...

Introspective: Looking Deeper into CONSCIOUSNESS

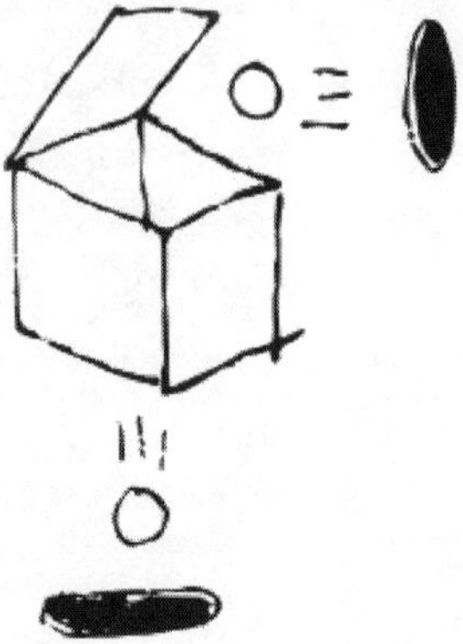

Reading and accepting lucid descriptions about advanced Consciousness doesn't equal attainment of it. That is, if I explain just what is meant by Clear Awareness of the Oneness of things, and the reader – you, for example – would grasp it, understand and fully believe it, that is not at all equivalent to the state of mind of *seeing the inner-outer connection clearly*.

Just accepting – as an **idea** – *the Oneness of things*, while still holding within deeper mind stores a broad array of ideas, definitions, religious declarations, subtle notions of ancient origin and flat-out wrong beliefs, produces confusion and inner conflict along with a mere semblance of overt understanding.

The purpose of what I've been calling an inner journey is to delete and dispel inner garble that restricts vision. Adding yet another idea, however clear and succinct it may be, to pre-established stacks of belief and definition only serves to muddy the water in which you would seek pristine clarity.

Still, directly regarding Consciousness itself can provide perspective by clarifying the nature of the intended, depicted mindset – providing something of a target mindset for the sincere seeker to aspire to, that is, to move toward. So, let's address questions pertinent to the main focus here…

Q40 – Is "cosmic consciousness" real? ... a type of consciousness posited by some psychologists and theologians, in which the universe is perceived as an interconnected network of individual consciousnesses, each one of which is connected to every other one.

And…

Q41 – How can you attain Cosmic Consciousness?

Cosmic Consciousness is a term coined by – or at least made common by – Richard Maurice Bucke in a book of that name, published at the beginning of the last century.

Bucke differentiated levels of consciousness, loosely, into three categories:

- **Simple Consciousness** in which the entity regarded is aware of the reality surrounding it. All animals, indeed microbes and even plants to some degree, are aware of their surroundings through various senses.
- **Self-Consciousness**, where the individual life form is aware that he/she exists. Included here are humans, chimpanzees and other apes, dolphins, etc. These look into a mirror and recognize their own being associated with the image they see. (My old, trusty golden retriever, Monti, smart as he was, didn't recognize himself in a mirror.)
- **Cosmic Consciousness**, a higher form of awareness in Bucke's observation, wherein, in his words, one perceives: "the cosmos to consist not of dead matter governed by unconscious, rigid, and unintending law" ... "on the

> contrary as entirely immaterial, entirely spiritual and entirely alive..."

In his book, Bucke listed numerous key visionaries and philosophers from history, some, like Walt Whitman, contemporaries of his and reflected on quotes from them. He showed how their words indicated they had attained/passed into (or whatever) a level of that Cosmic Sense.

The journey to that level of awareness – from my perspective – requires only one attribute, accompanied by persistence: ***open-minded regard for Reality***.

Indeed, you encounter daily a meaningful, cohesive unfolding of life events and relationships. This flow of your life inviolably reflects your own inner mindset – you are connected to all things that happen to you, not separate and apart.

But our common, modern thinking invariably sets us apart from encountered reality. Science looks only at the material universe as valid, ignoring consciousness as an innate driver of things, disregarding love, emotion, joy, fear and all other inner elements of real life. Religion fabricates out of myth and lore deities and devils, and assigns them powers. Luck, fate and fortune also clog your awareness with phony definitions of projected causality...

What stands between you and Bucke's Cosmic Consciousness *are mere ideas*. You absorbed a plethora of traditional notions while growing up – some taught to you explicitly, others simply absorbed from movies, cartoons, parental attitudes and treatment.

What keeps you from seeing the functional Oneness of you with the life you engage are the many beliefs and definitions – plus subtle assumptions that undergird them.

So, how you attain Cosmic Consciousness is to begin to delve inward, using at first meditation, then later techniques like self-hypnosis, dream analysis and ideomotor responses so that you can clearly discern exactly what all you hold in your subconscious. Having gained some clarity when regarding your own belief structure, you can begin to dismantle it.

You encounter a Oneness of all things – a reality that unfolds in meaningful patterns always associated with your own mindset. But you only perceive a cold, disjointed collection of objects if you hold science as the true explanation. Or you can only see a realm dominated by and controlled by a deity of any set of attributes – if you believe in it.

Behind those conceptualizations is an interrelated, cohesively functioning Oneness. You become aware of it – you gain Cosmic Consciousness – by eliminating beliefs, because beliefs ***only ever*** distort your perception; they never clarify it.

If you, yourself, are open-minded – the only prerequisite – do check out my YouTube videos, website and books. The videos and website are all free and without commercialization. Books cost a few bucks – but, ultimately, will be worth far more to you and your journey, I might suggest, than one Bucke, however helpful his book on Cosmic Consciousness might be.

Unlike preachers, priests, gurus, imams, researchers, rabbis, yogis, self-help experts and academicians, I'm not out to make money off sharing insights into life. When you really grasp Cosmic Consciousness, you don't need to extract money from those who don't, but seek to.

Q42 – Do you think consciousness survives the death of the brain?

It certainly does, whether or not you or I – or society's self-acclaimed experts, or large segments of the population – think so. Consciousness is not a function of the brain, but rather the basis of existence itself.

The brain is a highly complex organ – well over 100 trillion synapses between its 100 billion neurons. But these do not store memories or the many other qualities of consciousness. They only communicate the vast complexity of the subconscious with the physical world, including the body. They only pass information in the present moment.

If the brain were the basis of consciousness, all of your visual and other sensory encounters in life would have to be somehow codified and stored as memories in that physical medium for future reference. A computer, for example, in order to store photos and text information, converts all data into bit/byte combinations for storage in a physical medium for later retrieval. Any photo or other graphic image is converted into a long series of graded pixel colors, point by point along its length and width. Those binary numbers are what gets stored in memory – and the image is reconstructed from the stored data whenever it is to be displayed later. Even text in a word processor along with formatting and associated data is converted into a set of numbers for later reconstruction to recreate the text document.

The brain, if it were computer-like – that is, the only basis of your consciousness – would have to convert all visual experience as well as spoken or read language elements into some kind of codified data for storage. But also, your hopes, fears, thoughts, wishes, creativity, love, emotional engagement, music expression, poetic constructs, architectural creations, etc. – all aspects of the mind in the life experience – would have to be somehow reduced to a representative code for storage in the physical brain.

But there is no such storage mechanism in the brain.

By age 25 alone, you've lived over 500 million seconds of waking time. All of these moments of complex experience can be recalled in an instant – often casually with little effort, but minimally with practice and perhaps concentration techniques. That includes not only visual memories, a phenomenally huge amount of data to begin with – but other information and sensory recall in addition: thoughts you had at the moment of the memory, conclusions and impressions, emotional content, smells and tastes involved, etc.

Your memory contains a *vast array* of information – everything you've ever learned and lessons derived from how you were treated, emotional responses and precise triggers for them, connections of immediate experience to meaningful definitions, all language definitions and associated connections, etc. Add to the complex of experience, the inventive nature of thinking: creative capacities for things never imagined or produced before, of music and art, of mechanical and engineering solutions, of cooking varieties, of athletic competitions and game playing – the list of mental capacity is nearly endless.

Memory, considered just by itself, is based on meaning and can be recalled in detail decades later, beyond the original event – and often recalled in an instant. There simply is no physical mechanism within the brain to do that. But other of mankind's personality traits, of interactive philosophy, legal, artwork, design, psychological variations, are even more complex – and less possible to reduce to some code able to be stored in a physical data storage system.

Memory and the full, meaningful engagement of life are aspects of *Consciousness;* the total psyche/Self simply transcends the physical plane. Its complexity and diversity could not possibly be reduced to a mechanical, material-based system.

And that conscious Self you experience yourself to be *spans many lifetimes*. This is obvious when you recognize that many characteristics of your own personality were apparent at birth, customized qualities you bring with you into an incarnation – your taste in music, your creative abilities, your sexual orientation, your preferences for color and clothes. They aren't a result of either learning or genetic structure.

Consciousness certainly, absolutely and without question survives death. That becomes overwhelmingly obvious when you discard popular notions of religion and science that separate you from reality. You are fully connected to a meaningful unfolding of events and relationships in life...

Most obvious in indicating this connection are Near Death Experiences. Here, many people who died and were revived report exactly what happened – viewed from above – during their resuscitation. Consciousness leaves the body upon physical death. NDEs couldn't happen if consciousness were simply a brain function, fully oriented to reality exclusively through the senses.

Again, holding religious or scientific explanations to life distorts the picture. Memory processes, personal character traits and NDEs clearly indicate that Consciousness survives the passing of the physical body. A simple understanding for how data would have to be stored in a merely physical system along with a recognition of the unfathomably huge amount of data you've accumulated during a lifetime precludes the notion that the brain, as a physical, computer-like system, is the basis of the mind.

Q43 – Is awareness part of education?

This question presents something of a paradox. Standard education in a way *should* include perspectives on awareness: younger generations should be exposed to consciousness as the key aspect of their own being. It would be highly beneficial on an individual level and ultimately for society as the generations grew into life roles.

This sort of focus, though, is practically nonexistent in practice: both religion and science (as institutionalized, dominant elements of the Western world view) preclude presentation of ideas not consistent with their core tenets.

And therein lies the paradox...

Life's encountered events and relationships manifest in a reliable, predictable fashion: they unfold in an ongoing, patterned flow whose meaning reflects the total content of the mindset of the individual who experiences it.

Each person is intrinsically connected to that flow: he/she attracts life's qualities, both good and bad.

Clear Awareness of life's innate flow, though, is restricted and distorted by held beliefs and accepted explanations – not clarified by them. In that regard, education in effect *deters* growth in awareness; it doesn't promote it. Religion generally projects creative power to some imagined god while science attributes causality to real-world forces and sources.

Unhindered awareness involves shedding these popular definitions that project such causality – leaving a recognition that one attracts life situations oneself.

Thus, first, it is difficult to teach "Clear Awareness", as the process involves shedding beliefs and definitions that are commonly held as truth. Teaching generally promotes *absorption* of authoritative ideas. These ideas, even if they accurately portray the inner-outer connection, only add to the knowledge store in the subconscious. That differs significantly from dispelling contrary notions and thereby enhancing awareness.

So, generally, education promotes common thinking, not growth in awareness. The paradox is that common nurturing of young minds should involve stimulating approaches to deeper perspectives – but hardly could, due to the innate distortion to awareness that absorption of definitions and shared beliefs invariably creates.

Q44 – Is God a single consciousness, or is God an ever-burgeoning collection of Consciousness?

The word "God", with a capital "G", is just that: *a word*. Words are used to represent things, like the noun "table" is a series of letters which represent sounds (t, ay, be, el) which symbolize a generally wooden structure with a top and legs that people sit at to eat. If I say the word *table*, you can picture it and know what I'm talking about.

But words can also be invented that represent imaginary things. Unicorns and sprites, for example, don't exist and never did. And words, often commonly used, may symbolize things that don't really exist, but seem to *because* they are named. For my third book, I invented the term ***"noncept"*** for that purpose.

Based on my customized definition for *noncept*, the common cold, government and, say, friendship are all noncepts. The sniffing and coughing cold doesn't exist in itself, but is rather a condition of some person's sinus and throat. Without the requisite human, the cold is nonexistent. Government is illusory in this sense: what **is** real are big buildings and people doing tasks they were elected or hired to do, plus recorded laws and agreements. Those are all visible and tangible. But the government, *per se*, is a noncept – a collective of other real things functioning (more or less!) in coordination.

Likewise, friendship is a relational status between people. Minus the people, friendship can't and doesn't exist on its own. A noncept.

The notion of "God" with the capital "G" is a noncept in that sense. Forged as a long-evolving English word for a generic, imaginary deity, the word *god* was applied in early times when the Hebrew Bible (or more likely the Septuagint, an early Greek translation of the Hebrew) was translated into English. The really deceptive part of that is that various Biblical gods from different time frames – all mythical and nonexistent – are all translated into English and capitalized, thus producing "God" as a name.

El (earliest Old Testament god of Abraham), Yahweh (later deity of Moses), Alaha (the Aramaic name for a deity likely used by Jesus) and Theou (Paul's god in the Greek his epistles are composed in) are four different gods with different imagined characteristics. They are all deceptively translated as the same word.

There exists in this Reality or even outside of it, no entity who remotely resembles any of the creator characteristics assigned to El, Yahweh, Alaha or Theou. God, as depicted in Christianity, simply doesn't exist. He seems quite real to the Christian believer, however…

But any god or any other mechanism that would describe how life works seems real to the dedicated believer. That's because, as I've often clarified here, the mind is predisposed to confirming its held beliefs. You interpret the world through your beliefs to make sense of it – thus any mind-image will confirm its own definition.

So, a valid answer to your question requires first that the term God be dismissed as a functional being, real in any way. It is simply a word applied to an idea – one demonstrably false in this instance: a noncept, seeming to exist if you've already accepted the ideas.

That reduces your question to a more appropriate, simpler query: is there just a single consciousness or a growing collection of conscious entities. And that is a good question indeed, rife with deeper implications and collateral possibilities…

For sure, I exist as an individual, self-aware entity. Writing all of these words, plus doing all the other things I do (eat, drink, sleep, travel, observe, conceptualize, joke, think, love, question, create, laugh, cry, expound on occasion, etc.) are pretty good indicators that I exist. Given that you posited a question, I'll presume you exist in that same sense. And 7 billion others seem real in that same fashion – along with several trillion trees, a quadrillion ants, etc. I've seen and otherwise encountered quite a few of all of those – plus a myriad of other living entities...

The question then becomes, are we all tied together such that there really only is One Consciousness, kind of broken into pieces that only ever encounter other aspects of itself? Perhaps the single Conscious Self fuddles through one incarnation at a time, experiencing all sorts of good and bad things, because it's boring just being all-powerful and eternally conjuring up ice cream, orgasms, sunny beaches and other good stuff.

Alternately, are we all fully independent, individualized points of Consciousness that wander about encountering other such entities?

Once I realized – starting with that mystic experience at age 24 and regaining a full recognition of the innate connection between Self and Reality by my late thirties – that I was connected to all things, I began to leverage that Clear Awareness (as I call it) to improve my life. I found that all external, real issues – all situations I faced in life – were rooted within. When I delved into my subconscious, found the inner roots to real-life problems and changed them within, life always without exception improved.

We do encounter a metaphysical realm wherein our total mindset is realized, manifested into a flow of events and relationships that, with meaning, reflect our own basic nature.

So, here's what I can tell you beyond standard thinking: *You exist.* You attract relationships and manifest health or illness, success or failure, based on your own nature. In terms of your life, ***you are*** that god Christianity looks for up in the sky.

And your conscious Self will exit your body at death – you'll go on to create more lifetimes, experience more things, enjoy your creativity and physicality in many more instances.

But I am not you. We each now represent (i.e., symbolize) meaningful aspects of each other's life – you asked me a question and I'm providing some perspectives on it. So we interact. But in this moment of being – and there is only ever this Now moment of being – you are engaging an incarnation wherein you label your Self with a unique name and I myself as Tom Nehrer. You have a particular and highly complex set of characteristics and propensities – and I have a different set. We play roles in each other's lives that fulfill specific, meaningful needs.

That same can be said for all entities you encounter, from a yeast cell digesting sprouted barley to put out alcohol for your beer to the bartender who serves it. All elements of reality have a conscious nature about them. And they are all tied together in a fashion. But the details of how that interwoven, morphing collage of life events and relationships impacts you depends *only ever* on you yourself (whether you recognize that or not – most don't, but project causality to defined noncepts).

So, what appears to be the God you speak of is only you manifesting your own, complex inner self into a flow of life situations. And Reality is full of others doing so as well – but their impact on you *only* revolves around your own nature.

Thus, there is a Single Consciousness in that it's all interrelated, but it functions in an individualized nature with a huge collection of discrete, functionally separate Selves. We all interrelate in a complex fashion with virtually infinite possibilities laid out in potential events. But only those events manifest into actuality that realize – from your viewpoint – your own unique blend of value and inner meaning.

So, dispense with the noncept of an external deity as a One or Multiple essence. But recognize that what you encounter is an integrated Oneness, experienced from a multitudinous set of viewpoints – realizing practically infinite variations of main-line possibilities...

Some seemingly simple questions do indeed require complex answers...

Q45 – Is consciousness subjective or arbitrary?

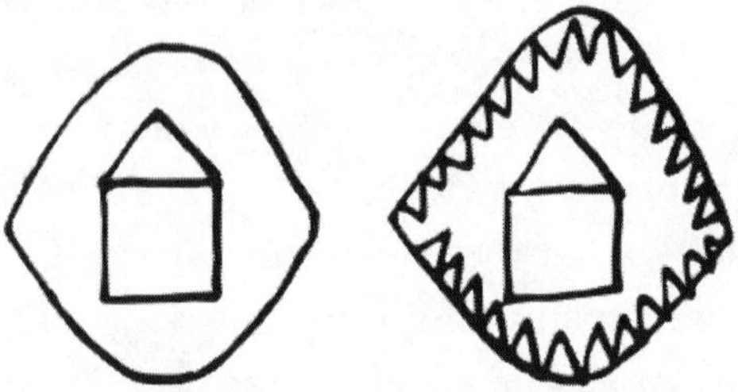

The simplicity of that question implies consciousness itself either reflects an individualized nature *OR* a capricious, non-reasoned nature.

Consciousness itself just *IS*: the nature of what it encounters, though, varies across a wide spectrum of positive to negative, that is, desirable and unwanted, events and relationships.

I think you mean to ask whether the conscious Self experiences a daily reality which is subjective – that is, that life is personalized and meaningful based on that individual alone. Or whether life as it unfolds is kind of randomized, unfounded, not based on determinate, predictable elements.

If that is your question, yes, indeed, you as a complex conscious entity engage a life that invariably reflects your own nature. It is purely subjective in nature in that events and relationships you attract are neither random nor inflicted on you by some external force or source – like a god or real agent (such as other people, bacteria, conditions, luck of the economy).

Life may *seem* to be arbitrary, powered by things *out there,* happening to you despite your will or hope. But that impression comes from ideas we share culturally which you absorbed growing up – religious elements, science, fear, chance and so forth. But if you can delve into your deeper mind content and delete common notions you were taught – like common Christian claims, science's objective implication, luck, fate, etc. – you will see that all things you encounter are woven into patterns. And those patterns reflect you and your total mindset.

Indeed, you can change them all by changing yourself, within.

The trick in life – a very useful and beneficial effort – is to become aware of the inner-outer connection we all experience, but few notice.

Without gaining an awareness yourself of how life flows in meaningful patterns, you will attribute causality in life, generally, to external forces and sources: it will appear arbitrary. When you come to see the connected quality of all things, you realize it is more than subjective – you not only interpret meaning in life's elements, you manifest them.

So, "consciousness" itself isn't subjective *OR* arbitrary. But the life an individual conscious entity – like you – engages *is* subjective and more. It not only pertains to you personally, but is driven by you – not, however, through action taken but by your own, realized composite nature.

Q46 – How is false consciousness promoted in society?

"False consciousness" as a *phrase* has a particular meaning in sociological terms. It observes, fairly accurately, that people are unaware of widespread effects – like exploitation and oppression at the hands of controlling classes – as those situations really exist.

That is, most aren't conscious of what they themselves really are, but rather attach their own self-image to common beliefs promulgated by common thinking.

That useful phrase, however, comes up short in considering

your question for the words *themselves* – i.e., not issued as a defined phrase, but for the meaning implied by the words "false" and "consciousness".

So, let me first explore what *consciousness* is. Without that clear view, you can hardly recognize what "false" consciousness might be.

Consciousness is the very basis of your being, the essence of what you are. Whether in the waking or dream state, you are aware of an environment surrounding you. From Near Death Experiences, people even report being totally aware, viewing in a lucid state, surrounded by an environment.

You *can* gain greater depth of awareness of the operative process of that reality – how it relates intimately back to the composite of inner values and meaning as they comprise your expansive subconscious. In effect, *you are connected,* in terms of meaning, *to the ongoing outer flow* of events and relationships that constitute your life: you attract patterns in your life quality.

At a "higher" level of consciousness as a quality (lower case "c") – attainable but not common – you will recognize that all encountered outer effects are rooted in your own mindset. Problems you encounter, typically repeating as noted in patterns, always have inner roots. You can find and change the inner, negating mechanisms and your life's outer patterns will improve in response...

That inner-outer connection is an inviolable feature of your *Consciousness*. The totality of your Consciousness, your essence of being (upper case "C"), is seen in both the composite mindset you hold and the quality-experience of your unfolding life flow.

So, from the outset, Consciousness is *what you are.*

However, common thinking in most Western settings rests on traditional, but archaic, religious declarations and old, but historically more recent, scientific definitions (empiricism). Standard views of life also generally contain subtle but effective belief in luck, fate, fortune and chance as contributing factors in causality.

The major hindrance to understanding is invariably this twist: your belief structure, i.e., your personally held set of accepted beliefs and definitions (quite complex if you examine it) *inherently distorts your perception of reality*. Indeed, whatever you believe in will appear true: you interpret experience based on your beliefs – and they invariably warp your evaluation to support their tenets.

If you believe in a god, it seems like he/she exists. If you exclusively trust science as your model for reality's function, it appears to be unquestionably valid.

Either of these traditional explanations, religion (any of them, doesn't matter) or science, can be seen as instituting and solidifying *false consciousness*. One leads you to conclude that there's a god out there making things happen – when there isn't, but it seems so based on your conviction of a deity. The other makes you think that a trigger to an event is the cause – when it isn't, as the cause in your life is you, via your collective mindset, attracting a pattern.

So, to answer your question: **false consciousness is nearly universally promoted in society by the widespread sharing of common, fallacious notions**, and more specifically, the indoctrination of children into those popular fallacies of religion and science.

I would quickly point out that science, unlike religion, at least has some use. It allows for better manipulation of real matter. But in ignoring the inner as a valid, inherent element of Consciousness, science sets up false consciousness by eliminating the core, causal element to your life: You.

As society promulgates its false view of consciousness, it passes about without question its synthetic "truths". Religion is regarded by its adherents as unquestionably true. "Scientifically proven" has come, through advertising and the domination of academic influence and scientific organizations, to mean "fact".

Both, though, are fallacy-based. Both create *false consciousness* by distorting the perception of the adhering mind to confirm their stated tenets.

So, Consciousness is the basis of your being. You don't recognize that so long as you hold beliefs to the contrary – and those beliefs are commonly and widely circulated as truth by widespread cultural institutions and indoctrination of childhood thinking. It should be understood that movies, literature, stories, news items in reporting, etc., all are expressed with the same background, shared beliefs and mutual assumptions – a commonality that only helps to reinforce the innate fallacy.

Thus, false consciousness is promoted in virtually all means of interpersonal communication and media expression.

There are, however, in our time, other voices oriented toward presenting a clearer, far more in-depth look at the real nature of Consciousness. But you have to go looking and, through open-minded regard, discern valid perspectives on the Oneness of things from the age-old explanations that substitute ideas for direct perception.

Q47 – If free will doesn't exist, why am I conscious right now?

Your question twists two concepts into a pretzel that might taste good, but doesn't have much nutritional value, realistically speaking.

You are conscious right now based on the nature of your being. Indeed, all life forms are conscious of their surroundings. Referring to that recognition of a Reality surrounding you (whether in the waking or sleeping state) as Simple Consciousness, clearly all life forms are aware of their surroundings: simple cells move toward food supplies, plants extend roots toward water, flies land on dung, etc.

Humans, though, along with the great apes, dolphins and a few other life forms are aware of their own being. That can be referred to as Self-Awareness. However, that level of consciousness in humans, qualitatively, is highly distorted by beliefs held as to the nature and functionality of the surrounding field of existence. Effectively, whatever the beliefs you hold, you will judge Reality to work in ways consistent with those beliefs.

This *"whatever you believe in will seem to be true"* effect is because you interpret your experience *through* your beliefs – which strongly tend to confirm their apparent validity, whether or not they are really true.

OK, so you are conscious in any case of a surrounding Reality. And you color and flavor that Reality based on your beliefs.

Interpreting Reality in a philosophical or religious context that includes the notion of Free Will – that is a whole other consideration. In philosophy, Determinism, imagining that Reality cascades through time with current conditions and forces invariably leading to set situations, which then proceed to lead to other set outcomes, would tend to disavow Free Will. But the argument could easily be made that you have a choice to do as you wish, thus you have Free Will. The Determinism adherent would argue that your choice is predetermined by your propensities and the situation – so you really don't have Free Will; it just seems like it.

To answer your question: whether or not Free Will exists...

You are conscious of a surrounding Reality. The latter state of awareness is not dependent on the philosophical construct or its counter-construct.

If you are interested, though, in how life really works, I will mention this: Consciousness is directly connected to the Reality it manifests. This plays out in your life in that you attract and create patterns. You'll find patterns of meaning in your health, relationships and level of success at endeavors you undertake – patterns that echo back through your life, recurring repeatedly.

People and situations come and go, but their nature and their impact on you remains with certain regularity.

There are always inner roots to those patterns – finding and changing them, eliminating the negative inner mechanisms, brings improvement in life.

You won't be conscious of that connection, though, if you learned to attribute causality to gods and/or external forces and sources.

So, you are conscious, or you wouldn't be reading this. What you are conscious *of*, though, depends on your belief system. And that may or may not feature Free Will.

In effect, you have free will to do what you choose to do. But you will unconsciously attract those patterns regardless of your chosen actions, which renders your Free Will moot. That is, unless you use your Free Will to go into the subconscious, find the exact roots to life problems and dispel them there, within.

E48a – In an effort to search out the meaning of my thoughts and experiences the question occurred to me, could it be that when a desire is fulfilled, the joy that we feel is the result of clearly perceiving reality? Maybe we knew something on a less than conscious level, and so thought of it as a desire rather than a knowing. It's hard for me to believe, yet... it nags at me.

There is an interrelationship among the prime values: Love, Joy, Peace, and Freedom. While approaching these major aspects of Consciousness/Reality in depth will require a more elaborate explanation, let me illustrate enough to present a background in which Joy can be seen more clearly.

Love in its purest form is acceptance. To be attracted to someone or something is to accept the values and qualities that comprise that person or thing. Of course, it's not really that simple – you may love someone, but yet want to change some aspects of that person. But that has to do with the many, varied complexities of people that make life so rich – rich in joy should love be supported by inner peace, or rich in pain should the inner state be rife with conflict and struggle. In any case, you can see Love as acceptance of a person or thing *in its essence*.

Peace is a quality of acceptance in another vein. Peace is an inner state, but yet comes about when one's desires become realized, when one's will is fulfilled by manifesting intent into real experience. Peace, in a way, is the state of being accepted – in terms of the events and relationships that constitute real experience.

Freedom – real, essential freedom, not ostensible religious or political freedom, which are illusory – stands at a slightly different angle. When you begin to see that your life's content reflects your inner state, you begin to free yourself from the many apparent forces that seem to make things happen to you. As you continue this path, you become more and more *free*. And therein Freedom consists of being able to act or think or proceed in any direction, and having the real events you experience support and sustain your intent, not oppose it or neutralize it.

Thus, *real* Freedom rides inner Peace as its facilitator. You become free from external chains when you recognize that those shackles are put into place by your own inner conflict and other negating mechanisms – and proceed to dispel the inner binding.

Now, what is Joy? Joy comes at the fulfillment of your will, the realization of your desires. At once it embodies the essence of being loved, the Peace of encountering a reality that is in tune with your chosen values, and a core Freedom wherein your intended direction is supported by realized events.

So, is Joy a result of Clear Awareness? Not necessarily – and not brought on immediately by that state, upon achieving it. But Clear Awareness allows a direct pathway that can clear out the many restricting inner mind elements – aspects of mind which cloud awareness and conjure up events and relationships that negate the will – *these* will lead to a greater and greater frequency of Joy-eliciting encounters in life.

E48b – I am beginning the effort of clearing away limiting values, and becoming aware of how far away my childhood memories really are. It seems that "Concentrated effort in coming to see the inner values" which have been blocked from awareness, but are suspected due to their effects, is the key.

In the interest of getting through the "blocks" it's been suggested that the "trick" is knowing that I haven't wanted to see them before now. Does this perspective from a psychology student agree with the principles you set forth in EoR? I just want very much to take the most direct path, as I am already at midlife and this looks like a very long road I am starting down.

Thanks so much for the time and effort you have put into EoR...

You will find many of the specific Elements of Mind that I illustrate in the Your Path sections of EoR online and my first two books consistent with Psychology studies. There are, however, subtle boundaries to our standard scientific ways of considering the world that limit clinical psychology as a movement from reaching the core of existence, the unfettered understanding of Self, and an awareness of the Oneness of Consciousness and Reality that allow me to penetrate deeper.

If you are wading across a stream, slogging through the mud and debris in the riverbed, and somebody offers you a boat when you are halfway across, would you turn them down? It doesn't matter how difficult or long a journey it may be, or seem to be, to realize Clear Awareness. However far you get realizes a significant gain in life quality – the elimination of fear, the improvement of health, the promotion of peace and freedom, etc. To back off in delving inward for the purpose of gaining understanding because it seems too long a journey would be a foolish rationalization.

I must add that, like each of us, you are a continuum, however terminal life's end might appear to be. What you gain during this lifetime in terms of awareness and life's multitude of lessons, *you take with you* – in fact, growth of character is the only thing you take along into subsequent conscious ventures into the Reality format.

I would also note here that, having set your mind toward awareness and clear understanding, the most direct path is the only one you CAN take, though it might not seem so direct!!

E49a – If I am the consciousness that experiences this reality (as every individual when considered from their own perspective) and if all the things (fears, beliefs, etc.) in my mind that make me feel that I'm somehow separate from reality are only my own constructs this would mean that I AM ALL, that there is ONLY me, at least in my own reality.

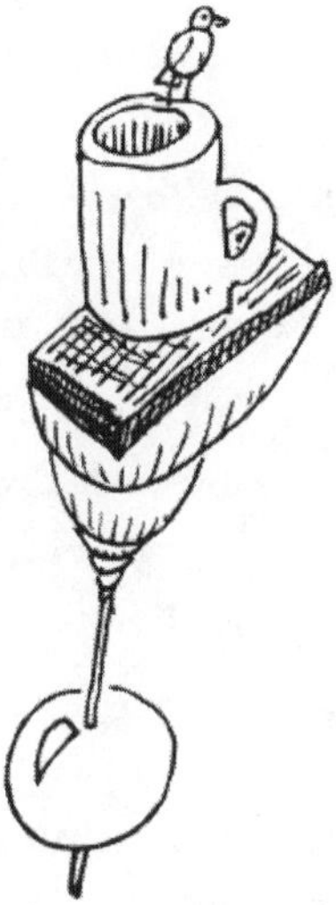

Reality, just as a dream, can only be experienced from the central point of view. You ARE the central focus of all the events of your life. In just that same centrist attitude, each individual engages reality as a series of events and relationships that impact the Self in certain distinct ways, with certain, specific values.

Actually, the same arrangement is the case from any conscious entity on any scale, and there is certainly an element of consciousness to all things on any level. But rather than philosophize about how reality looks to an amoeba or to a hydrogen atom, since you clearly aren't one of those currently, it is much more advantageous to consider aspects of the existence of your Self – aspects which are experienced directly and can be related to elements of mind, which can be perceived directly, as well.

So, looked at from one angle, *there is only you,* and you attract others into your life as role players, to act out roles in the fulfillment of your personal values. From another angle, of course, they are as real as you, experiencing life in the same fashion, but from their own personal perspective.

Essential to see, too, is that, from this moment onwards, there are many potential, possible outcomes to current scenarios – a vast range of variable consequences that might ensue. Exactly that one which corresponds to your inner propensities is the one that will manifest. No element of life emerges either randomly or adverse to your composite nature…

E49b – Everybody has a consciousness and experiences a reality. But I only know of my own reality. I don't know anything about another individual's reality. So if I'm only my reality I MUST somehow be separated or limited. Or is it possible for me to know everything about everybody's reality? Are there many realities and consciousnesses or is my consciousness/reality the only one?

You can interpret somebody else's reality based on your observation, but meaning and understanding derived by you will not be the same as that person makes out of it, since your own mindset is unique to you. Through communication, you can probably piece together a view of how somebody else's reality is being affected by that person's beliefs, fears, etc. Psychologists do that all the time. But the depth to which you can venture into somebody else's psyche is certainly limited, whereas with your *own* mind, in your own life, you can see as deeply as you have the fortitude to delve.

How could there be a limit to Realities/Consciousnesses?

The consciousness which currently finds itself realized as You (designated by your named self) encounters a reality which is constantly changing and therefore is not really a single thing, but a vibrant, flowing essence. Of course, your consciousness is changing as well. So how do you want to look at it? Is there one consciousness/reality essence, this one, occurring right now? Or many, since each moment brings some change? And since everybody and everything also exist in this consciousness/ reality essence, how many does that make?

Numbers are not relevant here. Numbers and quantification create illusions. What exists is You. You are not "the only one", but you are the only one who is you and who attracts your customized version of life quality.

E49c – Are you me?

Insofar as you encounter me, I fit into your life in some fashion – I play a role. Whatever that value embodies is the aspect of me that is you. By the same token, your e-mails to me are a part of my life, just as all the other people I encounter fit into roles and realize values in my experience. To that extent you are a part of me. It is not correct to say that I am you beyond that. We are different entities, each unique to ourselves, differing in quality and impact, even though sharing an interactive realm.

Each of us experiences life events from our own unique perspective. But the "mechanism" of our existence is the same.

E49d – If clear awareness isn't the end of the road for man's consciousness, what happens next?

"Clear Awareness" as I depict it in EoR is a small first step, actually. Once you realize that you are the only power source, you will very likely strongly desire to use that awareness to create a life which is enjoyable and fulfilling to your Self – and beneficial to others. That second phase, the tidying up of inner sludge, self-deprecation and other self-defeating elements, can be a journey unto itself, since it requires delving into all the limitations that you carry in your mind, and clearing them out.

All in all, there can be no arrival at a place of "perfection" – but rather attainment of Peace and Ease. If you climb Mount Everest, thinking you've achieved the greatest summit of all, you only need regard Olympus Mons on the planet Mars: it is much higher yet. There will always be a higher mountain...

Consciousness and the unlimited nature of quality and experience will never provide an end station where you will disembark from change and growth. Buddha's Nirvana or Jesus' Kingdom of Heaven – these are not places where your consciousness no longer encounters reality, as in an undifferentiated state of blissful orgasm. That imaginary sort of ongoing, meaningless fudge would be boring and without value.

But a state where your creative urges lead – for you, once you've reached full awareness of your connected nature and worked out your inner negatives – feature interactive realities that don't carry the pain, rejection, and failure of earlier life formats. You will still experience a Self-facing-Reality format, but your creative intentions will elicit success, bringing joy and fulfillment.

E49e – I can see that man has been projecting creative power into money for a long time and thus creating a society in which power expresses itself as money. And my question is: why, when and how did we start doing this?!

Man has been projecting creative power outwards onto all sorts of objects, both material and intangible, for a very, very long time. Yes, money is one of them, and is just as illusory as all the others. Clearly, our ancestors began to pin causality to imagined external targets very early on.

To grasp "why, when and how did we start doing this?" – that is, projecting creative power to money – let's first look at when man began attributing causality to any external source or force. In that case the **when** would be in truly ancient, prehistoric times. One can easily postulate that early Stone Age humans, once able to name things and communicate via language, began to not only conceive external elements of life – trees, hills, wandering herds of wildlife, weather and seasonal conditions – but to attribute the instigation of real events and outcomes to them.

What followed *that*, then, was assigning a certain will or cognizance to the element, thereby turning it into a god-figure.

The Sun, with its life-giving warmth and season-driving movement – bringing summer yearly as it climbed higher in the sky – doubtless was one of the first assigned power. Sun-gods appear commonly in ancient cultures: Ra and Aten to the Egyptians, Helios to the Greeks, Ravi in Hindu traditions, Wi to the Lakotas, Belenos to Celts and Hors, Sol, Koyash, Shamash, Amaterasu, Inti, Istanu, Yuyi, Surya to other cultures along mankind's long trek.

But other natural elements doubtless became causal in the growing imagination of early man, thus also being assigned some power. If storms damaged your hut, you could easily attribute negative consequences to a demon or even god of weather or the wind. You might attribute it to a Fortuna-like deity, a goddess out there, willing to zap you just for kicks. Fertility, war, success, love interest – indeed any aspect of life could be deemed driven by external forces, by deities or unseen spirit-realm entities. These features of life all merited godlike status in various cultures over the ages...

So, the practice of projecting power onto external forces and sources certainly originated in our long distant past. It grew and evolved through untold numbers of generations – honed by priesthoods, presented to superstitious nomads, then farmers, then industrial-age workers, built on and exaggerated by each generation of human. Ideas of causal power, presented as stalwart, unquestionable *truth*, simply enhanced the illusory notions common folk had been taught already as children while growing up.

It's easy as well, and doubtless an equally aged tradition, to attribute causality to real things: other people, conditions and, later on, things like bacteria or the economy.

But for *money* to receive tribute as the source of power, a lot of things had to evolve – principally, money itself. Doubtless ancient nomads of tens of thousands of years ago developed barter to exchange goods and work effort to make things. This cooperative exchange kept the tribe fed and functional. At some point a commodity probably began to take on a common value – arrowheads, fishhooks, scraping tools, fashioned from stone or bone, could have, by general agreement, become correlated to food preparation or clothes fabrication.

Eventually, as man developed agriculture and settled in fixed locations, set, defined value was assigned to items such as salt, seeds or livestock. That is, common, needed material goods could help gauge the value for barter equivalents: a pair of fashioned sandals would fetch a cup of einkorn at the town marketplace.

It was only about 7000 years ago that metal objects began to be used as value-equivalents – and it took millennia after that, until about 700 BCE, before coins were invented to hold a certain value.

Even then, however, coins held *intrinsic* value: the metal they were made of had a value just for its worth in usage. It was only in near modern times that money became issued that had neither intrinsic value nor gold or silver backing its inherent worth – only the reliability of the government that issued it. At some point money became more conceptual than real: most money now exists as numbers held in computers, not even as paper or metal representation. How much of your own money, for example, is real at the moment, that is, tangible? The overwhelming majority of money, easily 90%, exists in bank and investment accounts.

So, how did money come to be worshipped as a source of power? That conceptual leap came along with the invention of time and the notion of sequential, overt causality.

From the most ancient of times, it has appeared that an action that brings about an event actually ***causes*** it to happen. This appeared to be the case when gods were deemed to be inflicting their will on mortals – or the wind and floods, earthquakes or droughts seemed to purposely impart damage on people. Life appears to flow from action as cause into result as effect. So, it looked – and for most still looks – like the former *causes* the latter, rather than simply triggering it...

Money only joined or displaced gods, physical actions and sources as the cause of things. If you had money, so it seemed, you could do or obtain anything you wanted.

Of course, all of that is illusory. The real world each of us encounters is a result – a finished product of a qualitative nature initiated by each individual. That personal manifestation of inner value constitutes the subtle flow in life that few are aware of – for the notion that money or other material or intangible forces and sources drive life is widespread and so common that it's difficult even to question.

But questioning is the first step to seeing beyond the illusion...

E49f – I was wondering if you could confirm this. I am the ONLY power-source in my life, the sole creator of my life. There is absolutely no real external power-source affecting me and my life. My attention is the energy beam that shapes my life.

What will it gain, I have to query, for me to say "yes" to that? Will it make it so if it is not the case? You cannot rely on my words as a great authority to push yourself into a state of awareness of that status.

You must see that situation clearly by perceiving how your inner nature affects the outer events of your life. If you need my confirmation, then you don't see it clearly, but have only created an artificial belief that covers over a bed of doubt and other conflicting beliefs that would still hold afterwards.

E49g – All other apparent power-sources (god, fate, coincidence, luck, time, money, bacteria, virus, vitamins, DNA, experts, information, knowledge) in my life are just my own constructs, that I was conditioned to create during my childhood. I powered up them and drained myself. This is the way I feel. But since I think I've given away some power to you, your approval would boost me up.

Then, as I said, you'd have yet another psychological construct to distort your awareness. I've given my words as aids to your growth, not as words to be revered and deified. You must come to see life as it is, not how I tell you it is. Awareness is awareness, not philosophy. In other words, I can't boost you up.

If you lean on crutches all the time, your legs become weaker, not stronger.

Scrape away all the definitions of external power sources and forces for making life work, and you'll see it for yourself. At that point, you won't need me or anybody else to confirm what actually is.

E49h – Your perspective on things matters a lot to me, since it was mainly your words that gave me confidence in seriously changing my life, for the better of course. Is that bad?

It wasn't really I who gave you confidence. I can't do that. It was you, yourself, in your quest for understanding and your rejection of all the other philosophies and religions that abound in Western and even Eastern cultures. If my words mean anything to you, then you already had the kernel of self-perception – reinforced by open-minded pursuit – within yourself.

At earlier times of my own journey, I gained much from reading others' words – the great teachers – Jesus, Lao-Tzu, Buddha – and others like Krishnamurti, Watts, etc. But gain was attained not by following them, making them authorities and holding their teachings as flawless, but by breaking down older, more synthetic understandings. And I outgrew their messages, because, by seeing myself and reality clearly, I came to see even their limitations.

When you come to the point that you don't need to ask me for confirmation for something you perceive to be true, then your awareness will be of utmost value to you. It is only ever you and your perspective that count. Never mine.

Without a doubt, the greatest single hindrance to expanded Awareness is the complex belief structure you've formulated by the time you reach puberty – and likely solidify from then onward.

Always, to illustrate perspectives needed to ply the sincere seeker off base consciousness levels and help advancement take place, I must present deeper insights into Christian conjecture and fantasy declarations. Thus, let's shift focus to look...

Beyond Belief: Exposing CHRISTIANITY

In preparing my third book, *The Illusion of "Truth"*, I did considerable research on the roots of Christianity, historical details of the first two centuries and the lead-up to that time in the Middle East and Roman Empire, the traditions of Judaism, and scholarly writings on the New Testament. So, questions I've answered over the years concerning that religion are well founded on a broad understanding, not only of the nature of life and Consciousness – so that I recognize a distinct level of awareness in Jesus' viewpoint as expressed in his parables – but also in all aspects of Christian conjecture and its origin.

Becoming aware of Christianity's lack of substance and the damaging effect of holding it as true is a critical element for anyone who grew up in a Western culture and who desires to come to see life clearly. The subconscious mind holds and references information in a reliable and inviolable way. Simply coming to a rational awareness that Christianity is fantasy and invalid at its core beliefs isn't enough to remove it and its damaging effects from one's total mindset...

And until that Old-Time Religion is fully deleted from the psyche's accumulation of details, it will continue to contribute to inner conflict, likely self-punishment and other negatives – all of which then get woven into real-life problems.

So, in the following questions, I address specific points raised concerning Christianity, refuting them or otherwise illustrating life in ways that reveal the flawed core of Christian thinking. If you now recognize the journey you are on towards clearer thinking, the following answers to posed questions should help...

Q50 – What are the most common misconceptions about God?

Of course, the greatest misconception is that the Christian god, named "God" with a capital "G", actually exists – *or ever did.*

If you would explore Biblical manuscripts in their earliest forms, written in Greek (New Testament) and Hebrew (Old), you would never, not in any instance, find reference to a god named "God". In the oldest accounts (first few books of the Old Testament), the god worshiped by Hebrews was **El** – a god commonly regarded by various Canaanite peoples.

El, generally in the ancient Middle East/Mesopotamia, was part of a pantheon which included Asherah as his consort. But in time, through the era of Moses, the Hebrew deity switched to Yahweh. This is actually noted in Deuteronomy 32:7–8, where El Elyon (Most High God) assigns the children of Israel to Yahweh (generally translated as the "Lord"). Yahweh or YHWH from that point became the popular deity up to Jesus' time. So far as can be construed with some degree of agreement – much less so of actual reliability – Abraham, if he really existed, lived about 1900 BCE. His time frame of Hebrew history featured El as its primary god – likely at that time, still featuring Asherah and other gods in a pantheon.

Moses likely lived about 1300 or 1200 BCE – and his "burning bush" deity was already YHWH. So the switch came somewhere in between – again, so far as can be surmised. Archaic Biblical references are highly unreliable due to considerable change over the ages as its stories were passed only through oral traditions, then writing – as even written accounts would have changed over time as interpretations and religious notions evolved.

The Bible is thought to have been first rendered to script only by about 600 BCE. Even if writing stems from earlier, the myth and lore on which even Old Testament accounts are based are far short of reliable documentation of history.

In any case, El and Yahweh were depicted differently – gods evolve in the minds of believers over generations, so that isn't surprising. El to Abraham seemed to be more of a personal god – appearing to him in the form of a human at one point. Yahweh, however, by the time of Moses, had become a grand and powerful war god – look upon him and you die!

But Jesus spoke of a different god – a loving, caring one, not the vindictive, judgmental deity of older times. He would have referred to his described deity as Alaha or Elaha – Aramaic terms for "god". But Paul created Christianity, not Jesus. And Paul's imagined god would have been called Theou in Greek. And he bore no resemblance to Jesus' loving deity. Theou, still in the mythical traditions of Yahweh, was to come down from his realm in the heavens to establish control over things – *any day now.*

(In those days, gods were imagined as real, physical entities, living up in heaven, a place above the big, blue dome "firmament" that spanned the flat earth. Paul really thought his big, authoritative god would come flying down to earth in physical form, accompanied by angels and Jesus. People had a really, really primitive view of earth back then.)

Anyway, "God" is never mentioned. The Christian deity is an amalgam of all those earlier deities – a product of deceptively translating various gods' names all into one English term. He contains, as imagined by Christianity, qualities that can't possibly coexist within each other: forgiving, yet vindictive (can't be both), beneficent, yet willing to damn you to eternal Hell (can't be both), loving, yet judgmental (can't be both). The Christian deity, named "God" with the big "G", not only doesn't exist – but *could not possibly exist,* based on the mutually exclusive characteristics he's supposed to have.

My point is that God, ***itself,*** as a word, is a misconception. It's a smoothed over, puffed up, grossly generalized conceptualization of anything and everything the superstitious Christian mind wants it to be – picking and choosing among all those characteristics to suit the current needs of the deluded believer.

Any other misconceptions – and there are many, as a cascade from that major one – are less significant:

- That God judges you after death is absurd – a holdover from ancient times of Zoroastrian belief in a deity named Ahura Mazda.
- That God makes things happen in your life or on earth is banal – another relic of a big, intrusive deity above the firmament.
- That God will change his will as implanted into real life in response to prayer, *your* prayer nonetheless, is phenomenally silly – yet another remnant notion from archaic belief in an intrusive, small-minded, egoistic creator god.
- That God wants all people to worship him – thus imposing on *you* the need to convert and spread "His" word among all mankind – again beyond silly...

All of these misconceptions stem from the main one: that a deity named "God" exists in the first place.

Q51 – Who really wrote the New Testament of the Bible?

According to critical studies of the 27 New Testament "books", Paul almost certainly wrote seven of the books attributed to him, and possibly an eighth – based on writing style and content. Biblical scholars have concluded (in general, as some doubtless differ) that the other books attributed to him were written by someone else. Their style and content differ considerably.

And all of the other books of the NT, 19 or 20 of them, were anonymous – with names attributed to them either attached later or applied at the time to give greater believability to the work. These are logical conclusions based on scholarly research. For example, whoever wrote Matthew drew heavily from the writings attributed to "Mark" – many passages are copied, some revised a bit to correct errors or eliminate accounts deemed uncomplimentary to Jesus.

If Matthew were indeed written by the tax-collecting disciple of Jesus, he wouldn't have had to copy the older writing. And he would have recounted the stories as "we" did such and such, or "we" then went to so-and-so. In fact, these gospel writers' names and all the rest of the NT documents were assigned names, i.e., made up to lend credibility to the works.

In ancient times, you could write anything you wanted to – provided you were literate, which most (a good 90%, including all non-wealthy peasants) weren't – and *put any name to it you chose*. There was no publishing standard, no such worry that someone would find out – who could or would be able to check? There weren't publishing houses or copyrights or even libraries (outside Alexandria and Pergamon) to check against. Putting your own name as title would garner no authority, but falsely applying the name John or Peter, noted disciples, or Jude or James (brothers of Jesus) – now *that* would get your epistle read and accepted, get your own ideas heard.

So that's what they did – unknown characters, putting their own ideas into play.

NT books were all written in Greek, with the gospels dating maybe 70 CE, 40 years after Jesus' time (Mark) to 60 or more years (John). Paul's letters actually predate the gospels, as his travels and communication took place in the 50s CE. Other letters and Revelations date from late in the first century to perhaps 110 CE. These are difficult to date precisely, as the original copies are all long gone and the authors as well as date and location of composition are unknown.

Clearly, the illiterate peasants who followed Jesus, including his disciples, couldn't write in fairly good quality Greek, so none of them, including the disciples, were authors of any of the works – including letters attributed to James and Jude. Again, these had names of Jesus' brothers assigned as authors to give the works some credibility.

The point: outside of seven or eight Pauline letters, names of writers of the other 19 or 20 New Testament works are unknown. While you don't know their names, however, you *can* conclude who they were.

By 70 CE, about when Mark was written, the Romans had invaded Jerusalem and most proto-Christians had long since fled Judea. Early proto-Christianity was still stuck to Judaism, but had started to attract non-Jews – thanks in part to Paul introducing to Greeks and others in the region the notion that Jesus was divine. Few Jews bought into the idea – their notion of a Messiah wasn't a guy strung up as a common criminal, but would be a great leader come to free them from external control (like the Romans).

But when Mark was composed, reliable info on Jesus was sparse. That was four decades after Jesus' likely crucifixion. His Galilean culture was illiterate, so only personal stories of his travels and teaching survived. But those tales passed by word of mouth *for 40 years*; they were retold among illiterate, uneducated, superstitious peasants. Consequently, they grew in myth and added special effects – miracles and astounding feats – drawn from other traditions, enhanced at each retelling. That process carried on over several generations, as people didn't live long then.

Early proto-Christians – particularly the Greek contingent intermingled in the population of Syria, Asia Minor and Egypt – had only the Septuagint (Greek translation of the Old Testament) to reference for their meetings and discussions. And they had those old, exaggerated tales of Jesus. About the year 70 CE, then, some fairly literate follower collected stories he'd heard and wrote them down. These eventually were reputed by later generations to have been written by Mark, companion of Peter – but that was simply added myth. Earliest manuscripts have no byline. But the writer, clearly, based on style and fluency, was Greek, not Galilean.

Scholars don't reliably know even *where* Mark was composed, let along by whom – Syria? Asia Minor? Nobody knows. What it contains, though, is clear. It contains the viewpoint of that anonymous writer and his community – stories they'd heard and believed. What it doesn't contain are biographical *facts* – ancient writers weren't objective reporters: they wrote to pass along ideas, not report true events.

Both Matthew and Luke – similarly, written by unknown Greeks – take Mark and expand on it. Of 660 verses in Mark, Matthew practically copies some 600, Luke 300; but each revises Mark accounts to clear up errors and make Jesus appear ever more heroic and divine.

The author of Mark, writing in 70 CE, knew nothing about a virgin birth or resurrection. (Nor had Paul, writing his letters around year 50.) Matthew and Luke both had to make up those stories to glorify Jesus – so they invented stories to get him to grow up in Nazareth (which people generally knew, as hometowns were often used to differentiate among people long before family names were invented) but yet come from Bethlehem (where lore claimed a great teacher would come from).

However, those two writers *weren't aware of each other's fiction*: if you read both accounts of the birth of Jesus, they couldn't both be true. Same with the death and resurrection. As Mark knew nothing about these stories, undoubtedly, they were invented later.

So, clearly, exaggeration and myth-growing were at work here. By the time John was written, likely around the end of the century, the Jesus myth had grown even greater – he was now equated with god, had been in existence forever, etc. (This certainly wasn't written by John, son of Zebedee, who would have been about 100 by then, in a time when age 30 was already old.)

And, of course, the Jesus depicted in John is radically different from the man in the Synoptic Gospels in many ways.

So, who wrote the New Testament? Superstitious, credulous, extremely naïve Greeks.

Everybody in the first and second centuries – outside of a small group of sincere, searching folk in Alexandria and maybe a few thinkers remaining in Athens – was in that category: superstitious, credulous, extremely naïve. They had no idea they inhabited a planet orbiting a sun, no recognition of weather patterns, continental drift, economics, political science, world cultures, history, pre-history, geography, mathematics, bacteria, objective thinking, critical thinking – or much of anything else we take for granted.

The New Testament writers were stating their primitive notions, based on generations of accrued myth, exaggerated lore – and *a total misunderstanding of Jesus' parables*. Where Jesus spoke of a Kingdom "within" – find it within yourself and you'll be blessed, i.e., good things will happen to you – the NT writers latched onto and expanded Paul's archaic ideas: God would be coming any day now to establish his kingdom on earth.

Who they were is unknown. *What* they were, conversely, is easy to see – if you look with an open mind: first century, superstitious believers in primitive deities and lurking evil spirits.

Q52 – Are Jesus of Nazareth and Paul of Tarsus the two most important individuals in Christian history?

That, of course, is a judgment call — but looking at the emergence and development of Christianity objectively, with a sound knowledge of its early development, I would emphatically say: **NO**.

If you seek two key people in the creation of Christianity, Paul of Tarsus certainly was one. Christianity is so built on Paul's viewpoint, that it could be accurately called *Paulism*. Paul's ideas displaced anything Jesus alluded to in his parables – and affixed notions like a judgmental deity, that Jesus, dubbed by Paul as "the Christ", was god made flesh and would return, that belief in Jesus as Savior was key to eternal life, with all that fantasy woven into a post-death Heaven/Hell…

("Christ" is the Greek translation of the word *Messiah*, but it took on a greatly different meaning, thanks to Paul – no longer a great, anointed leader who would lead the Jewish people to freedom from their oppressors, Christ now meant a superhuman who would save you from your sins and inherent failings…)

Paul was the principal driving force to the development of Christianity at its beginning. Pinpointing any other *real* person as more important in "Christian history", relying primarily on actual contribution to its scriptures, therefore, is futile.

Jesus of Nazareth, the real man – actually named Yeshua in its original form – had amazingly little to do with the religion later formulated based on myth and lore about him. I'll get to that shortly…

Peter, a key disciple of Jesus, and James, Jesus' brother, are mentioned in the Acts as crucial players in the early movement to convince the ruling Jewish hierarchy of Jesus' status as the long-awaited Messiah. But that effort ultimately failed, as Jews in general were looking for a heroic leader to rally them to defeat their numerous, domineering enemies – Rome at that time. Peter and James simply disappear to history as Paul came to spread his own message out to gullible, superstitious Greeks and other ethnic groups.

So, Jesus and his contemporaries had little to do with proto-Christianity and its ultimate emergence as a religion separate from its original Judaism.

A case might be made for one of several early church patriarchs as critical to Christian history – the shaping of the religion out of a plethora of doctrines promulgated by early movements, distinctly different in various regions. Second century contributors were:

- Polycarp (69–155), supposedly a disciple of John (doubtful, as John, Jesus' apostle, would have been long dead), was martyred for refusing to burn incense to the Emperor.
- Marcion (c. 85–c. 160), bishop in early Christianity, created a rival branch to what became orthodoxy.
- Valentinus (c. 100–c. 160) was an early, successful Christian Gnostic theologian – also a rival doctrine to orthodoxy.
- Justin (100–c. 165) was an early Christian apologist who interpreted the theory of the Logos.
- Irenaeus (c. 130–c. 202), a bishop at Lyon (then Lugdunum), refuted Gnosticism and emphasized traditional elements of the Church, such as scripture and tradition.

Into the third century some others contributed to development of Christian ideas:

- Tertullian (c. 160–c. 225) basically invented the idea of the Trinity and fought against "heresy" – basically anybody who differed from his interpretation of things.
- Origen (185–254) believed in the preexistence and transmigration of souls.

Into the fourth century, you find Athanasius (296–373) who fought against Arianism at the Council of Nicaea, thus helping to establish orthodoxy as the accepted doctrine, and Augustine (354–430), whose contribution strongly helped formulate Christian thinking.

But none of these was really critical to "Christian history". Had any one of them not lived, the ancient religion wouldn't be much different. You have to look outside the ranks of the faithful to find one other individual who shaped Christianity: the main character who *really* contributed to the course of Christian development was **Constantine the Great** – the Roman Emperor who gained control over the entire empire and called together that First Council of Nicaea in the year 325, where Christianity was wrangled together from various, divergent ideas.

Thus, the two most important individuals in Christian history were ***Paul*** and ***Constantine***. Without either, it simply wouldn't have evolved as it did.

Aha, but **why not Jesus?**

The real man we call Jesus, Yeshua, whose words survive in sayings – the parables of the Synoptic Gospels and the Gospel of Thomas – had a message totally unlike what became Christian doctrine:

- The real Jesus spoke of a Kingdom "within" – that is, within the psyche of each individual: see it and you will be blessed, i.e., good things will happen to you. Paul and others twisted that inner Kingdom 180 degrees to point to an imagined external power source, a grand, dictatorial deity up above the firmament. To Christianity, he is the cause of all things, not you – as Jesus implied.
- The real Jesus taught of how this Kingdom existed ***right now***, in this very moment – all you had to do was see it. Paul – and thus his religious movement – projected the Kingdom to be coming in some future time, when his big, tough deity would come down and establish an earthly realm, favoring believers in his existence.
- The real Jesus decried the elite establishment of a priesthood and organizations that could only distort his message – the blind leading the blind. Paul helped

establish *exactly that* same clueless, self-serving religious hierarchy, based on his "Christ" superhero incarnated deity: countless bloated organizations which have since imposed their fantasy-based ideas on untold millions.

- The real Jesus spoke of healing based on inner trust and belief. The church, based on Paul's archaic thinking, projects healing out to its imagined deity or to phony, faith-healing quacks.

So, no, Jesus of Nazareth, the real man, did not, in any way, shape or form, contribute to the history of Christianity. That man, the real Yeshua, would have been appalled at the bogus, fantasy-based superman Paul and others turned him into in the decades and centuries after his lifetime.

Christianity was built on Paul's archaic ideas and was first hammered into an artificial set of beliefs only three centuries later, thanks to Constantine's dictates. It was based on myth about Jesus' superhuman nature – not his deep insights – and on exaggerated lore about his otherworldly miracles and god-nature. These fantasies had accrued in Jesus stories only after his death as they were passed by word of mouth through oral traditions over several generations – and they grew even further in the generations and centuries after his death, ever magnified by individuals listed above and many other small-minded, superstitious followers of fantasy ideas…

So, the answer to your question is resoundingly, **NO**. Jesus didn't contribute to the history of Christianity. That religion formed only long after his death. Paul did, though, and Constantine the Great aided and abetted in the formulation of its baseless, invented doctrine.

Q53 – What do you find to be the creepiest aspect of the Christian Faith, as practiced by Christians?

A lot of good answers were posted on Quora for this question, as Christians are known to do a lot of really oddball things in practice of their archaic beliefs:

- Transubstantiation – the belief in the Catholic church that, during communion, the wine and the bread offered in the ritual literally turns into the blood and flesh of Christ. (Pretty disgusting if you think about it.)
- That there is a Hell to which you would be relegated for eternity just for being what you were created – and that, somehow, God is *good*!?!?
- The beliefs that evil spirits exist and make bad things happen.
- The indoctrination of children.
- Honoring a tool of torture and execution (the cross) as a symbol of devotion.
- The notion that Jesus died to alleviate human sins – when God was supposed to have created the whole system in the first place.
- The connection of morality to religion – in light of the history of Christianity with its murderous crusades and torture via the Inquisition.
- Saint's body parts as relics displayed in churches.
- The notion that, if you wrong somebody, all you have to do is ask God's forgiveness and everything is OK – which brings up "Confession" as a Catholic ritual.

But in my answer on Quora, I questioned whether readers ever wondered **why** Christians do or believe these things:

Ask a preacher why he wears a robe. Ask why he/she performs communion or blesses people. Ask a believer why he/she goes to church or believes in redemption or sin, in a judgmental god. Ask a Catholic why he/she gets a smudge of ash on the forehead or does confession.

You'll get lots of answers as to reasons for those and any religious gestures or rituals. But none of them are accurate.

Here is the real reason for any of these goofy practices: people do those things solely *because somebody told them to.*

People build up beliefs and definitions early in life, indoctrinated and fully programmed by adults and proclaimed authorities. If those experts in various practices are wrong, the rituals are worthless – but people, gullible and programmed with their phony truths, won't know that, because *most don't question*. Indeed, most seem incapable of questioning.

Anyway, it's worth understanding exactly ***why*** people do or believe these absurd things. Only because they're told so!

Q54 – How can I get Christians to believe that I am the true messiah – I have finally come back as I have promised, but I am not taken seriously – J. C.

You never would or could, even if you really were. Christians are looking for a magical, mystical happening and have been for two millennia. But their dreamy intent has no basis in reality: it is pure fantasy. You, on the other hand, are real (even though your question may be less than serious). As a real human, you don't fit into their expectations...

Years ago, as a young guy, 24, I had just begun a year-long adventure hitchhiking around Europe; I'd started out in Ireland. Traveling through Belfast, the original home of my mother's parents, I was engaged in deep discussion in a pub one night. A local, a great guy, commented at one point in his Northern Irish brogue where the sentences always finish on an upbeat, "Ya know, Christianity has been in a state of masturbation for two thousand years..."

"Yeah," I answered. "And they're still waiting for the second coming!"

Jesus of Nazareth, actually named Yeshua (they couldn't even get that right), was a visionary. As all such seers, he could sense to some degree the interactive Oneness of Self with experienced Reality – an awareness that simply escapes those whose perception is heavily distorted by beliefs. (That, by the way, includes most people and all Christians – which is neither a criticism nor a slam, but an accurate observation.)

He tried to illustrate a "Kingdom of Heaven ***within***" in his parables, attempting to show in ways colloquially attuned to farmers and fishermen how each of us engages life with an intimate connection: how your life would work well with trust and belief rather than contention, how this recognition was a very valuable thing, how this "Kingdom" existed *NOW* if you could only see it, not in the future or elsewhere, how this level of recognition doesn't fit into old thinking, etc.

In my third book, *The Illusion of "Truth"*, I point out nine indications of his insights into the functional Oneness of Consciousness/Reality. To grasp what he meant, though, you have to be able to see through your own restrictive beliefs and discard them – beliefs only serve to distort perception of reality; they never clarify it.

Christians wouldn't be able to do that.

Jesus may have reached a few open-minded individuals in his lifetime – but probably not many in the rigid, traditional society he encountered. Ultimately, his peers, spurred presumably by the established priesthood (whose privileged lifestyle would have been threatened by a new, charismatic teacher), did him in.

Other, far less perceptive people (the clueless disciples, superstitious, Zoroastrian-thinking Paul and others) thrust Jesus into mythical, otherworldly status and established, based on that myth, a religion that had/has nothing to do with his insights.

So, if you really were a visionary of the status of the real Yeshua, who railed against the excesses and blindness of the entrenched priesthood of his day, you would find no fertile ground among Christians to plant your seed. And you would find nothing but resistance and scorn from any and all priesthoods, all of whom, however sincere in their beliefs, are even more deluded than their flocks – *PLUS*, they have a vested interest in keeping those tithes and offerings flowing into their own pockets, not yours.

Kind of like planting seeds on rocky soil, where they won't sprout – sound familiar?

You would need to seek out open-minded people who were sincerely looking to understand life. They are around in the 21st century, but they're not to be found in churches.

That, of course, doubles back onto your question as a revealing disclaimer. If you really were the reincarnation of the character who played out the lifetime of Yeshua of Nazareth, you wouldn't have to ask how to go about things.

Oh, and Jesus' initials wouldn't have been *J. C.* "Christ" is the Greek equivalent of the Hebrew "Messiah". The real Yeshua of Nazareth would have had no interest in either title.

Q55 – Was there any physical evidence about the true existence of Jesus Christ?

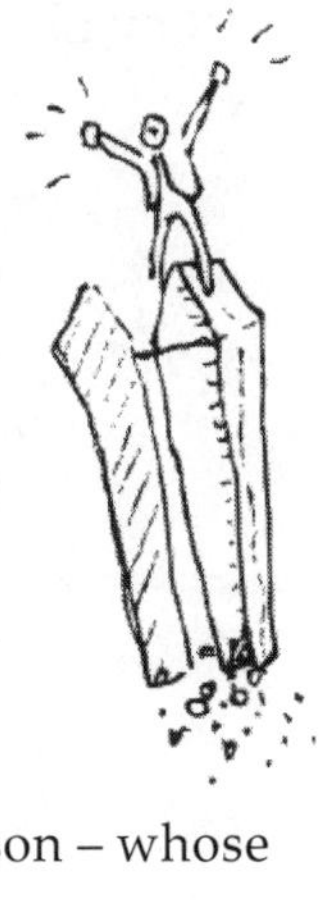

No and/or Yes, depending on what you might define as "physical". So far as I've ever read, there exist no reliable archaeological remains that stemmed from Jesus of Nazareth. (Various religious icons, including the Shroud of Turin, are all phony.)

Before I go on to illustrate real evidence in the form of meaningful ideas, let's first distinguish the difference between a likely real, flesh-and-blood person – whose name would have been *Yeshua*, not the Latinized/Anglicized "Jesus" – and the mythological fantasy created by Paul, named "Jesus Christ".

The term "Christ" is a Greek translation of the Hebrew "Messiah". *That* term, in Jewish lore, meant an "Anointed One" – that is, a religious or military leader who had duly, through official ritual, had oil poured on his head. The ancients associated evil with foul-smelling things – and they were highly concerned with evil spirits, which they deemed to cause mental and physical health issues. The ritual of pouring a sweet-smelling oil onto someone symbolized the cleansing of Evil by overcoming it with Good in the form of pleasant fragrance.

In general, the traditional Jewish people were long looking for a grand leader (who had been duly anointed) to lead them to freedom from oppressing neighbors – of which there were many.

Judah, i.e., Roman Judea, was stuck right smack between the Persians (later Parthia), various empires of the Mesopotamian region and Egypt. By Jesus' time, Rome had joined the queue and made its way to the front.

The long-awaited Messiah was to be a great leader to bring freedom from Rome and anybody else.

When the disciples and Paul, then other church founders, proclaimed Jesus to be – in retrospect, as he'd been issued a criminal's death by crucifixion – that Messiah, they fabricated a mythical story to sell the very gullible, superstitious peasants of the time: Jesus would lead a rebellion by coming down from the sky with heavenly host and crushing the enemy and saving true believers. Paul preached at first that this was imminent, but as time went by, it never happened. So, Paul and others had to change their story – which they've been very good at for the intervening two millennia. (They all do need to keep themselves in business – keep those tithes and offerings flowing…)

That mythical fantasy, *Jesus Christ* never existed – except in the fervent imaginations of millions of superstitious dupes over centuries.

Yeshua of Nazareth, however, was certainly a real person who did leave "physical" evidence in the form of his parables – if you'll consider valid, well-illustrated ideas that were passed on, eventually in written form, as *physical*. (I'll refer to the real human as *Yeshua* to differentiate reality from myth.)

To grasp that as conclusive, irrefutable evidence, you first have to understand how life actually works. Yeshua was offering a visionary recognition of the flow of life, trying to get his listeners to see past the rigid Jewish and myth-based beliefs of his time.

Please note: that same difficulty exists in *anybody* seeing what the parables meant – *personal beliefs interfere with perceiving life's real function.*

Reminder: *whatever you believe in seems to be true* – whether 2000 years ago or this very minute. Your belief system, featuring modern notions of science as well as primitive thoughts of a manipulative deity, luck and fate, invariably distorts your personal perception to confirm its precepts. If you aren't willing and capable of questioning your own held beliefs, you'll not grasp my illustration to follow – nor will you understand what the parables were saying.

Your conscious Self is connected to the flow of events and relationships that constitute your life: you attract patterns. Life is based on meaning, and the meaning woven into your life stems from your own comprehensive mindset. Problems you encounter in life always have inner roots.

You can delve inward to find and change inner mechanisms – such a venture will revise the patterns you encounter and bring improvement.

Stated otherwise, you encounter in unfolding life a *reflection of your own nature.*

Yeshua (the real guy behind the Jesus of lore) became aware of this inner-outer Oneness. He tried to get his peasant peers to see beyond the Law and Prophets' declarations of his traditions. But he couldn't explain inner, psychological elements to uneducated, superstitious farmers and fishermen – he had to illustrate life perspectives in metaphor, in simple stories that reflected the agrarian lifestyle of his contemporaries.

At least nine elements expressed in Jesus' parables show his significant level of awareness of the inner-outer connection. They include:

- That the recognition of life's functional Oneness is a powerful, exclusive realization that precludes other explanations – hidden treasure in the field, pearl of great value, yeast to leaven flour, mustard seed, etc.
- That clearly perceiving the Oneness of things required getting rid of old ideas that masked it – seeing life as a child, being born again (i.e., without all the beliefs and indoctrination already in place).
- Greater Awareness doesn't fit into old ideas – new patch on old material, new wine in old wineskins.
- That patterns form in life – the rich get richer…
- Where and when the "Kingdom" will come – now, as it's already here, but people don't recognize it, some won't die before they see the Kingdom…
- Love your neighbor and enemy as yourself – others aren't the source of your problems, so loving them will help revise life issues away from continual realization of conflict.

Again, seeing the insight in these observations is deterred by one's personal beliefs. When you come to see for yourself how your life reflects your own composite nature, how you can revise your life's flow by changing your own inner, subconscious elements, you'll grasp his parables' meaning.

Historically, though, neither Jesus' peers, the disciples, Paul, church founders nor two millennia of deluded believers grasp his core message. That's not surprising when you recognize how the mind is deluded by its own beliefs.

My point, then, is this: parables noted by those who had heard Yeshua speak stuck in their memories – like jokes remain intact during retelling to keep the punch line, parables all have unique twists to them. So, decades later as accounts of Jesus built into myth and lore, his deeds exaggerated into miracles at every turn, his words were preserved when they were written in the Gospels by about the year 70 and on.

And those descriptive accounts of a pearl in the field, a new patch on old garment, that the Kingdom of Heaven is NOW (not in the future or somewhere else), that you should love your neighbors and enemies, that you should see life with the innocence of a child, etc. – these are all irrefutable evidence of the existence of a very aware person.

But that person was a real guy, Yeshua. Not a fantasy superman titled Jesus Christ.

You can't get better evidence than that, conceptually, for the existence of the real Yeshua. But many layers of religious fantasy and cultural notions hide and distort the meaning that man tried to express.

Q56 – What is the biggest scam you've ever seen?

My first impression of this question was that the biggest scam ever – was Donald Trump's campaign running for president. He made great promises, pushed all the hot-buttons to incite gullible people's reactions, got them emotionally involved – and said of all the problems the country faces, only he can fix them. Yet he had no experience in such things, no temperament or intelligence to take on a highly complex job and offered no realistic plan to accomplish anything.

That was a monumental scam from the beginning. The trouble was, there were just enough suckers around who bought into it – fools by the millions were conned into his wild claims and Fox News propaganda.

However, that Trump con pales in comparison to Christianity. A plethora of Christian churches propagate the greatest con ever foisted on mankind – far longer and somewhat more widespread than its rival, Islam.

That Old-Time Religion makes a wide range of unfounded declarations, claims them as true, then has pure suckers, generally brainwashed since birth, donate their legitimately-earned money to support its dedicated priesthood, often in luxury. The number of evangelical frauds, worth millions conned from the gullible, is in the dozens. Popes, not unlike TV evangelists, for ages have lived in luxurious decadence, all paid for by – is there a good synonym for "sucker"? I hate to overuse that word. OK, dupes…

Doubtless, some unprincipled portion of mankind figured out millennia ago that it was much easier to spout off popular beliefs and take in donations than to actually work for a living. Their philosophical descendants, spouting some religion or other, have been living off the ignorant, literally for ages.

Christianity's tenets (a judging god, post-death heaven or hell, sins, artificial morality) are more deeply rooted in Zoroastrianism than in Judaism. Otherwise, they're just made up (Trinity, Savior, miracles) and foisted on gullible, fearful believers.

It works.

There are two billion Christians, plus unfathomably supreme suckers for pseudo-Christian movements like Mormonism, the Amish and Jehovah's Witnesses. Where Jesus spoke of a Kingdom "within", they buy into a big deity in the sky – pure myth and lore.

So, ***without a single doubt***, lacking any peer (outside of its close competition, Islam, which is even a worse hoax in cosmological and ethical terms, but not quite as widespread), Christianity is the greatest scam ever perpetrated on mankind.

Q57 – How do I stop being religious? I recently became an atheist, but find that some religious traits in my character hinder my growth.

The subconscious, that deep realm of your mind, stores information, memories, definitions, conclusions, hopes, fears and many other aspects of consciousness in a structured way. It can be quite convoluted, in that many of your deeper beliefs and accepted definitions contradict each other, yet are woven together in meaningful strains – as learning them, absorbing them during childhood, tied them together with meaning. Held beliefs, including religious tenets, claims and synthetic values, can be quite inaccurate, in that many of your cherished cultural notions simply aren't true.

But your own psychological store of a vast array of information and interwoven notion will persist with its current belief structure indefinitely – if not explicitly changed. In effect, the subconscious is timeless. It forgets nothing; even if you can't recall details effectively, they remain stored deeper within the mindset.

The consequence of this is that to fully outgrow, i.e., to completely and effectively release bogus religious claims and declarations, it is necessary to delve inward with focus and, point-by-point, release all the lessons you learned about your old, worn-out religion.

The mind stores details. You likely learned religion as a child, when lessons about Jesus and miracles, notions of myth as fact and impossible events as truths, were all set deeply into your naïve mind – and reinforced by parental love and need for acceptance. To fully eradicate these phony declarations of such deep-seeded religious tenets, you have to focus inward, find each point of misunderstanding, and "rewrite" the subconscious. Repeatedly and pointedly focus on and release all the artificial Christian (or whatever) "truths" you absorbed, which aren't true, but were given to you as such.

I discuss techniques for doing so on my website and throughout my books. I have also created demonstrations of these tools, e.g., self-hypnosis and ideomotor responses, on my YouTube channel.

If you don't fully scour the subconscious of its religious programming, *you'll still have issues*. You may outwardly have come to see that there isn't any deity like the god with the capital "G", that Jesus wasn't a superman, that popes, priests and preachers are just deluded con men passing along an age-old hoax – and still have the distinct feeling there is an external force out there, dictating your life.

There isn't.

But there ***is*** meaning in life, with you at the center. To see how that works, it is vital to flush each and every tenet of your previous religion from your mindset. If you don't, it will remain in place. And it will affect your psychological stance, your peace of mind – and the flow of your life.

Q58 – Why do many Christians not know the Bible/Biblical scripture very well? When trying to discuss the Bible in general or particular passages of scripture many Christians seem to be completely out of their depth. How can they profess faith in something they seem to know so little about?

One principal reason why Christians don't know the Bible and its contents very well is that churches and their priesthoods rely on gullible believers to keep coming back and dropping their tithes and offerings into that old, well-worn collection plate. If the sheep were actually educated, told realistic points about the New and Old Testaments, who wrote them and what archaic ideas they promulgate, a lot of them would leave.

This is one of the most damning (figuratively!) features about Christianity: young people, when they go to seminary to study to become ministers or priests, learn a lot of major reasons to question the religion. They study the Bible in its historical context and look critically at its conjecture. They learn that the New Testament wasn't written by the people listed as authors, but rather was composed decades later by unknown Greeks, not the disciples or *anybody who ever heard, saw or knew Jesus*.

They learn about internal conflict in New Testament passages – where it says one thing in one place, just the opposite elsewhere.

They learn of impossible reports, where the gospels report events that the author, writing a good half century after the event, *could not possibly have known what happened*. They learn how exaggerated accounts, basically myth, are simply accepted as truthful. Young, would-be preachers learn how early Christianity had many opposing sects – competitive groups brought together only in the fourth century to form a single orthodoxy, by the emperor Constantine (of all people!).

They learn how the church pretends that orthodoxy was predominant from the early days – which it wasn't. In short, clergy in training learn of all the flaws and distortions, exaggerations and revisions of history perpetrated by unknown writers decades after Jesus' death and added to by Christian sects over centuries. They learn many, many reasons to doubt ideas put forth by every Christian denomination...

But strangely, even though they hear all of the fantasized dogma and myth, its lack of substance and basis on really, *really* blind faith, when they go out and get a job as preacher, all they talk about is the same old stock ideas that the flock is used to hearing.

Most Christians aren't very curious. They don't want to know anything more than their reassuring myth: God's out there and he loves you, but, boy, if you don't do what he says he'll damn you to eternity in Hell. And anyway, go do what you want – cheat, rape, pillage, screw people, lie. It doesn't matter, because you'll be forgiven if you only believe that Jesus was your Savior!

That fantasy is laughable, with much of it, actually, pulled straight out of Zoroastrian teaching about a judgmental Ahura Mazda – thanks to Paul's import of common myth. But it's the schlock Christians learned from childhood, so they're happy with it and socially accepted, so, hey, ministers and priests are happy to feed it to them. And collect their pay for doing next to nothing.

In writing my third book, *The Illusion of "Truth"*, I did extensive research into scholarly writing about the "historical Jesus". To see the depth of the fallacy, the extent of exaggeration and myth-building that went on, was amazing. First, exaggeration of events and invention of miracles grew rampantly in the forty years after Jesus' death until Mark was written by a writer who isn't even known in a location also unknown. Then it continued to expand in fantasized, totally impossible accounts as Matthew and Luke were written probably 15 years later. Then, as John took shape a couple decades after that (scholars recognize at least three different writing styles in the fourth Gospel, so it was hammered together from different accounts), the fantasies grew to new heights.

In effect, the Gospels are fictions – demonstrably so, as I do detail in my book, *Illusion*. Elements, many of them, were simply invented by superstitious peasants and overtly pious priest-types over the first two or three centuries. The Trinity, for example, is never mentioned in the New Testament, but was practically invented by Tertullian around the year 200. Doesn't matter that all three, the Father, Son and Holy Spirit, are fully fictitious, mythical inventions – the Trinity got woven into Christian tenets, so it became **real** in the eyes of believers.

Anyway, the answer to your question is twofold. Christians don't know much mostly because they don't want to. Those who *do* start exploring the shallow, insubstantial Christian tenets often just jettison the religion.

And the dedicated priesthood is highly motivated to just keep piling on the old dogma and mush. Their paycheck depends on keeping the dupes in line and attracting new rubes into the social club.

Q59 – What are the differences between a believer and a nonbeliever?

While growing through childhood, each of us was presented with cultural values and norms. Some of the understanding passed on came through explanations by parents: religion, science, old pagan notions like luck and fate, etc. Some came from stories you were told, cartoons and movies you watched, television shows that you were exposed to – all of which share and reinforced cultural standards and popular beliefs. But also, you absorbed many values and impressions, subtle conclusions and emotional responses through the behavior of and your treatment by parents – how you were loved or rejected, praised or punished.

During the process of absorbing the explanations and treatment, you, as all humans have done, built up a *self-image* and *world view* – a complex, interrelated set of values and concepts woven into the huge complex of subconscious mind that holds complex explanations of life (that is, how it *appears*) and underlies core thinking.

For some, the ideas and fixation on them as real and valid becomes rigidly frozen into place. Declared conceptualizations displace any logic or reason proposed later – held, indoctrinated ideas *become* reality in the perception of the believer, when in essence, they are only concepts, mental images, nothing more.

Other people, inherently open-minded and inquisitive, are capable of evaluating ideas they were indoctrinated with as children. They look at the same declarations a religionist believes in and sees that they *don't correspond to reality*. People don't walk on water. People don't have withered hands restored in an instant. Multitudes aren't fed on a few fish and some bread. These things never, ever happen – and never did.

The believer in Christianity, though, hears these stories and accepts them as though they actually took place – it fits into the conceptualized world they imagine as real, the fantasy one they learned.

The nonbeliever quickly concludes that those old stories, based on ancient myth and accounts exaggerated over generations of superstitious peasants, never actually occurred in the first place. The book that reports such myth as fact is questioned when its stories explain events that simply and reliably *could never happen*.

When the nonbeliever looks into things, he/she finds that the stories about Jesus doing such nontypical deeds date from decades after the fact. They are based on unreliable lore, exaggerated over decades, further inflated through time by self-serving priesthoods and organizations, translated into an altogether different language, recorded by anonymous authors who had never seen or heard Jesus...

And they conclude there is no validity at all to the accounts: people 2000 years ago were very primitive and irrational in their thinking – their stories offer little or nothing to help clarify how reality really functions.

So, the main difference between a believer and a nonbeliever is that the former accepts ideas as valid, falling completely for any illusion formed by his/her belief structure. The nonbeliever in Christian myth may well fall for some *other* religious explanation or the scientific paradigm (also forming illusory effects). But at a minimum the nonbeliever does not substitute the fantasy explanation of a judgmental deity ruling over his vast herd of duped humans.

Q60 – What is some advice for a debate about religion as an atheist? I am the only atheist of the class and we'll be having a religious debate next week. The amount of stupid things I've been hearing for a whole year is unbelievable and this is my time to make my opinions be heard, but I'd like to get some advice on how to handle the debate.

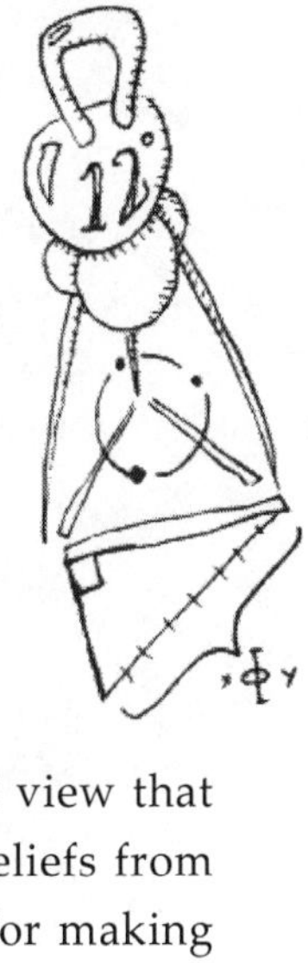

If you follow classical atheist arguments, you will have little impact on your religious classmates. Strong believers don't respond to reasoned argument because their beliefs impose a strongly held point of view that can't be rationalized away; they've absorbed their beliefs from a young age and those tenets form their very basis for making sense of the world they see.

And that presents to you a basis of argument that undercuts their limited, archaic thinking: *whatever you believe in seems to be true.*

The Christian holds and relies on a set of unfounded declarations (god exists, he created people, he will judge them after death, he sent Jesus as a savior, etc.) as true. They, and many other Christian "truths" have absolutely no substance:

- The "Holy Spirit" is an imaginary fabrication, an early invention that likely predates Jesus. But the Holy Spirit notion gained credibility (among the gullible) by being rolled into the Trinity – an invention of second century theologian Tertullian. It has no basis in reality. (You might query your debate opponents on what the Holy Spirit does all day, every day, since it doesn't seem to have accomplished anything since impregnating Mary. [Which, of course, it didn't do anyway, as it doesn't exist.] Does it eat? Run errands among angels?)

- The judgment of God after death is a carryover from archaic Zoroastrian notions of the god Ahura Mazda – Paul apparently injected this deity's imagined nature into proto-Christianity. And it stuck. That a deity sits in judgment of **150,000 people** who die every day is utterly and totally absurd. You might ask if God ever gets a day off from his heavy load of judging people. Or could God do tens of thousands of judgments simultaneously? That would mean pantheism, wouldn't it? Not monotheism…

- The Christian deity imagined in the first century was a real, physical entity – thought to live above the firmament (a big, blue dome in the sky) and above the water that surrounded it. Heaven was thought of as a physical location outside that small earth model – dirt with water underneath and the firmament above. Sometime after courageous, brilliant men like Galileo, Bruno, Kepler and Copernicus showed the imagined cosmology of the church to be totally wrong, the Christian deity (named "God") was shoved into an imaginary "Heaven" in an intangible, other-dimensional realm. (That is, imaginary.)

- You might ask your debate opponents where the firmament is – up there somewhere? And where Jesus went during the Ascension? Into orbit? The point here is to indicate how primitive the Bible is in its cosmology.
- In ancient times, God – that is, Yahweh and El – were pictured as real, physical beings. It was imagined as frightening unto death to look upon Yahweh. Yet, the modern notion of God is that he exists in some other plane of existence. You might ask, where is God? In what dimension? You could note that there are two realms you know of – the real universe and the imagination. If God isn't to be found in the real universe – here, but invisible? – he must exist only in imagination.

- You might query your opponents whether their imagined god, named "God", has a penis and legs and such things – like a nose. The Bible says man has been made in the image of God. Thus, the deity should be similarly equipped.
  - If so, what need would he (or "He" with a capital "H") have for a dick – sex? With whom? Urinating? Then he must drink water – so, where'd he get the excess?
  - What would he need legs for? Walking around – if so, on what surface? Where?
  - Such questions won't be received lightly, as it exposes the total imaginary nature of the believed-in deity. If they question that, then they don't believe the Bible on a key claim of man being made in his image – which, of course, is false anyway.

In any case, Christians simply buy into archaic, primitive ideas they learned as children to be true with little or no regard to viability. Simply point out that whatever beliefs your opponents hold will completely inhibit their ability to objectively judge any argument outside their artificial beliefs.

The above points, though, ought to provide some unusual zingers to, at the very least, provide you the fun of watching your Christian opponents squirm to rationalize some concocted explanation – which they likely will, to the satisfaction of others equally deluded by Christian fabrications.

Have fun! Christian conjecture is so phony, it's really easy to poke holes in it. But regardless of the expanse of the hole, the typical Christian won't see it.

Q61 – Why do people in smaller cities seem to be more religious?

This is a longstanding tendency where people in less populated areas tend to be more conservative in views – which lines up well with religion.

Religion, you understand, is nothing more than a set of ideas that were taught to people as "Truth". For those who believe in those defined notions, they appear invariably to be valid. But that is due to the way the mind interprets information it encounters: it compares situations, events and relationships back to its favored beliefs. Thus, any set of ideas, believed in as true, will seem so.

People in smaller cities, towns and rural settings tend to encounter fewer and fewer different ideas as the population decreases. Their peers all tend to think, basically, the same way – open-minded folk can't take the small-town mentality and move elsewhere.

Television never really introduces new ideas to people –

viewing audiences only watch what interests them. And mostly new ideas don't. In and around cities, though, you can't avoid different points of view. Other ethnic groups have different standards. People from elsewhere move into cities where jobs are to be had – not to less populated areas. Ideas mingle and mix...

Thus, larger cities tend to be more liberal, more open-minded and more diverse in thinking. And smaller cities and towns, not in close proximity to major cities, tend to be more fixated on old, traditional ideas – like religions.

This, as noted, is a tendency over ages. When Christianity became first acceptable as a religion in the Roman Empire – 313 CE, by Constantine's Edict of Milan – then later became the state religion via Theodocius I and his Edict of Thessalonica in 380 CE, it was first more fashionable in populated areas. Rural folk resisted the new explanation – they relied on their trusty old gods and goddesses like Demeter to provide an abundant harvest.

They had been taught the old ideas; breaking them away from rituals and assurances they'd learned growing up took a lot of time. And, of course, organized Christianity helped pave the way for acceptance of its ideas: it simply adopted old Pagan rituals and retrofit them into Christian practices to accommodate. Christmas was placed on December 25th, the date when the sun starts to noticeably rise in the sky, indicating rebirth of the growing season and Saturnalia. Easter was established to incorporate spring fertility rites offered to the Old English goddess, *Ēostre* – rabbits anyone?

Indeed, the word "pagan" itself stems from Latin *paganus* – country dweller/peasant.

Eventually the "new" ideas took hold. As time went on, rural thinking solidified around Christian dogma and fantasy. The rural contingent is by far more Bible-thumpingly religious than city dwellers.

As new ideas emerge – like the recognition that there is no silly judgmental deity sitting up there interfering with 7 billion people, ready to send poor schleps to Hell for eternity just for doing what comes natural – they find poor conditions in the rocky mindset of rural folk.

So smaller population areas don't just ***seem** to be* more religious – ***they are!***

Q62 – Why does God create us and put us with so much suffering to grow and be enlightened? What if I don't want to grow or be enlightened? Can't we be just free of life, death and suffering enlightenment cycles? Can God just leave us alone and let us be?

You exist in a status you are unaware of, else you wouldn't be asking such convoluted questions. Direct answers to your questions would only further the illusory understanding you hold concerning the nature of existence and help keep you embedded in a fantasy sort of existence.

So, if you don't mind, I'll answer your complex entreaty with an illustration of the essence of being – and do so with a clarification of the various elements of your queries.

First, let's get beyond words: **"God"** is a word, *not an entity*. The ideas you assign to whatever that word connotes will lead you to confirm your own notions. No deity created you and stuck you with whatever characteristics and propensities you currently have. No esoteric, external conscious entity inflicts suffering on you or requires anything of you. It would help your apparent quest for peace to jettison such notions to begin with.

You yourself are a timeless, essentially transcendent, conscious entity currently engaged in an incarnation. The nature of this Reality is *certainly* not a collection of happenings that some deity forces on you. Nor is Reality a collection of objects and materials floating in a matter-based universe, blindly interacting based only on forces exerted by those physical objects.

The Reality you face is a **meaning-based flow of events and relationships** that always, *inviolably*, **reflect your own core nature**. Nothing happens to you by sheer chance, through causation by an external force nor by decree of any sort of deity. You attract and thus manifest the events and relationships you encounter; you create, qualitatively and innately, the life you encounter by virtue of the complex nature of your total mindset – not directly impinged by action you take, which actually only fits into the overall scheme.

You are connected to the Reality you encounter, not separate and apart, not a powerless, unwilling recipient of outside manipulation.

You have grown into your current status, starting with a distinct set of character traits you brought with you into birth, and having changed to some degree from this life's encounters, from lessons learned through your experience to this moment.

Within that context, now, let's look at your questions:

1. God... suffering... enlightened: there isn't a god, as noted. But life does contain good and bad – things that feel good and stuff that hurts, physically and/or mentally. But none of it was imposed on you – rather is attracted based on inner propensities, which are likely quite complex.

2. Much of the purpose of an incarnation is to grow in awareness of your real nature – to gain in attributes of love and empathy, to explore the wide range of creative life undertakings. However, you do not need to do so! Rather than learn and grow, you can close your eyes, believe in silly, obviously flawed religions, avoid any lessons or greater awareness. It's entirely your option!

3. Yes, you can be free of life/death cycles. After this

incarnation, just float off and find the underside of a barren planet endlessly circling some non-distinct dwarf sun in any of a hundred billion galaxies in this universe. Roost there as long as you like: no incarnation, no suffering, no problems. It might become a tad boring, but go ahead and do so.

4. Again, as duly noted "God" doesn't exist. You engendered this reality and are interacting with people doing lots of interesting, creative things – art, music, child-rearing, business, sports, hiking, water sports, etc., etc. Nobody is imposing these things on you – do nothing if you like!

Your questions crumble into idle chatter if you understand that life can be extraordinarily interesting and rich, creative and fulfilling – or not. It's all up to you. It just happens that the more enlightened you become – that is, the more clearly you see that you, the total Self, incorporate all you encounter, not just your inhabited body – the better you can enjoy life, the more creative and meaningful you can make it.

So, forget the notion of God and dismiss the worry of death – it isn't an end, but an opportunity to switch playing tokens, to take on a new life with new possibilities. Begin to recognize that existence provides enormous potentials of great interest and fulfillment.

One need only embrace that Oneness, to proceed with curiosity and an open mind to gain ever more clarity in viewing the nature of existence and the Self – rather than dwell in frustration by seeing life through the blinders of phony notions...

Q63 – If Jesus was born from the Virgin Mary, then how were his other brothers and sisters born?

Do you want a superficial answer that fits within the confines of Christian fantasy and myth? Or a realistic answer that reflects what likely happened along about 4 or 5 BCE prior to the birth of Yeshua of Nazareth – whose name was only much later anglicized to "Jesus"?

I'll approach the latter, as I did considerable research on the historical/cultural situation of that time frame while preparing my third book, including extensive reading of scholarly research on the origins of the gospels and the stories they tell. It helps as well that I recognize how reality works – and how totally fantastic stories can be believed by naïve dupes...

Just what happened in the betrothal of Mary, daughter of Joachim and Anne, to Joseph can be concluded – and it has nothing to do with virgins conceiving, miracles or impregnation by the fantasy "Holy Spirit", none of which happens ***in reality***...

First and foremost, you have to recognize the source of the virgin birth story: it was fabricated by two anonymous writers about the year 85 CE. The gospel stories that appear as Mark, Matthew, Luke and John of the New Testament, you should understand, are the only pseudo-biographical references to Jesus – *at all!* There are **no** surviving historical or personal records that refer to Jesus of Nazareth from Roman, Greek or Jewish writing – not only during his lifetime, which likely ended about year 30, *but for 60 years afterwards*. So the gospel stories have no corroboration – no other *objective* confirmation to, in any way, support their content.

Also, critical to judging veracity *in any story*, ancient or modern: the four gospels are anonymous – the oldest surviving manuscripts have no author name attached. No one knows either who wrote them or where. These gospels had names attached to them only much later, primarily to give them some credibility: claiming, for example, that the traveling companion of Peter, named Mark, had written that first gospel (c. 70 CE) gave it some authority in the minds of early church fathers – unable to confirm or disprove the claims. But that claim was bogus, as is now known by Biblical scholars.

Worthy to note: as the canon became fixed, between the time of Origen, early third century, through Athanasius and to Augustine in the late fourth century, the gospels and other works were included – **principally based on false authority**, *fabricated centuries earlier* but unknown to later generations who believed the phony traditions! Amazingly, many to this day still believe that the gospels and other New Testament books were composed by the listed names! Indeed, outside of eight letters of Paul, the other 19 books are not written by the people whose names are claimed – James, Jude, even some books attributed to Paul weren't written by those people.

Likewise, the disciple of Jesus, John son of Zebedee, didn't write the gospel with the name John on it. Scholars recognize now that there are three distinct writing styles, indicating three different authors. And it was written in Greek, likely about or near the end of the first century. John, Jesus' follower, would have been long dead – and, Jesus' peasant fisherman follower was illiterate *even in Aramaic*. (As noted in the Acts.)

Point: if you don't know the author, you can't judge reliability or bias. Oh, and if the author's identity is already phony, what reliability can be given to the work?

Further, Matthew and Luke were both copied pretty much from Mark. About 90% of Mark appears, often slightly changed or corrected, in Matthew. Luke contains about 300 of Mark's 660 verses – again, revised to suit the anonymous author's purpose.

In any case, all of the gospels relied, when written, not on authentic, recorded accounts available 40 to 70 years after Jesus' demise or even on personal reports from people who had heard Jesus speak. People didn't live very long then. Farmers and fishermen, ignorant and superstitious peasants, who had heard Jesus speak in the Galilee countryside were long since dead. And certainly the Greek-speaking writers who assembled stories about Jesus decades later didn't get any direct info from Aramaic-speaking peasants, indeed, from any first-hand accounts.

All gospel accounts are based on *oral traditions* – stories told and retold over a couple generations, exaggerated and enhanced in mystical impressions by highly credulous peasants. And it passed though the inevitable distortion of Aramaic to Greek.

So, gospel accounts are very shaky by any rational judgment – if taken at face value. But, understanding the mindset of first century commoners, one can deduce what likely actually happened. Clearly, at the time the gospels were written, people knew that Jesus had come from Nazareth and that he was not the real son of Joseph – that would have been common knowledge, with or without the exaggeration and added elements of myth and miracle woven into accounts.

Mark was written about year 70 to pull together various traditions for the author's local audience. And that consisted of a small subgroup of the local Jewish community, a batch of people who believed Jesus, this already aggrandized teacher from four decades earlier, was the long-awaited Messiah. The real author of Mark, unique in that he could read and write, pulled together various stories he'd heard so his and neighboring Christian believers had something to read when conducting meetings.

But he wasn't writing the Bible. That initial collector of stories was simply assembling lore he'd heard and recorded it. And according to ancient standards, he wasn't really writing a biography – he was telling a story to illustrate points he felt were true. That's what people wrote back then – they concocted stories of high praise, not objective accounts of what really happened…

It is very important to note that, by 70 CE, 40 years after Jesus died, *nobody had heard anything about a virgin birth*. Paul, writing in the 40s and 50s – his letters are the oldest documents in the New Testament – says nothing about a virgin birth. That would have been an important selling point as Paul traveled widely to impress his views on the early proto-Christian movement. With neither Paul nor the writer of Mark aware of any sort of miraculous birth, **clearly the virgin birth myth was invented between about 70 CE and 85 CE** when the writers of Matthew and Luke concocted stories about Jesus' birth.

How do you know they were made up? Because the two stories are fundamentally different in content – mutually exclusive. They report things that couldn't both be true. In fact, they report things that *nobody could possibly even know* 90 years after they supposedly happened in private settings!

Why would they make such things up? Only one possible, rational conclusion: because Yeshua had been an illegitimate baby. Marriages were arranged for girls starting about age 12 as they came of age. Betrothal took place at about age 13 and the actual ceremony – a walk from the girl's parents' house to the mud-floored hut of the groom – took place not long after that.

Having many children was highly promoted in the culture. Soldiers and workers were needed – and women to make them. With life then circulating during daylight hours, people withdrew at night and sex was just about the only pastime, particularly in a male-authoritative culture.

Clearly, it was widely known that Jesus had been conceived prior to the arranged marriage of Mary to Joseph. Two writers, who expanded accounts from the earlier Mark, had to somehow justify that. So, they simply embellished the situation with a fiction worthy of a great figure – an offspring of a god, straight out of common myth of ancient times. And since sex had heavy negative overtones among the overtly righteous figureheads of early church development, it was a natural step to make Mary into a chaste virgin, untainted by sex.

There you go: wonderful, miraculous story! The great Yahweh-god impregnates a pre-selected human and a grand superhuman is procreated. It only took another 15 or 20 years from the already exaggerated accounts of Matthew and Luke to where Jesus is even proclaimed God incarnate or God-equivalent in the fantasy mind of the writers of John.

So, to answer your question: James, Joses and the other four siblings of Jesus were born ***just like Jesus and all other people at all other times***. Mary got pregnant and nine months later, a baby was born. Jesus' father wasn't Joseph; the others' father was.

Now, is that conclusion absolute and unquestionable? Of course not. But given all logical indications from the setting, shaky reports from the gospels, a bit of insight into human nature, a recognition of how the human body works and a reasonable modicum of common sense, it is most likely.

Gospel accounts are not merely unlikely; ***they are fully, totally impossible***.

Those stories fabricated by two unknown writers in the late first century – which later got to be included in the canon of 27 New Testament books based at least in part because of the bogus names attached to them – clearly are fiction.

Well, that should suffice for leveling Christianity down to "see" level. In honoring fair play, let's switch attention to neutralizing that other pillar of modern thinking, *science*. Given that "scientifically proven" has come to serve as a synonym for "valid", it behooves the sincere seeker of understanding to explore some chinks in the always well-polished armor of modern science – which deems itself, as have Christianity and its brethren religions always and unfailingly, to be the only truthful way to see things.

Empiricising: Quick Look at SCIENCE

Roots of science lie in 16th century exploratory techniques launched to a significant degree by Francis Bacon: if you want to explore reality to make sense of it, you have to test ideas put forth, i.e., hypotheses. That testing procedure must cover all variables in the process being tested, so that no question could remain as to veracity of the hypothesis – even providing that there is a possible failure route for the experiment.

Within the technique of empiricism, if a hypothesis passes the test, it must also, subsequently, be reproducible by other experiments and other scientists to be fully confirmed. And it is held as valid only until the time when others might prove it to be false via additional testing.

The scientific method – along with ultimate technological advancement – has led to remarkable advancement for mankind in many areas: communication, cosmology and astronomy, travel and material handling. Basically, the whole of mankind's way of living has revised itself over the centuries since early adoption of science and subsequent expansion of the understanding of the material world that it affords.

However…

Why do I always have to throw in a caveat? Actually, the caveat is already there – I just happen to notice it when I regard science as a technique to discern how reality functions. Most don't.

The core problem with science is that it is an objective model – rendering validity and importance to the material world of objects. Problem is: this is a subjective reality – an experiential engagement of meaningful events and relationships in which objects (including other people) only play a role in the unfolding environment of each individual.

And that simple problem, in end effect, means that science assigns causality to illusory forces and sources – finding creative power in real-world features that are actually only triggers.

My education as an engineer and ongoing curiosity and interest in various sciences gives me a unique clarity in the realm of science – I can deal with its principles of physics on a molecular scale or galactic level. And, given my awareness of the metaphysical aspects of life, I can equally put science into perspective as a useful tool, but not the ultimate answer to how reality works.

Let's regard three science-related questions I addressed in Quora. They can provide some insight from a different angle...

Q64 – How can scientifically-minded people believe in a god?

Understanding life on a personal level has to do with interpreting the nature of daily experience. That interpretation rests, *not* on purely objective, rational conclusions as to the operative process of reality, but on a wide range of beliefs and definitions one has absorbed while growing up.

Many in our Western culture grew up inflicted with declarations about life put forth by Christian sources. For most, even quite intelligent individuals, those declarations serve as definitive points of fact: God is a real entity who created and will judge you, Jesus was his offspring here to save you, sin is bad, the priesthood is all-knowing, give your offerings to the church to help the cause, etc. Once such ideas are put into place within the naïve, young mind of a child – a phase we all pass through – for most, they become the standard of **"Truth"** by which to evaluate encountered reality.

The difficulty arises due to this standard state of things, oft reinforced by my observations: *whatever you firmly believe in seems to be true.* The mind compares experience to its complex belief structure for interpretation. If you strongly adhere to the tenets of Christianity you were handed as a kid, they will seem absolutely valid – indeed, you will be puzzled at others who deem them as primitive, false or even silly. According to your strongly believed-in definitions, such negative comments are blasphemous and wrong – maybe prompted by the devil!

Many people simply aren't open-minded enough to question the rigid dogma they hold as true – notions dictated by the church, those firm declarations they were brainwashed with during childhood. Very intelligent people will grip their beliefs *even more firmly* than their less endowed brethren. They will have committed to memory more details and connected those dots more firmly.

Now, science provides an alternate explanation about reality very much in the same way religion does. That is, it's a different means to approach understanding, but its notion of exclusivity in being correct is very much in line with the aloof, self-assured, unquestionable attitude promulgated by Christianity.

In empiricism, reality must be tested to prove or disprove a theory, a hypothesis – rather than the foundation of religion, where the statements and declarations of the religion's tenets stand simply on their own self-made claims of validity. Regardless of veracity or support for it, regardless of technique to prove truthfulness, science and the procedure of empirical testing will have been absorbed into the mindset of the scientist precisely in the same fashion that Christianity or any other religion was absorbed into the mind of the believer.

Now the kicker: a given individual can absorb *both* paradigms as true. Indeed, if indoctrinated during the naïve, fully open phase of childhood, a particular individual can absorb, and confidently believe in, any set of ideas, regardless how demonstrably false they are – because those ideas have become the basis of judgment, the standard against which subsequent critical analysis is measured.

I can point out contradictions in the gospels, false reports, made-up stories and myth presented as fact, impossible events reported as real, phony authorship and a plethora of other reasons to dismiss the whole Christian fantasy. But the true believer, no matter how intelligent, simply can't process my rational argument. He/she will remain, frozen in old belief held in his/her mind as fact.

Likewise, I can show significant, foolproof argument as to how science doesn't fully describe the human experience – near death experiences that indicate survival of a transcendent Self beyond death of the brain, psychic connections and "para-normal" interactions that defy scientific probability, obvious mind-body connections that circumvent medical science healing expectations, etc. But the scientific-based thinker will not question his/her held notion, but rather simply disregard the argument.

So, for the individual who holds both scientific orientation and belief in a deity, the same effect is in operation: because both paradigms are considered true, there will appear to be no contradiction between them…

Christianity attributes all causality and all-encompassing meaning to a creator deity. Science assigns causality to blind, real-world, i.e., material sources (mass, momentum, etc.) and various forces (gravity, electromagnetic force, strong and weak nuclear forces). It posits a reality that has no meaning, no ultimate purpose – only superficial, derived meaning based on fleeting, temporal values of life forms that will, ultimately, pass out of existence.

Rationally, the two notions are *mutually exclusive*: either there is an external, driving intelligence to the universe (a creator god) or there isn't (an objective, material universe).

But the mind accepting both paradigms can "believe in" both

and simply not perceive – just be totally blind to – the rational inconsistency to its own belief structure.

Intelligence, by the way, is no guarantee of an open mind. Some very intelligent people base their world view on firmly implanted Christian conjecture and simply cannot see out of their boxed-in view. Others affix veracity to science. Some accept both, totally oblivious to the contradiction.

Of course, belief in either system doesn't make either Christian claims or scientific proofs true – a rigid belief system will only make either, both or any other accepted explanation ***seem*** true when firmly believed in.

Q65 – What is the biggest lie in science you know?

There are two great distortions resulting from science, both rather subtle. Applying the word "lie" to either is a bit harsh. But, in that both effects create false impressions, either *could* be so termed – or the cumulative effect of the two working together. I'll list both – you can take your pick as to which is bigger.

Science, of course, is a process: propose a hypothesis, test it (allowing for falsification), reproduce test, evaluate/publish results. Science doesn't lie, per se, although it can be distorted by many twists: fudge factors, need to obtain funding, p-hacking (selecting results that suit your purpose while disregarding other data) and outright subversion – corporations (e.g., cigarette, energy) paying scientists to come up with preordained results to promote their products or obfuscate reality to hide their products' damaging impact.

Beyond that, though, the first great distortion is *implied*. Conducting an empirical test will indicate falsity if the hypothesis fails the test – or validity if it passes. Reproduced testing by others further supports the conclusion that the hypothesis is "valid". Indeed, in our modern culture, pulling away from ancient *revealed truth,* the line of conjecture that underlies religion, it has become a strongly positive claim that something is "scientifically proven". In common thinking, though, that claim has practically become a synonym for "true".

And that leads to the first distortion. Many aspects of life – real, cornerstone elements of the conscious engagement of daily living – are simply **not testable**: intuition, obvious emotional connection between remote situations, psychic phenomena, beauty and its effects, etc. – plus, a plethora of human qualities such as hope and love, creativity and artistic talent, parental care (even in animals) and complex, abstract thinking...

These things are not able to be tested. In common regard, then – given the modern bent to rely on science for confirmation of validity – things outside the scope of scientific focus, things that can't be tested, are often shoved into the category of **invalid**, along with scientifically false hypotheses.

And that is a major detriment to life quality. Many aspects of life and living are simply not scientifically proven or provable, but are true and valid...

In effect, ***science doesn't define life*** – but it seems to, if you've bought into the scientific paradigm of empirical testing as the only test of real, true effects.

The second distortion is even more subtle: the scientific process only regards the material world as real. It assumes that the realm of matter, of objects from the subatomic scale to galactic proportion, is all that exists. This leads to a mistaken notion of causation, because science looks only to objects and their transfer of energy as making things happen.

You can measure the speed and momentum of a bullet, for example – and predict what it will do when piercing armor plates to damage a target. It seems the *cause* of the bullet's acceleration is the hammer's impact and the potential energy released from gunpowder.

But what really causes the bullet's trajectory isn't that physical activation at all. It is the intent of the person pulling the trigger, the purpose of the manufacturer in making the weapon and bullets, the mindset of needing such a firearm, the original invention of guns, etc.

So, the great distortion here is ***misdirected causality***. Real causes for things happening are primarily instigated by conscious entities – humans or animals making things happen. Indeed, the prime cause of science as a tool to examine reality in the first place is human rationalism – the invention of empiricism by Francis Bacon around 1600 based on much older Greek thinking.

Causality always hearkens back to intent, principally human, along with capability of fulfillment of that intent. Thus, causality stems from *Consciousness* – which, indeed, is a transcendent quality unto itself, timeless and exceeding the physical plane. Consciousness does not result from brain function – which is an illusory, incorrect scientific conclusion, based on science's wholly misdirected notion of causality.

So, regarding both of these distortions, the greatest falsity of science is the notion that we exist in an objective universe – and that illusory conclusion rides the thought that science is an exclusive tool to test validity of an idea.

The "biggest lie" of science, then? That would be ***implied falsity*** due to an idea not being testable or ***false causality*** due to misdirected attribution of what makes things happen – or the resultant of the two: the ***flawed impression*** that Reality is an objective realm fully described by the scientific method.

Take your pick!!

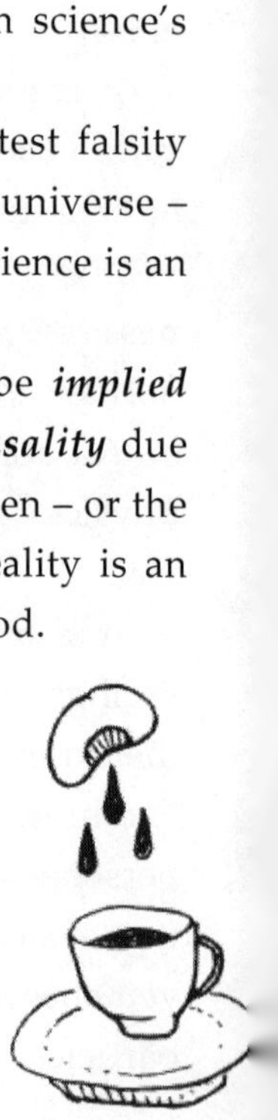

Q66 – How did all the matter in the universe come from nothing?

Most miss the point because they are only looking at the surface of Reality – and base their conclusions on science, which does the same.

To grasp the nature of the universe, you have to look at consciousness and the values on which it rests: this is not a purely material universe at its basis, with consciousness having emerged from complex brain function of advanced life forms which blindly or via fixed selection process (natural selection) evolved into its current state. It is not a fundamentally physical, objective universe at all. It only appears like that to the mind that has accepted science as its preferred explanation…

Life is based on meaning. What exists in essence is an interrelated Oneness of Self with experienced Reality – *a subjective universe*.

You can perceive that personally by recognizing that you attract patterns in life – that you can change those patterns by delving inward to find and change inner roots to outer problems. But you won't see it at all if you simply interpret reality according to the religious or scientific tenets you've learned.

Perception is invariably distorted by the beliefs and definitions you hold.

If you shed all of your held concepts, you will recognize this: your experience invariably reflects your own nature. Consciousness, which you are in your basic, core state, *manifests its own Reality*.

All accounts providing for a material Big Bang that rely on Physics and its "laws" are not only invalid, but misleading as well.

It is much more accurate to say that the material universe springs into being *in this moment*, reflecting the inner state of the experiencing conscious entity. Thus, it doesn't emerge from "nothing", but rather from value propensities held within your personal subconscious.

Physical matter has no real basis outside of consciousness. If you observe matter really closely, examine atoms and subatomic particles on a really small scale, you will only find energy bundles in complex relationships with surrounding non-substantial elements of a similar nature. The closer you look at physical matter on an ever-smaller scale, the less you find of substance.

Matter and its apparent solidity are illusions. Yes, they exist in this physical universe. But they aren't the driving basis of it…

The significant part of emerging states of matter has to do with life aspects – the meaning woven into the people and things you encounter, their relational status and resultant events. That, in terms of real experience, in light of the emotional response, the accomplishment, the creativity, the *outcome* – **that** is what, ultimately, is real.

Meaning. Value. Experience by Consciousness. These are real features to reality. The material universe is only a means to realize potential.

So, if you really want to understand life as it is, you need to shed common thinking, which will only deceive your rational mind. You need to look at your unfolding life and the patterns in relationships, health and success you repeatedly encounter. And realize that life consists of meaning, not randomly moving particles in wave patterns. When you see that, you recognize that there isn't a past that needs definition or tracing back to a Big Bang origin; *there exists a NOW moment*, this one, that emerges into being based on personal propensities and attracted values.

Given that recognition, you will realize that the "real" universe you continually encounter doesn't flow from the past moment through the present and into the future. The flow of particles through space in an apparent time-based scheme is equally illusory.

Think about that for a moment: I'm saying that the apparent flow of reality from one measured second into the next is pure illusion. Reality's fundamental flow is not through time – as time does not, in any valid way, exist. You are only ever soundly, thoroughly, unwaveringly embedded in a NOW moment. It was never not NOW. The universe of matter, unfolding in real events and relationships you encounter, is only ever emerging in this NOW moment from…

From where? There's a good question.

The answer is astoundingly simple: from within. Reality flows, not through time, from one moment to the next, coursing through hours, days and years. Reality exists in *this very NOW moment*, emerging – in your very own, personal, customized experience, manifested in sync with your own specification as comprised in your comprehensive mindset.

So, indeed, all the matter in the universe didn't spring into this state from nothing. That notion of past tense implied by the English statement is itself misleading. It emerges RIGHT NOW, springing into being in your experience (and a separate but interrelated experience on the part of all other conscious entities) based on the prefabricated spec *of your total nature*.

This, I might emphasize, is a highly significant recognition to grasp and perceive. When you recognize it, personally and intimately, you are gaining the Clear Awareness I often mention. At that point, your life and your mindset change…

All answers provided here are meant to facilitate the sincere seeker along his or her journey. The point is not to see things as I do – not to accept my various arguments for the Oneness of things, the functional NOW moment, the distortion of perception by beliefs. The point is *to see them clearly*. Truth, that is, Clear Awareness of How Life Works – as I like to put it – is not to be found in my explanations or perspectives, my illustrations or exposés. A clear view of life is right there in your direct gaze – to be seen by you when you've rid yourself of all the flawed ideas that cloud and hinder it.

Progression: Continuing on That INNER JOURNEY

So then, let's proceed with questions pertaining to a Personal Quest for unfettered understanding…

Q67 – When, where and how did enlightenment originate?

Discerning a legitimate answer to that question is very difficult, as individuals may have had deep insights into life's workings ages ago, but couldn't get their message across to contemporaries or simply didn't establish a meaningful description that was recorded and passed on. One can, though, deal with visionary messages that *did* persist – though you need to consider those accounts within their context and against any likely distortion built into them through time, cultural difference and translation of language.

But first, *you must understand the nature of "enlightenment" to begin with*. That term, chameleon-like, changes colors according to the viewer's estimate of his/her own level of awareness – and claims made by a guru or fancy-titled teacher who would gain your favor. So before tackling *when, where* and *how*, let's clarify ***what***…

In general, people are aware of a world around them – but for the most part only in terms they were taught. People growing up believing in gods or a single deity, who were taught notions like luck, fate and chance or were indoctrinated into empirical proof and purely rational thinking (regardless of the validity of underlying assumptions) – they all see and interpret the world around them within the confines of their beliefs.

And the core difficulty *there* is that trusty old tenet oft-repeated here: *whatever beliefs you hold* – any paradigm, any structured philosophy or religion – ***they will always appear valid***. The mind arrives at conclusions as to causality of events and the veracity of its own conclusions based on its own pre-established belief structure.

The nature of conscious existence is rather simple and quite apparent – but it becomes clear only *after* you see through whatever beliefs you hold *which invariably distort your perception*. You, as a conscious entity, are engaged in a meaningful flow of events and relationships that unfold through your lifetime. The substance of your experience consists of patterns whose impact is never random or caused by external sources or forces, but which reflect your own inner nature.

Elements like struggle and conflict, held within, will always be manifested in real life as physical health issues, relationship problems or failure in your undertakings. Patterns of your career and serious engagements on a personal scale will invariably, inviolably reflect your own inner propensity to the degree you hold struggle and conflict…

Most key features of common thinking project power out to seemingly external forces and sources – gods, other people, the government, bacteria, conditions, etc. But in reality, *you attract* situations, illness and/or failure *based on your own inner state* as held within your subconscious.

Enlightenment involves achieving a state of consciousness wherein you are aware of the full, innate Oneness of you with the complex world around you. It is fully deterred by beliefs you hold; you will invariably project causality to conceptualized externalities and be fully convinced, based on your beliefs, that something else out there is causing your issues.

Full awareness of the Oneness of things – the *enlightenment* you refer to – can be glimpsed briefly, yet leave a profound impression. Many (including me) have had a spontaneous mystic experience. Many others have briefly come to glimpse to some degree the connected nature of consciousness/reality through meditation or other techniques.

Another pathway is more effective: it's entirely possible to carve away your beliefs through self-hypnosis, wherein you can focus on the artificial tenets you hold and dispel them. This clarifies your awareness, as it scrapes away synthetic, deceiving understanding, allowing perception of your own being.

Caution: one can experience different levels of clarity. Through various tools of introspection, I had regained the clarity of my mystic experience (encountered at age 24) by my early thirties. But it took some time afterwards to really grasp the Oneness of all things. Some people gain some degree of insight through a particular discipline and assume they've attained the highest level – and thus stop looking.

But pure enlightenment is like climbing a mountain, where you think the summit is just above… But when you get there, to that higher level, it was only another outcrop, with more mountain to climb. You just didn't see it from where you were.

So, understand that true enlightenment is awareness of the timeless Oneness of you with all you encounter – with the vast, apparent universe of seemingly independent objects and cosmological entities. It includes, but isn't limited to,

- **Loss of fear** – for you fully realize that only you attract, and thus determine, events in your life. No external source or force is any longer a threat to you or an authority over you. How that "real" world impacts you depends *only* on your own inner composite, your own essence – not on any outside force.
- **Intensification of Love** – you gain a full, rich, engaged feeling of love and acceptance for others, without limit. Recognizing your own depth of character, good intent and broad, creative impulse, you see that same set of quality existence in others – only compromised there by the inner

conflict and struggle you rid yourself of already.

- **Full Trust** – in your body to work right and in others, as you know you will only encounter positive, helpful people into personal and business relationships. That trust in others, of course, stems from full, unbounded *trust in yourself...*
- **Creativity, Sense of Humor and Intelligence** – all facets of your own mental capacities are enhanced, as the mind is no longer churning through worthless worry and uncreative, repetitive thinking.

Pretty clearly some in ancient times achieved a degree of awareness of the essential interactive Singularity each of us engages. Siddhartha Gautama, so far as can be deemed, was first to recognize the interdependence of all things – how Reality all fits together in meaningful ways. Li Er, the old philosopher "Lao-Tzu", recognized the *flow* of all things experienced – how your rational action could only *interfere* with the flow, not improve it. These sages date from around the middle of the first millennium BCE.

Heraclitus, an early Greek philosopher from about that same time frame, certainly grasped the flow of things – noting that no two people ever stand in the same stream, as it's always changing. Plato, too, a century later, gave indication of recognizing the nature of things: his Allegory of the Cave is a clear indicator of his insight. Plato, though, apparently chose not to write out his most piercing insights, sharing them only with trusted contemporaries through spoken accounts.

(This is understandable from my standpoint: no description put into words can fully depict the integrated, meaningful flow of life. Thus, Plato was reluctant to attempt to do so, as it could only be misconstrued and lead to further confusion and distortion. That, I would note, is why I provide techniques and guidelines, plus exposure of faulty ideas that permeate common thinking, so that the sincere seeker can gain first-hand recognition of the reality he/she encounters daily.)

Beyond those key, visionary sources, a half-millennium later, appeared Yeshua of Nazareth – the real person behind the Jesus Christ facade of the religion that grew out of myth and lore about him. That man, as expressed in his parables, obviously came to distinguish a "Kingdom within", a status replete in the now moment, which, when recognized, would lead to blessings. That is, life would work well…

But the message of all of those individuals was distorted through time and translation – as well as total misinterpretation by people, contemporaries and subsequent generations, who certainly didn't grasp the Oneness of things, and thus couldn't grasp the visionary's accounts…

So, as to the *when* part of the question: when did enlightenment originate? Probably 2500 years ago or so. I've found no earlier reference to substantial insight into life's real functionality. The Bible, with its Old Testament full of archaic myth in attribution to El and Yahweh-style deities, provides no enlightened perspective until Jesus' parables. Paul, who really established Christianity with his own common and unenlightened ideas, was notably unaware of the connected nature of things. His distortions obliterated Jesus' insights, propounding a Zoroastrian notion of a judgmental deity and spouting unfounded declarations.

The Vedas have fascinating references that set up notions of reincarnation – an obvious element of existence – and the thought of karma, carrying one's nature onward into subsequent incarnations. This thinking does indicate some early perceptiveness – but without any specific individuals pinpointed as to initiators of those insights. But Hinduism carries other primitive declarations and distortions, thus diminishing its level of perceptiveness.

Zarathustra, called Zoroaster in the West, presents a unique case for possible clarity. When he lived is impossible to pinpoint, it seems, with claims of his historical existence varying from 500 BCE to a millennium before that. His ideas featured considerations of free will, the ultimate choice between Truth and the Lie, indicate some degree of thinking outside the generally superstitious, myth-based deity stories of early times. But it would be difficult to select him as enlightened, with the original notion of a judgmental deity, thought to send people off to a Heaven or Hell, attributed him – fantasized ideas that ultimately made their way into Christianity.

Any earlier characters – Akhenaten around 1350 BCE tried to move Egyptian worship towards a selected sun god, Aten, while Moses about 1300 BCE pushed deity worship towards Yahweh – can scarcely been seen as enlightened. Their ideas were doubtless significant – but their being remains unspecific in lore and meaning.

So, as to *when* enlightenment first emerged, I would point to about 500 BCE with the emergence, however clouded in myth and uncertainty, of Heraclitus and later Greek thinkers, plus Gautama the Buddha in India and Lao-Tzu in China. These all had a demonstrable glimpse of the Oneness of things.

Of course, it is possible, likely even, that individuals gained personal clarity from earlier times – or others did so in various more primitive cultures across the earth but simply left no trace of their insight.

So much for "when". As to where…

There seems to be no specific location that fosters a tendency for clarity. I grew up in a stalwart Christian environment, but could see through its flimsy tenets as a ten-year-old. Others, seers and sages of old or latter day, emerged in various locations, grew out of diverse environments. Location doesn't seem to much matter: you bring a certain individualistic flair with you, essential to outgrow limited ideas of the surrounding culture…

But "how" – now that's the most important part of your question. I spell that out in my books, my website and my YouTube videos – look 'em up. Personal growth from standard thinking to a clearer state of awareness requires a personal journey inward – to clear away distorting notions and negating inner elements. Traditional procedures are limited. Common, popular disciplines will only get you to see the world and yourself in the terms of the leader and the discipline. If you have to pay money for some version of enlightenment, you can be sure the vaunted leader offering it doesn't have it to give.

In any case, your path, if you are sincere and open-minded, will be unique to you, yourself. And it may require passing through various failed gestures, down numerous dead-end trails – growing from the experience at each step.

When you have arrived, you will recognize in all of life that good and bad, all of your health, relationship and success experience reflect your own core Self. Beyond the recognition, you will, step-by-step, reorient your life toward great health (without need for drugs or vitamins), wonderful relationships (without need to manipulate the other) and success in all your endeavors.

In that regard, enlightenment originates *when **you** attain it*. That's the only significant when and where. The how is up to you to pursue...

Q68 – What are some of the ways you teach your children in regards to faith, the universe and life?

There are two significant ways in which you pass meaningful impressions to your children as they grow up:

1. **What you say:** ideas you explicitly teach them – or more accurately, indoctrinate them with, and...
2. **How you treat them** – that is, interrelate with them.

Of the two, the second is much more important in terms of positives.

The first, generally, *what you say*, consists only of ideas – and most of them, particularly in terms of religion and life, are full of fallacy. It appears true only because you believe in it. Adding multiple "faiths" to the mix only adds to confusion.

Christianity, Islam and practically all other religions claim vociferously that they each offer the one and only truth. Teaching these can only result in confusion and inner conflict within the deeper mind stores of any child exposed to such insubstantial, yet uncompromising "truths", neither of which really is.

But again, more important, *is how you treat your kids*. Love and respect in treatment of children are far more important than old, myth-based religious dogma and fantasy.

Kids grow up to be loving and successful themselves when they've gained self-esteem and confidence. Teaching them that there's a judgmental deity hovering over them, nitpicking their actions for sin and ready to render them to eternal Hell if they just follow their impulses – that is a guarantee to powerlessness, struggle and self-doubt. You couldn't possibly install inner conflict more effectively than to explain that the world is dominated by Satan and his power, such that you need God's help to survive.

Espousing religion, any of them, but particularly the myth-based Western varieties, is certain to pass along struggle and conflict as ways of life.

In this reality, you manifest the meaningful flow of daily life by what you are – the composite of your total mindset. You are metaphysically connected to the events and relationships you encounter – neither separate from life happenings and subject to random or ill-willed acts, nor a powerless bystander to a deity-driven life flow.

You attract patterns. And those patterns invariably reflect your own nature.

Thus, projecting power out to an imagined deity – be assured, each and every one of the 2500 gods concocted by mankind are purely imaginary – can only create diminishing effects within the mindset of each believer. And that doubt and fear result in negative and ineffective encounters in health, relationships and success – invariably.

So the best way to positively impact your children is for **you**, personally, to dispel and jettison all the phony lessons about sons of god, saviors, merciful deities and means to please them. Once you see life clearly, the interactive Oneness with which you interface with reality, having rid yourself of all the myth of ages, once you see clearly that you alone attract and thus create the life you encounter – only then can you pass along trust and self-confidence, unmitigated love and optimism to your kids.

The more you "teach" them of the religious schlock propagated by self-serving churches, eggheaded, unimaginative preachers and self-proclaiming religions – all of which want your money – the worse off they will be.

E69a –Your site has certainly been a challenge to my "world view". My perspective aside from having experiential knowledge of several spiritual paths is, most recently, involvement with Sufism and *Course in Miracles*. I have sat with your communication and seen exactly how it jibes with my perception. For the most part I am impressed by what you have to say and delighted that you exist; your consistency is impressive.

Consistency comes from being descriptive of the pure function of reality. Philosophical treatments invariably deal with their underlying illusory paradigm. The rational twists that are necessary to make such philosophies conform to the preconceived paradigm inherently lead to inconsistency.

E69b – There are some intriguing variations between what you communicate and my perception, specifically as modeled through *Course in Miracles*. Fundamentally, I think the Course, with a different language, communicates what you are saying, that Reality is a singularity and the outer imagery reflects the inner state. Where your system and the Course system diverge, from my understanding, is in the meaning of it.

My main point – which you can't have avoided if you've read EoR to some extent – is not to model your mind image after *ANYTHING*. Whatever structure you put to your understanding immediately creates artificial objects and synthetic boundaries between those named things – both of which only lead to distortion.

The divergence you mention between my expression and *A Course in Miracles*, of course, is a highly *significant difference!* I haven't read that book, but there's one lying around here somewhere that a friend gave me once. As I recall, it talks a lot about a god in the third person. It seems to project itself as a modernized Christianity and an upgrade of its viewpoint. Indeed, it appears to me to be little more than an extensive money-making gesture that attracts fairly gullible believers in one belief system and sucks them into another – sort of a classic frying pan-into-fire deal...

There *is* no judgmental, external being out there pulling strings and interfering with the flow of reality. That is an illusion based on being taught that there is such an entity. What exists is YOU, and you consist of values and images, all mind-held and intangible. That totality of mind content becomes the real events, health and relationships you encounter daily.

Whoever wrote *A Course in Miracles* is tied up with his/her old beliefs and hasn't cleaned them out adequately. Miracles can't happen – nothing exists outside the smooth flow of Real into Consciousness, and all events are within that flow. You do well to see the flow clearly, and not partially, in which case some events seem to occur over and above the normal.

E69c – My understanding is that you are saying through continuing cleansing of the doors of perception, one will achieve a clearer and smoother outer world. The Course, to my understanding, is stating the outer is not real, let it go, in an ordered, gradual manner, and come to know something that is Real, beyond a description that can be given.

The outer is a reflection of the inner, an illusion in a fashion, but quite real in effect – much more vivid and rigid in its essence, for example, than the symbolic dream state. To dismiss it, to "let it go", is to trivialize the grandeur of the vivid life setting, with its enormous spectrum of feeling and experiential diversity, sensual intensity – as well as to underestimate its absolute reflection of your values. One needs to recognize it for what it is and how it emerges.

E69d – Strangely, as I write this, I am not so clear there is any difference between what you or the Course are saying. This is not bad.

Whether judged good or bad, it is not accurate! Don't try to hold onto *A Course in Miracles* as your reference source, because ANY such standard will form your basis of comparison. By the same token, don't grasp what I say and hang onto that. You must come to see reality clearly, personally, not grab a filter, which, intended to help focus your sight, only distorts it.

There is, again, a significant difference between my perspectives and *ACIM*. But details of either depiction are not so relevant to your life as your own perception, your own journey toward awareness of what is. This involves not absorbing what somebody has expressed, but coming to see what is as it is, for yourself, regardless of what I or anybody says about it.

E70a – I am excited with your work. Could you clarify the definition of values or "value fulfillment" as related to beliefs and conceptualizations? I just can't seem to get a clear feeling about values. Are values the same as beliefs, the results of beliefs or cause of beliefs? Can they in different context be all three? What am I missing?

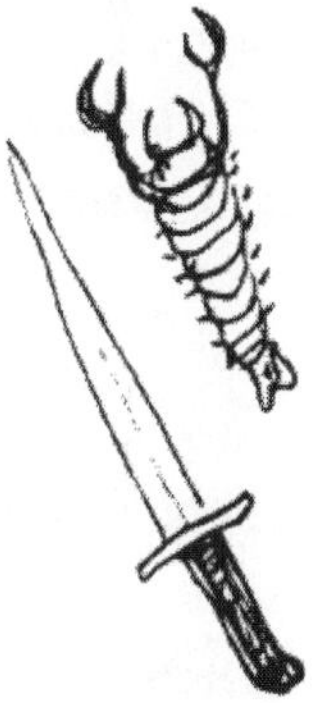

The mind contains a very large array of elements that can be considered as several commonly understood concepts.

You hold a self-image, already complex in its definitions, as to what you are in many ways: physical attributes, roles, personality, abilities, interests, appeal to others, self-confidence, etc. You hold a world-image, also complex, which contains many, many beliefs and evaluations as to how things work in reality, but also has extensive constructs as to political, biological, astronomical, physical, cosmological, etc., attributes.

Based on the extremely complex relationships of those images, you hold to other paradigms (models) as to structures and roles things play, philosophical and theoretical notions concerning intangibles and lots of other aspects of any angle of life.

The word "values" can be used as an overall indicator of these complex mental structures, because each element of each image carries an implicit "value", or meaning. The term "value fulfillment" can be used to indicate how these values, held in mind elements, combine to become realized in the events, health and relationships you encounter. Your inner values, in other words, become fulfilled in your experience.

So, beliefs are constructed values that ascribe certain meaning to the mind images they depict. Values, then, as a rather general, overall term for elements of mind, could be the same as beliefs, or could be the *results* of beliefs. But I don't see how values could "cause" beliefs, because beliefs are rather accepted definitions – complex constructs now held in the mind as true (whether they are or not).

I use the term "value" in a very generic sense, to cover meaningful elements of regard, as held in mind. I don't know of any other term that might cover that. Maybe I should make one up.

E70b – Being totally aware, I assume one can create any circumstance or participate in any actualized event desired. Not in the context of good or evil, is there a responsibility of creativity with such people and can you comment on that?

I would separate Clear Awareness from what might be called "Absolute Determination".

Clear Awareness is an ongoing, unquestioned perception of the Oneness of Self with Reality. Realization of this is a major step in consciousness, and a powerful impact in one's life. But, once attained, the journey then evolves to another phase.

When you understand that your health and your life's events and relationships emerge into experience from the inner realm of your mind, based on its values and images, then you continue the journey to clear out the negating elements – values, beliefs, fears, conditioning, concepts, etc., which go into events and relationships that contain negating, self-defeating effects.

That "second" journey can be a great deal more arduous, because the mind is extraordinarily complex and interwoven. But, as progress is made, one's desires flow more readily into real events. Even at that, though, what one *thinks* one wants is not always what one really does, indeed, want to have happen. That is, fulfilling one's exact intent is not always conducive to spurring the happiness or joy in fulfillment as had been imagined beforehand.

That can be better pictured in regard to large, overall values, like peace and freedom, joy and love. Often you might picture an event you are convinced you want to have happen and are disappointed when it doesn't – only to realize later that the desired event wasn't really what you wanted! But what did actually happen led to greater freedom, greater peace than the earlier, targeted event would have.

Basically, though, if you put your mind to a goal, however great, you can reach it with determination, given innate limitations to your capacities. Even with Clear Awareness, though, the realization of this goal – because it might require clearing out many negative values within – can take a while. In the meantime, what gets realized might contain apparent failure or pain.

As to "responsibility of creativity", I would mention that even attaining a budding Clear Awareness level of perception brings along an element of character in which you don't blame conditions or other people for things. If you realize that only you, in terms of your inner nature, are causal for the events in your life, old feelings of hate and distrust just evaporate. "Good" and "Evil" change as well in highly significant ways.

In any case, once clearly aware of life's real flow, you enter any particular episode of intent seeking peace and ease – not a particular object or specific outcome. When you are at peace, the object of your intent will manifest and bring fulfillment and joy. If you aren't at peace, either the intent you hold won't be realized or it will, but it won't bring the contentment and fulfillment you sought.

E70c – I know my conception of the reality created by the events I choose to encounter is biased by my beliefs – do values cause me to choose the events, and if so do beliefs give me my values – isn't that circular?

I don't understand this question. The values you hold certainly would lead to your choice of particular events, but your overall belief structure may not allow you to realize those chosen events. Moving toward Clear Awareness, then clearing out negating mind elements would allow creativity to manifest success and accomplishment. This would realize peace and joy, which are the overall values that are inherent in the journey.

In a fashion, that *is* circular, but only in the sense of consciousness, growth, and self-realization, based on desire and intent. The "circular" part is the loop between inner self and its intent – and the outer manifestation of either a peace-inducing outcome or one which brings disappointment and travail.

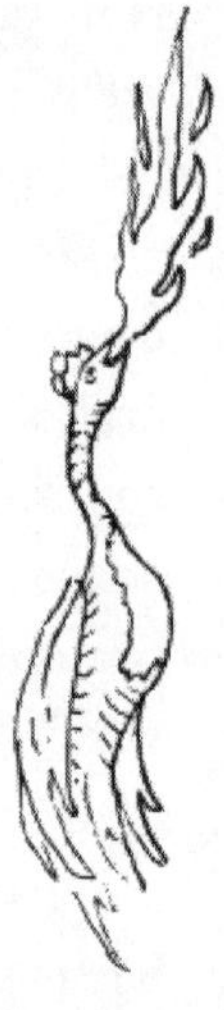

E71 – Maybe I'm missing the point. But you create your own reality? Through your beliefs, desires, expectations, and day-to-day thoughts? And Religion had a kernel of truth (all religions) at some point, before priests and scribes changed the original intent?

It's hard to reduce the complexity of content of EoR and the whole of human nature to just one point.

But that's certainly a central theme. I avoid the phrase, "you create your own reality", though, because it seems to imply that you have to turn the crank, that you consciously do something that makes your personal reality happen. In the current time frame, our culture is pretty much into rational control, intellectual override of what could (and should) be a free-flowing system.

It's more like: your reality (the series of events and relationships you encounter) results from your inner state. You "create it" only by virtue of its being a reflection of your Self, of your total value state. You can become effectively causal only in coming to perceive the inner values you entail, and changing them.

As to religions having a kernel of truth, it depends on the religion and its precepts. Take a kernel of corn and grind it down to flour, and, while you have the same stuff, you haven't much left of the original character. Accuracy in depicting life is much more fragile! Religion can – and almost invariably does – crush validity under the enormous weight of synthetic beliefs, interwoven myth, artificial definitions, and useless, outdated rituals.

In Christianity, as an example of religions, there is a profound level of perception illustrated in some of the phrases attributed to Jesus of Nazareth. But others were clearly not uttered originally by the same person. And all of that is laced with mythological stories and fantastic accounts that were doubtless added to make the whole package more appealing to converts through the ages.

Of course, powerful individuals through the ages – within any religion – have significantly changed the message offered originally. Everything evolves, and certainly such stories and their interpretations do so greatly over the course of centuries. While this change comes partly through a natural change in cultural conditions, much of it comes by deliberate reinterpretation to satisfy the agendas of overzealous officials within any religious political structure.

Does that add a bit of clarity to your impression?

E72a – In my own explorations into life, mainly via J. Krishnamurti and the Seeing perspective of Douglas Harding, but also reading the teachings of many other teachers within the "non-dual" view, I have arrived at my own experiential understanding of many of the things you write about.

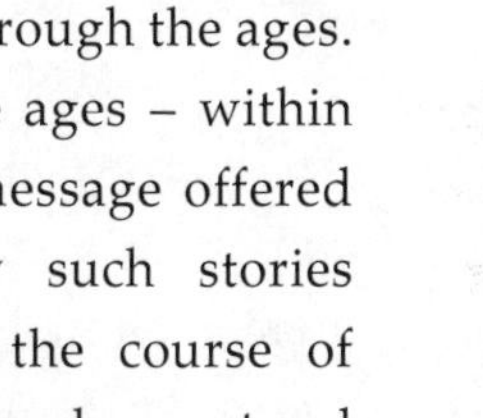

That is the key, of course. It doesn't matter what I say, or what Krishnamurti said, or the claims and prophesies of anybody – but you. Your own understanding is the only significant measure...

But of course, for any particular individual, that personal understanding can be clear or loaded with distortion based on beliefs. It may well, though, appear highly valid and correct – but, based on the distortion to perception leveled by beliefs, that may be highly illusory...

E72b – However, you raise a point that has been part of my consciousness for some time now. Simply put it is this: If you see who you really are, that is, the awareness that gives rise to manifestation, and begin to live life from this, then Life "happens". But there is also the sense that so-called negative events can still happen, except now you will not be troubled by them. This I am constantly experiencing.

The odd twist to life's flow is that sometimes things seem negative at one point, but later a positive, very meaningful value can be perceived in the experience. Life, in regard to the experience of events and relationships, can be exceptionally complex, such that there is rarely the black and white evaluation of positive and negative.

That said, however, it is not so much that one becomes dulled to the negative, but that one can understand that events with an immediate negative quality are aspects of one's essential Self – perhaps inner values that need to be perceived, dealt with, and eliminated, or perhaps they involve lessons that are there to be learned.

Generally, though, negative events – pain, disappointment, failure, emotional trauma – are symptoms of something within that needs to be sought out and removed. Those negatives are never really outcomes of intent that stems from a state of inner peace and ease – but rather of conflict and struggle.

And that is an indicator you haven't cleared away the inner sludge completely. Experiencing painful events in health, relationships or failure and not being disturbed and hurt by them is a study in stoicism – not a desired state where you become dulled to failure and pain…

E72c – But you seem to suggest that even these negative events can change as we uproot conditions of mind that give rise to them. But this implies an entity that feels apart from these conditions, an entity that wants to exert control.

Are we not back to what is already the case with so many New Age people, and indeed Old Age people, who all want to manipulate reality?

Clear Awareness and subsequent removal of negating and neutralizing inner values is a self-contained movement toward *not needing to control* – not needing to manipulate people and situations via concocted plans and action. As you exist in this moment, you are a blend of complex and varied values that lead and will continue to lead you into various meaningful events. Your experience of those events will elicit pleasure and pain in a broad spectrum of feelings.

Undoubtedly, you, as I, are familiar with many levels of pleasure in accomplishment, creativity, physical pleasures, successes of family and teams, etc. Likewise, we have likely had our toothaches and other pains, illnesses, failures, rejection, etc. Very likely, we agree on preferring the former.

The perspective I would communicate is that the pathway toward the positive, manifested with pleasure and fulfillment, the creative, the successful, etc., is coming to understand the Self and being able to shape a Self of peace, freedom and other qualities, so that the positive is encountered with regularity – so reality doesn't have to be manipulated in order to try to squeeze happiness out of it.

That pathway is not one of manipulative control of the "real", of DOing, but a dedicated venture into meaning within, seeking real change in status of BEing.

By the way, many people claiming to be "New Age" haven't a clue what that status really consists of.

E73 – I spent some time reading material on your EoR pages. In my wanderings, however, I failed to find a clear definition of what you consider reality to be. There were several statements about religions and philosophies getting illusion and reality mixed up, but this doesn't do much good if you don't define what these two concepts are…

I hope you never find definition in these pages! Religion and philosophy, both attempts to explain how reality works, are founded on definition – logical conclusions based on expounded explanations. But the mind invariably latches onto definition, and then, predisposed to that model, turns it into "fact" and ceases to see Reality clearly.

My primary point – and I hope that, whether or not you continue to delve into EoR, you will proceed with life recalling this singular perspective – is simple: whatever you accept as true, whatever definition, whatever paradigm, whatever rules or gods or astral planes or forest nymphs or powers or *anything* contained in that stated explanation will take on veracity in the mind that accepts it.

So, my point is that Clear Awareness (a nice, clean phrase, totally lacking in definition) is never attained by philosophically clutching any such defined model of reality, but by *clearing* the mind of such definitions. My words focus on pointing out the illusion and fallacy to all the overt and subtle definitions the reader already holds. That, along with a sincere determination on the part of the reader to clear away that mental debris, will lead to an ever-clearer conscious view of life.

If you want a definition, you'll find ten thousand of them out there. Take your pick. You can agree or disagree and debate your whole life long on those various defined truths. But regardless of the definitions or anybody's agreement, life functions in a certain way. But you will never perceive that function clearly so long as you accept any explained definition of it.

E74 – Question in response to my personal comments about delving into past events connected to a current problem, "But I cannot see how recalling my first incident of shame, which I related, can be affecting me today, or how reliving it will free me."

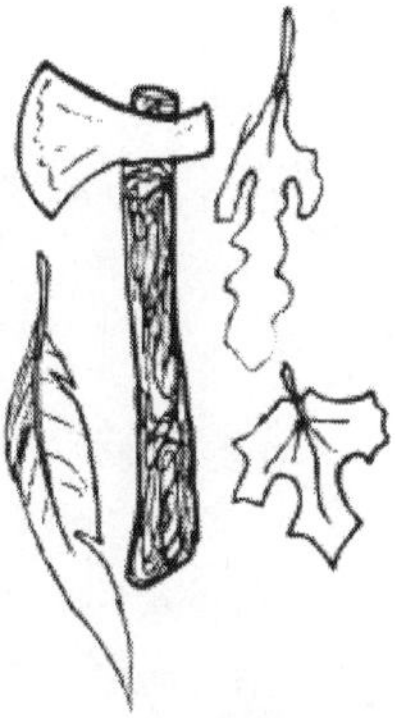

Either that event was a lot more devastating to you than you related in your story, or there were other events and other connections with your parents or other significant people in your life that resulted in what you describe as "shame". Work your way deeper to them. Anyway, if you've come clearly to a view of even that incident, you then "reprogram" it, by telling yourself something like this once or twice a day for a few days: "I see clearly how this event embarrassed me and degraded me in front of others. But now I leave it in the past. I no longer need this shame. Now I release it."

You see, *time doesn't exist*. A connection like this (and probably many other connections you haven't focused on yet), forming a pattern which can be related to past situations, is still in effect, and will remain there until you deal with it. As you begin to do so, you come to realize how these values, held in mind, affect your life – and further, how you can deal with them.

The point is that such connections, forming patterns throughout life, will continue to repeat until you rid your mindset of their twist, their meaning. Whether you focus on the current iteration, the situation you face right now, or on the same pattern as it played out earlier in life, you are dealing with the same active mechanisms of mind. Finding that earlier situation in childhood is often less stressful than dealing with other iterations, like the current one.

But the key is deciphering the inner mechanisms involved and deleting them from your subconscious.

If you have trouble with that particular pattern, laced with shame and other negatives, start with less powerful, less intimidating effects in your life. As you proceed you become more at ease with the effort, more confident with your power over these events and effects.

E75 – After wrestling these past two weeks with my newly acquired belief systems of the last three years, the Internet/Universe has indeed again provided me with what I needed to see. For it drew me to your articles today... they are indeed what I needed to learn/see/absorb today. Thanks so much for having them here.

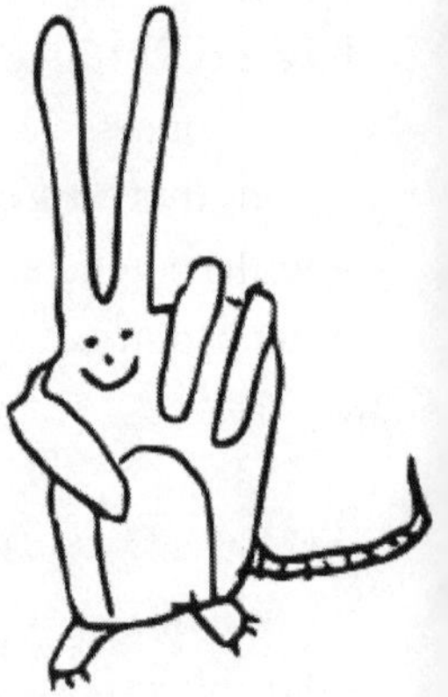

You will find in the course of sincere, intent inquiry into life that you will happen upon the "right" thing to provide your next step or steps. From my angle (bearing in mind that reality can only be clearly examined from someone's perspective, never from a neutral, "objective" stance) the Internet provides a means of free expression ideal to my message. I can write as I wish without need to filter my perspectives through the limited vision and vested interest of an editor.

I will be continuously adding pieces to EoR (this question being one of the first posed by a reader of my website in 1996, when I first posted initial writings), so stop back at your leisure. The only limit is that the day will come when I will no longer be focused here (i.e., dead). From this juncture, though, that is a long way off, with very much to write, considering that I can illustrate virtually any aspect of reality and communicate some message. Effectively, it's not what I write about, but the angle I view it from that carries the significance.

Well, at this point, 21 years later, now 70 years old, I'm still presuming my eventual departure from this realm to be quite a way off. One conventional method to speed that exit up – a longstanding potentiality – is to be critical of Islam. Next are three questions I answered on Quora some time ago. My critique hasn't yet had any negative repercussions, so I'll include them here.

Noteworthy is that, having eliminated fear from my repertory of responses, I have no worry that a vindictive Muslim will do me in. It is, after all, quite silly to be afraid of powerless people – which is the effective, personal consequence of believing in a creator deity…

Regressing: ISLAM and its Declarations

I'm often amazed at how reasoning, intelligent people can look at a set of ideas – such as those put forth by a religion – that are obviously contrived, clearly fantasized and overtly fallacious, and simply nod in agreement and comply with their dictates without question. I never could do that. From age 9 onwards, I protested the Christian bunk my parents and Sunday School teachers presented. From my middle 20s, I could point out shortcomings of science.

And in recent years, I've looked at, researched, analyzed and debunked any manner of statement that would pretend to describe reality: philosophy, Eastern mysticism, religion, esoteric disciplines, self-help gurus and everyday gurus. Islam has not been free of my attention; both in my first book and in my YouTube videos, I level its grandiose claims to being unquestioned truth to a much more pedestrian level of primitive conjecture and unfounded declarations…

Q76 – What technically went wrong with Islam?

Oh, that's easy! What went wrong with Islam is what goes wrong with all artificially concocted declarations as to how life works: Islam simply *doesn't describe Reality!*

As with all religions, its "holy" scriptures, the Koran and hadiths, make various declarations and claims. For those who believe in them as unquestionable truth, they seem profound and irrefutable.

But that's the case with ***all*** religious tenets and, indeed, any philosophical statement. The mind adheres to its accepted tenets, interpreting the world it encounters through those definitions and resultant beliefs, yielding my oft-repeated observation: *whatever you believe in seems to be true…*

Those growing up in an Islamic environment will only ever hear the same message – parents, neighbors, literature, stories, etc., will all echo the same impression that this is the way of things, most merciful Allah, must submit, must do this and that…

Few will question – learning early on the negative consequences of such free thinking.

Islam is particularly discouraging of dropouts: the remedy for apostates is to kill them.

One could go through the points declared by Islam and refute them with rational thinking, point out the primitive viewpoint, political ramifications, shortcomings of its originator, Muhammad, etc. One could reveal conflict, inconsistency, the changing nature of its tenets from early on (rather peaceful and condoning) to later ones (aggressive and intolerant). One could point out the stunningly primitive nature of many declarations, and detail how the illiterate originator didn't write down any of his words – but they were only collected much later from various accounts from those who had heard him…

But none of that would have any effect on true believers. They are already hooked on their own beliefs. And if they do question and shed the archaic notions promulgated by the "faith", they face aggression and rejection by their families and society – or death, if they can't escape their repressive culture in their Islam-dominated country.

So, yes, one could raise many issues as pertinent technicalities for just how Islam went wrong. But the basic answer is that Islam *fails to explain* to the slightest degree *how life works*. Allah, for example, doesn't exist and never did. He's an outgrowth of more ancient gods, like Il, El and the pantheon of gods believed in in pre-Islamic times.

Islam only *appears* true if you believe in it. It goes awry in claiming that it is valid and true – when it is neither. And many millions of people over centuries – a billion and a half today – pay the price of believing Islam's wild claims and primitive assertations.

Q77 – Is the fact that Muslims keep saying that Islam is not the problem perhaps the problem itself? Failure or refusal to recognize that it is Islam that is generating the global menace of Islamic terror absolves the need to do the necessary soul searching to unearth the root causes, and instead perpetuates the menace, as evidenced in the history of Islamic terror.

That's part of it for certain – the act of denial keeps any believer (and consequently, a group of them) from viewing the big picture and questioning the religion itself. But there's much more to Islam and its inherent tie to violence than simply not being willing to recognize the connection.

To grasp the deeper causes, it's necessary to understand how one's own belief system affects one's view of Self and the world – once again, it deceives the holder to confirm its own claims, regardless of what they are…

Principally, the psyche simply interprets the world *through* its favored beliefs and definitions – that is, by comparison to defined truths as described in those mental constructs. You make sense of all aspects of life by subtly and quickly relating life's events and situations to your "world view", which includes notions as to what causes things to happen. If you have been totally indoctrinated in Islam, you will have absorbed many beliefs as to the nature of Allah and values as to behavior and reward, etc.

This overall distortion of perception leads to extensive conflict in itself, as most people can't grasp that others arrive at different conclusions and hold other values than they do.

In terms of Islam, this fixed-mind effect can be very strong. Islamic cultures are rigid in customs and tightly knit in combining religious ceremonies with daily life, government and behavioral standards. That, in itself, is highly problematic in Islam – more so than for most religions – because of the religion's claims themselves. In defining the surahs as coming directly from "The God", Allah – and thus perfect and unquestionable – Islam sets up rigid, fixed standards that dictate one's actions, values and way of life.

And the problem becomes complex for several reasons:

- Demanded actions and values are mostly not consistent with human nature, particularly in terms of realizing one's desires and cooperative relations with nonbelievers.
- The definitions are concocted and do not reflect reality: Allah doesn't exist *and never did*. (Nor, indeed, did Gabriel, who supposedly delivered them to Muhammad in a cave – of all places – ages ago.) All declarations issued as though coming from this authority are no more than myth-based concoctions.
- The surahs became increasingly aggressive through time as Muhammad proclaimed them, with the last ones being highly intolerant of other beliefs and religions (as the Prophet gained power). Because of Abrogation (Naskh), later surahs are deemed to void out older ones. Thus, surahs that recommend fighting nonbelievers, even lopping off their heads, generally neutralize more amicable, tolerant ones.
- Much of the goal of the religion itself is to convert the rest of the world to its primitive, concocted declarations and tenets.

These points all lead to real problems, particularly when groups of people holding Islam as unquestioned truth encounter other groups who hold some other myth-based religion equally firmly.

But the "menace", as you put it, goes even deeper:

In life, we each interrelate to the world around us through our own inner set of values and, indeed, beliefs. In addition to formulating a world view, as noted, beliefs and definitions held as true combine into a "self-image" – what you believe yourself to be.

Holding sincere, strong convictions of powerlessness in your own subconscious will severely damage your own evaluation of your creative power in the world. It will foster fear and distrust. And it will promote conflict with the external world to try to fulfill your standard human desire to accomplish your intent.

Islam, its title actually *meaning* submission, innately creates a core powerlessness in the mind of any true believer. That adherent, if sincere, projects all creative power to Allah – thus rendering that person, *within his/her own self-image,* powerless.

And that simple, but profound, characteristic of human nature lies at the root of Islam's real menace to the world. 1.6 billion believers, all of whom suffer their own daily conflict and struggle based on indoctrinated notions of their own lack of power and worth in the face of an imagined – but nonexistent – deity spread that conflict outwards.

That effect, of course, is amplified by the point implied by your question: denying that the religion is the problem is *a major problem in itself.*

You, as an individual, will never fix the problem of Islam and religion in general until you recognize its negative nature. And Islam in particular prohibits that by threatening to kill any adherent who does want to reject the faith once it was held.

Q78 – What are some mind-blowing facts about Islam?

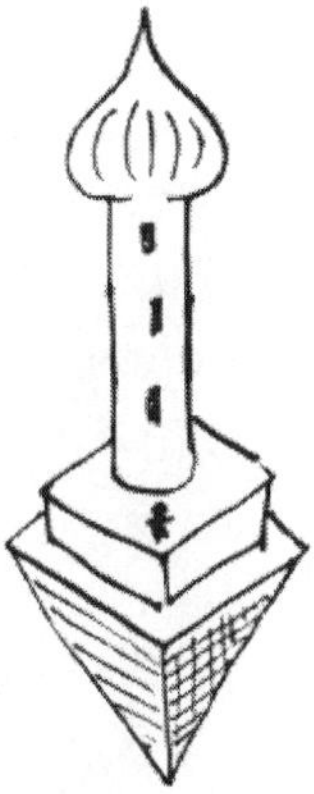

Clearly the most astounding aspect to Islam is that anybody with any reasoning power, with any faint recognition of the world around them and with the slightest tinge of intellect can actually believe the archaic notions promulgated by the primitive writings that constitute the Koran and Hadith.

I explain in my various books, website, hundreds of talks across the English-speaking realm, and now YouTube videos, the nature of Consciousness. By necessity I have to debunk various religions. It's tough enough to sludge through the Bible's ancient, fantasy-based thinking to expose their unfounded claims as claptrap. It's far worse to slog through the vindictive, contradictory, unfounded declarations that constitute the Muslim scriptures.

No religion describes reality *at all;* but all of them, by issuing declarations they claim to be true, inherently distort perception of reality to seem to confirm – to the believer – their own validity.

This is due to the ultimate gullibility of the human psyche – as often noted here, we compare experience to our current understanding, our held beliefs and definitions, in order to make sense of it. Conclusions we arrive at are *invariably* skewed by those beliefs to confirm the beliefs' claims.

Thus, *any* religion or philosophy, even science, appears valid to the individual convinced of its validity. Beliefs, held with conviction, distort perception and skew reason; they never clarify how life actually works.

Most people are unwilling or incapable of questioning their own beliefs. So, most are stuck in what I call "thought boxes" – unable to see past their held beliefs to recognize life's real, self-engendered process.

Islam, in a fashion even more extreme than the other predominant world religions, totally indoctrinates its younger generations with its age-old tenets. For most young, naïve minds, surrounded by authoritative parents and religious figures, hearing only one set of definitions, it's impossible to see the pure fallacy in Islam's claims and declarations.

Some, more open-minded and inquisitive, would question Islam's claims – like I (and many others) did with Christianity as we grew up. But shedding Christian bunk and discarding the whole religion is no big deal – except perhaps to still-deluded family members. Mormons and the Amish, for example, will shun any member who questions, doubts and discards the belief. In Islam, though, open questioning and declared dropping of the faith altogether is *remedied by death*! Death, of course, isn't inflicted by Allah – who doesn't really exist – but by some fundamentalist thug who believes he does.

Allah is a notion, a thought, *a mere idea*. This conceptualized deity is an outgrowth of earlier gods like Il and El. He doesn't exist now *and never did*. Gabriel, the imaginary angel who supposedly delivered the text of the Koran to Muhammad, never existed either. These are fantasy beings coming directly from ancient, superstitious minds, imaginary notions planted into naïve, young minds at an early age. They seem to exist to staunch believers precisely because the mind is deceived by its own held beliefs.

So, the most profound *and accurate* answer to your question is that the most mind-blowing fact – by far – about Islam is that over a billion and a half humans can believe that its 7th century declarations are somehow valid. Included in that number – and even more astounding – is that people, especially women, actually *join* the religion!

Now that is *really* mind-blowing!

I can't put it much more clearly or forcefully that religion *of any sort* distorts perception for the holder. The more profound lesson, though, for the sincere seeker is that religion and religious thinking very likely populates his/her own thinking – even if that person long since jettisoned the faith and no longer consciously believes.

That problem rests firmly in the nature of the subconscious in absorbing and holding ideas while young. Notions and definitions become woven into complex structures – often attached to other definitions, to vague impressions and other values. Ridding oneself fully and permanently of artificial religious tenets requires focus and concentration: finding the explicit notions in all components of one's subconscious, and pointedly removing them by auto-suggestion.

But let's turn attention away from religion for a bit, and emphasize a deeper topic...

Insourcing: MYSTICISM – Grasping Intangibles

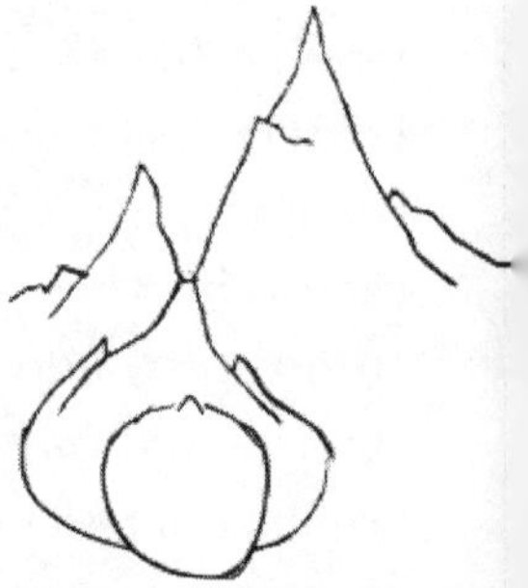

I don't look upon myself as a "mystic". Perceiving life unhindered by the common veil of beliefs is simply a, well, a state of clarity – no fancy bells and whistles, no aura projections and heavenly host chanting from above.

There is nothing otherworldly about it, nothing that would be implied by words like *paranormal, transcendent, spiritual* or other such esoteric-sounding phrases that many seek and apply to pump up their own status in the view of the potential acolytes. At most, if one considers a unique clarity of awareness special – which it is, both in a practical sense and one concerning peace of mind – one might apply concepts of traditional mysticism to a descriptor.

On occasion, for lack of a descriptive title, I've referred to myself as a grounded mystic – lower case, not a title, just an indicator. In reality, I'm just a guy who spent decades clearing illusory definitions out of his subconscious so he could see clearly what's going on here. But one does have to deal with the term, *mysticism,* with or without the "M" capitalized…

Q79 – Have you been through any mystical experience in your life?

Yes, and I can recall it vividly. And I would share it with readers, including the lead-up to it and its impact on my life – because such a personal epiphany doesn't pass without consequence.

I was always a smart kid – independent thinker, questioning things. My mother inflicted me with her

Presbyterian religion, and I dutifully said my prayers at night. I noticed, though, that things I prayed for, I rarely got. Something wrong with that procedure I'd noticed pretty early on.

I distinctly remember saying my prayers one night when I realized there was nobody there listening to me. The big, deep voice I'd imagined hearing back was just my imagination. Didn't take long to just quit believing. Of course, as a kid, you kind of have to go along with things…

As I grew into my teenage period, I just considered myself an atheist – and had no trouble admitting that. But, as is typical, I latched onto science – which seemed to explain everything.

That orientation facilitated obtaining a degree in Chemical Engineering (in 1969, that was enough to keep you out of the draft and the idiotic Vietnam War) and brief work as an engineer. But when it was clear I would no longer be drafted, I quit. Saved some money and took off to spend a year hitchhiking around Europe – kind of rare for a Pennsylvanian.

I was amazed at the freedom – traveled through Ireland and England, looked up some distant relatives. Worked in Munich a bit – realizing what good beer tastes like – and by winter headed to Spain and Morocco, then back up and across Italy. Too many adventures to report!!!

Heading toward Athens, I had taken the ferry from Brindisi but stopped for a few days on Corfu. It was spring and the Youth Hostel/campgrounds were loaded with young travelers. Great time spent hiking around a beautiful island! But after a few days, walking into town to check the ferry schedule, I stopped on the beach facing across to the mainland, with a scenic view of northwest Greece and Albania…

Sunny day, clear sky, crystal clear water, Cyprus trees, green hills set the scene – and I was very free. Spontaneously, with no real warning or unusual stimulus – certainly no Ouzo or Retsina – I had a mystical experience…

I could perceive, utterly clearly and absolutely apparent, that

I wasn't one thing looking out over a collection of other things – trees, hills, blue waters – but that ***I was a Oneness***, looking at itself/myself from within its/my own being.

That wasn't a quizzical thought, a speculative idea or a philosophical statement I'd heard somewhere. It wasn't a conclusion or hypothesis – but a clear, distinct recognition of my unbounded nature. It was much like a curtain of synthetic explanations that filled my understanding had parted and opened a view to the real nature of things – and I could see clearly **what really existed**, beyond my prior impressions. As I had long since jettisoned Christianity, I didn't hear heavenly host concertizing or see doves descending. I could just see clearly the absolute, undivided ***Oneness*** of all things – including what I regarded as *me*, at the center of it all.

I felt great, ebullient, energized! It lasted for days – I continued my travels on to Athens and other great adventures. But in time, that lightness wore off. Old beliefs and impressions settled back in…

But it gave me a clear view of life – like knowing the plot to a movie you hadn't seen, I was "tipped off" to life's deep mystery.

In subsequent years, during many more travels as well as settled times, too, I explored religions and philosophies – coming to see, through self-hypnosis and other techniques, how the inner, the psyche's interwoven content, was directly related to and ***causal of*** the outer: life's real events and relationships.

As I developed my ability to clear away inner restrictions, my health improved and I began to revise my pathway. I could identify definitions and beliefs I'd absorbed earlier – and rid my deeper psychic store of their distortion.

By my late forties, I'd created a website – a new means to communicate at that point in 1996 – to illustrate my views. By 2005 a British publisher contacted me and said he would publish a book of my writings from my website The Essence of Reality, if I wanted to write one. That and two later books, promoting them and communicating my viewpoint led to more than 250 talks (at this writing in 2017) across the US, UK and Canada – only ever to open-minded groups.

By 2015, I had geared up to create a YouTube channel to present my unique view – a full, unhindered view of life just as in that mystic experience. I developed skills to script episodes, stated clearly and somewhat less complex than my sentence structure in writing. I practiced and honed my presentation skills while reading from a teleprompter. I purchased a camera capable of HD quality recording. And I found and learned how to edit videos creatively.

My YouTube channel allows me to explore many topics – a much broader and deeper excursion than giving talks – which can generally only be an overview.

I think my mystic experience, way back in my twenties, was spurred by my independent, analytical nature. And it, in turn, led to a life of adventure and expression. In effect, readers and viewers can share my mystic insights by delving with me into the realm of mind – without hokey spirituality or new-age glitz and superficiality.

At this point, my entire spectrum of expression stems from an ongoing clarity of awareness just as vivid as that fleeting mystical experience on Corfu nearly a half century ago. My purpose is to share that Clear Awareness of perception and all of its benefits – freedom, trust, unbridled love, lack of fear, health, success – with all others with minds open enough and the determination to understand life…

E80 – Can you compare or speak to those prophecies found in Revelations (and throughout the Bible), Edgar Cayce, Nostradamus and the various prophecies of the indigenous

people, Hopis and Mayans in particular? So many of them seem to be following the same thread and are similar in so many ways. Could their ability to prophesy be something like remote viewing? or channeling? or what? Again, there are many contradicting statements, too. Some say we are in for a wonderful, healing period; others say the earth will be in turmoil, etc. Thanks...

There are two angles from which I would approach that question. First...

In the most brutal of wartimes, there are people who survive easily and prosper. In the calmest of peaceful historic periods, there are many who suffer great pain and failure. Suppose I would gather from my deepest perception a layout of the path of coming large-scale disasters and political change. How, beyond a certain academic interest, would that benefit you? Regardless of mass events taking place, your personal life may face anything from great success to inevitable failure, from budding health or mortal sickness.

The focus of *your personal life* is the format under which you intimately engage values, live them, experience them, react to them and ultimately learn from them. The mass events that grand prophecies focus on, while relevant to the direct focus of your personal life, are not *causal* to your personal quality of life. The main gist of all my expression is to show you that *YOU*, through the values you hold in the complex of your timeless, limitless mind, are the only determiner of your life experiences.

All the sources you indicate in your question were looking at the world, big events, some managerial, invasive god, mass effects, or whatever as being key to determining the flow of events in your life. They aren't. Only you are. So seeking out and focusing on such revelations is a rather futile effort, and self-defeating to boot, since it only reinforces the illusion that something else, something out there – mass events, cataclysms or historic upheavals – controls you.

I could be more abrupt and say that the writers of Revelations, along with indigenous shamans, Edgar Cayce, etc., were simply not aware of how life unfolds on an individual basis. Thus, their focus was distorted, and their intuitive output likewise bent in a direction that fulfilled their intent. I'll look further at those shortly…

Nostradamus is another subject, however. I will use him to illustrate the second point here.

There is no inherent limit to the reach of your conscious mind. A vast, truly unimaginatively vast, store of information exists within the realm of extended consciousness. For the daily, indeed momentary, ongoing function of your body, much information flows among all parts of your body, which, of course, maintain their own inherent consciousness – on a smaller scale, but no less interwoven. You have access to this information, as it's all stored in the subconscious. But for the overwhelming majority of pertinent data, you ignore the very existence of it.

Information abounds, likewise, within the Reality around you – an integrated whole, you should understand, with all events coordinated precisely to fulfill patterns of consciousness, in which your individual mind focus is primary beneficiary of value.

Amid all this information, your mind focus rides your lifetime – not unlike how you drive a car. At any given moment while driving from point A to point B, you are not aware of the myriad of mechanical functions taking place – the flow of fuel, the electrical triggering, the computer overriding function, the conversion of fuel to kinetic energy, the transfer of energy to drive the wheels, the friction of tire with surface, the lubrication of rubbing parts, spring action of the seats, the flow of air through and around the vehicle, etc., etc. You just drive the car, worrying about traffic, the proper turns and whatever else might be on your mind.

And similarly, your consciousness rides your body/Self through the daily flow of events. You ignore this great pool of information around you – partly because: A. it is not within the capability of your conscious focus to deal with a large amount of it; B. it is not necessary to deal with it, based on the nature of this life format; C. you've been effectively taught that such background info doesn't even exist; and D. your self-image contains little awareness that you actually have access to it.

Well, in actuality, you do have access to peripheral information. It's all there, available to your focus:

1. the specific, meaning-based *future* which will unfold based on your current mind value set,
2. the *present* as it exists in remote locations outside the scope of your awareness, and
3. the *past,* in a constantly reevaluated personal judgment you make about things.

And you can focus attention onto any aspect of it. Psychic mental ventures – "channeling", remote viewing, prophecy – are simple reaches into the readily available info that's always there ("here" might be a better descriptor, though logistical references are irrelevant in terms of consciousness).

I personally tapped into such information when I did psychic readings for a couple years during my thirties. I regularly explained key elements in the lives, expectations, hopes and issues of those who came. Thus, I assure you that information exists at many levels of consciousness, mixing extensive fields of related meaning with essences and proto-events poised to emerge, depending on yet other potentialities. However complex, however interrelated, however subtle, info surrounds the conscious Self and can be accessed under the right conditions…

(Sorry to be a bit cryptic with that: the deep interface within any person's mindset of *subconscious* information, directly accessible and important for unfolding quality of life, with *unconscious* information – for the most part remote, expansive and not usually accessible to conscious focus – doesn't lend itself readily to verbal explanations.)

So, what was the question? Prophecies from various sources? Nostradamus could apparently see clearly into "future" major events. So could you with some minor adjustments to your self-perception. So could I, if I chose that path. But a far more valuable step into awareness of "what is" would be to come to perceive precise elements of the Self, of one's own full-ranged subconscious, in its interplay with life, rather than rendering as grandiose the temporal effects of historical events, which most gestures of prophecy do.

The point is: if Nostradamus could and did foresee major political and other large-scale events lurking in man's inevitable path, so what? What he saw and reported, generally cryptic and open to varied interpretation of his quatrains, is at best inexact and unspecific – even in regard to the most seemingly fitting predictions. In effect, such prophecies are only ever retrofit onto events that have already passed – rendering them useless in personal life. The only real value to such prophecy at all is the indication it makes for the potentiality of a given individual to access proto-events – and that, as an indication of the transcendent nature of Consciousness.

As for others you bring up…

Revelations, the last book of the New Testament, seems to me an ongoing rant of cryptic beasts and numbers – with a specific preference for the number seven – that serves no useful purpose whatsoever. Superstitious, credulous folk may seek deeper knowledge and understanding from its grand prophecies. But the only real lesson to be gleaned from Revelations is to recognize the gullibility of such simplistic thinkers.

Edgar Cayce doubtless had a psychic antenna out for tuning into people and their ailments. But his proposed remedies reflect only his own limitations. For certain, a good psychic can access such information from others – and in some detail. But physical issues are *rooted* deeper, in inner conflict and other negatives. Proposing "cures" to these as actions to be taken to deal with the physical symptoms of what are actually deeper problems – that technique is not only superficial but also counter-productive. Cayce, visionary for his time, simply wasn't aware of the innate mind-body connection to be able to delve into real, inner-outer healing processes.

Far better is to enable each individual to delve into his/her own psyche, provided with techniques to discover and change the core, inner roots to problems – so they don't just keep popping up as other issues later.

As to Mayanism or Hopi prophecies – what does delving into this ancient or referenced lore expect to accomplish? Prediction of the future? Amazing revelations of the past? Loose affixation of ancient prophecies to known historical sequences? I suppose such paranormal projections from exotic peoples elicit some spooky titillation or evoke a vague mysteriousness to our being. But ancient lore is typically only interpreted in ways to elicit such occult, esoteric-seeming effects – often by people who mostly just want to sell you a book or something. Kind of like ancient alien myth and exaggeration – they'll affix a mysterious translation to some real document in order to excite people who are generally naïve and credulous.

If the Mayans or Hopis or any other ancient or modern cultural group were truly aware of great truths, they wouldn't have maintained primitive, early agricultural levels and eventually either died out or come to be dominated by other people.

So, in general, despite any offbeat predictions or paranormal readings, we are in for *both* turmoil and peace – as we (all of us) have always been – in varying portions. The vital consideration is whether *you* personally are to be living out the former or the latter in preponderance. And that little tidbit of data is within your scope to know, and within your power to determine.

Most communication I've received over the years directly through my website – where my e-mail address is prominently listed – has been of a more personal nature than Quora questions. These direct communications either pertain to one's own pathway towards clarity, directly question about consciousness or ask me about my own journey…

Onwards: Resuming the INNER TREK

Let's explore some more queries oriented to one's own inner search. These, as always, may easily reflect questions that occur to you as you seek to grasp my message...

E81a – Thanks much for your EoR website... I've found much of value with what you've put out there, and I feel that you are truly sincere and commend you for putting this valuable information out there free in the public domain. For the past year I've done a pretty much intensive study of Advaita Vedanta and feel that for me that system goes a bit deeper than your system. That's an opinion, of course, generated from my own mindset!

I'm not sure what you understand by the term "deeper". I avoid overt analysis of things, hoping to prompt each reader to begin to rely on him-/herself in personal awareness. In that regard, I don't really have a "system" at all. Indeed, I never will propose a surefire system to attain enlightenment, a structured paradigm or procedure, any sort of philosophical construction, or any guaranteed tightrope sort of pathway to walk to get there.

In that regard, your pathway is your own – and that of each individual is unique. If the Vedanta, i.e., any of its sub-schools' teachings, seem helpful at the moment, that's good for you. Most Eastern teachings I've encountered, however helpful, have an innate structure to them that is heavily influenced by the background Hindu/Meditation traditions they grew out of. Not that there is no value to their typical message, but any such set of declarations congeal to form a conceptual model out of their standard presentation that is ultimately just as restrictive as the one a person begins to shed when getting involved in Eastern thinking *in the first place.*

Often enough, ancient teachings and their esoteric terminology offer an impressive model that seems particularly appealing to the neophyte, seeming in their time-honored sanctity to be irrefutable – particularly, I imagine, in comparison to an upstart guy (e.g., *me*), not steeped in traditional movements, not spouting long-established, mystical truisms, not confirmed and verified by fancy titles or academic labels.

I would suggest that if age-old Hindu teachings were truly beneficial and full of valid insight, India would be a lot better off as a consequence – not overpopulated, not mired in poverty and excessively swamped with pollution.

Still, exploring Eastern thinking may be a useful and necessary part of your pathway – and that of others. It certainly contributed to my own growth. Some, though, get mired in it themselves, deem meditation and yogic traditions to be the final answer and never progress beyond it.

Others, though, learn much from the very act *of discovering its limitations*, so that Hinduism can play a key role in the journey while not being the end-all and be-all of awareness as it might seem – and as it might, effectively as do all other religions, present itself.

E81b – For example, you say that change is the key element of Reality. I tend to think that change is the key element of the phenomenal aspect of Consciousness, while in its noumenal aspect it is unchanging and unaffected. And this, of course, is only a concept, and not the Truth...

Is that how things really are? Or is that a philosophical description you read somewhere and accepted it on authority – so that it currently seems to you to be true? That's not really a question you need to answer to me, but rather how it sounds. A given philosophy always seems true if the precepts and subtle assumptions on which it rests coincide with your own.

Change is *obvious* in Reality (the phenomenal aspect of the Consciousness-Reality Oneness). Conduct of daily life is not as it was 100 or 50 years ago – or even as it was last week. Yes, patterns persist, but many things change – resources are extracted and used, life forms' habitats are impacted (driving some to extinction), conditions are impacted by natural forces and human activity, structures are built as others decay, etc. To think the material world is unchanging is rather absurd…

But change is inevitable in the inner makeup of each human as well, the noumenal. Each individual changes within the scope of a lifetime based on the values encountered and absorbed in the life experience. To imagine that *anything* remains intact, unchanging, static, is to be blinded to reality's essence by a structured belief that inhibits clear perception of that thing – whether real or noumenal.

You may agree or disagree with that observation, but neither case of your personal evaluation will affect the essence of how existence functions. However, either agreeing *OR* disagreeing can greatly affect *your ongoing perception* of how life works.

E81c – You say that complete rational control banishes fear. Another way that fear could be banished is that if the entity having the fear were to be seen to be an illusion, then the fear would necessarily disappear along with the illusory entity.

I never said that "complete rational control" accomplishes anything! The intellect really has no control over anything anyway. Where did you see that? Not in *EoR!*

Fear can be dissolved by coming to regard the source in mind content and more or less dismissing it. Once you come to see the roots, killing the fear is not such a task – but it has nothing to do with "rational control" – rather with revising values learned and held within the subconscious, so that the fear isn't triggered when the object of that fear is encountered...

E81d – I am not writing to quibble over points of view, to say my view is "more right" than yours. I believe what I say to be true, and am conducting my own experiments to see if they indeed are. Time will tell – possibly.

The perceived outcome of your "experiments" will be subtly distorted by the belief structure you hold going in. If a person believes in a god, he can attribute any sort of real outcome to be the result of that god's power. That didn't make it so, but just made it appear so to the believer. Any tests the believer conducts will unconsciously be structured such that the outcome confirms preconceived definitions.

All your conclusions will stem from and fit into your belief structure. They will certainly appear to be true if they coincide with your prefabricated beliefs...

E81e – Don't know if you're still interested in reading, but if you are, may I suggest the book *The Final Truth: A Guide to Ultimate Understanding* by Ramesh Balsekar, pub. by Advaita Press? Another couple of books I've found useful, these by an American writer, Franklin Merrell-Wolff, are *Pathways Through to Space* and *The Philosophy of Consciousness Without an Object*.

Both are available in one volume by SUNY Press, can't remember the exact title, something like *The Teaching and Philosophy of Franklin Merrell-Wolff* [actually, *Experience and Philosophy*].

I wouldn't say I'm disinterested in reading, but I clearly see the limitations to intellectual exchange in terms of personal awareness. Clear awareness requires a direct perception, an immediate consciousness of self, interwoven with the apparently external reality (the "phenomenal aspect" you referred to). That awareness is not to be obtained by reading, though it likely would be helpful to be exposed to other perspectives along the path – as I certainly was during my journey.

Reading EoR will not get you there any more than anybody's "Final Truth" ultimate declarations. The value to my writings in EoR is that, in recognizing that limitation, I focus on illusions, the false assumptions, the distortions created by beliefs, and other subtle pitfalls on the pathway. If those other books you refer to recognize that limitation, then that's great and cool. I don't have an exclusive copyright on insight. And perhaps my way of expression doesn't reach you as well as it might others.

But if those books cost you money, and the "teacher" is living off that money – that is, they are basic commercialized ventures – or if those books offer a concrete paradigm of truth, or if those rely on authority or doctorate degrees or time-honored, agreed-upon truths, then proceed with caution! They likely just present more subtle pitfalls to get conceptually stuck in.

By the way, I don't say that because they are somehow competition for me! I have no vested interest in whether you read my EoR stuff or not, buy my books or access my uncommercialized videos. Your life is yours, and your pathway is purely your responsibility. But those others may have a vested interest in your buying their books or buying into their teachings, much like all religions and most authorities, Eastern and conventional, esoteric or academic, do: *they live off your money*.

That is a pretty common occurrence – all religious organizations, cult leaders, scientific organizations, philosophical orgs, gurus, etc., live long and prosper from funding provided by others to whom they propose to teach the "truth". If Ramesh holds the "Ultimate Understanding", why does he need to sell you a book about it?

(I would add here, as that answer was voiced before my books were published, that my books, this being the fourth, are commercial items: books do cost money to print and publishers, printers and distributing systems need to profit to maintain the system. But I personally benefit little from books sales. Income only partially offsets my expenses. I personally fund my videos and my website maintenance. And I cover extensive expenses for travel to speak to groups – which I never charge for a presentation. Making personal profit from my venture is *never the point or priority or a necessity* – a situation that allows me to be totally candid and unrestricted in my expression, including criticism of popular viewpoints.)

E81f – The reason I have taken the time to write is that I think that you are very close, very close. I also think that you probably live your daily life in a fashion much more in the flow than I do mine.

However, I think there's something more primary than mind, and that's that awareness that includes "mind" and everything "else", if that sentence makes any sense! That which might be pointed to by the term "Consciousness-without-an-object-and-without-a-subject", Pure Awareness, Awareness not aware of Itself. Consciousness cannot be understood because there is nothing that is not consciousness.

"Mind" is a handy term that most people can at least relate to, if not perceive as I do. So I use that word to communicate. Since language cuts the undifferentiated Oneness that really exists into artificially severed pieces, it isn't really feasible to use it to describe the hyphenated term you refer to. Indeed Consciousness ***is*** the subject – the viewpoint of each observer enmeshed in a subjective experience. And each material item encountered, each object, is a portion of the animated experience of events and relationships that constitute life.

So, no – not only does that first sentence make no sense, but the second is even more nonsensical. The Self, the individual standpoint of each conscious human, ***IS*** aware of itself as a functional entity. Just exactly *the nature* of that existence – that is the question and its answer can be significantly skewed by beliefs that color and flavor cognition to conform to the definition.

But in terms of Awareness, there is only the Self to be aware of! Awareness of some ethereal nothingness is not awareness; it is the esoteric report of somebody who overdosed on meditation. Consciousness **is indeed** and **emphatically** understood when one becomes fully conscious of his/her essence as the personal perspective in the Consciousness/Reality Singularity.

Not to appear critical, but I get the feeling here that you are quoting one of your Eastern mystics with these last few comments. If you believe, because some teacher told you so, that "Consciousness cannot be understood" because of anything, then you can be sure you will inhibit your progress toward that very level of awareness.

E81g – As Ramesh continually says, "All there is, is Consciousness." He advised a person one time that he'd given him two things: "1). I told MN that the glasses he was looking for were already on his nose – there was nothing to seek; and 2). If the glasses were not on his nose, he would not have been able to look for anything at all, without the glasses." (From *Consciousness Writes*, by Ramesh Balsekar.)

A nice story, but where does it get you? To set that analogy straight, THERE ARE NO GLASSES. You don't need a "means" (like the glasses) to attain awareness, because every means of viewing, every supposed aid to awareness only serves to distort perception, not clarify it. For most Eastern teachers, meditation is a means, *the glasses*. Perhaps Ramesh is not aware of his own limitations. You should be, because if you treat him as the great expert, you will not be aware of his limitations, either.

E82a – I am not that widely read, and have a limited knowledge and understanding of the divine but what I do feel tells me that the dross that you have gone to all the trouble to share with us is mushy rubbish. I don't just think this, I know this.

In the years of my having The Essence of Reality available, yours is the first e-mail offered with an aggressively critical tone. (And well over a decade later, this is still the only such communication!!) I would respond to your specific comments below…

Most of one's intellectual interpretation of anything is based on predisposed ideas. And those ideas are invariably founded on cultural attitudes you absorbed while growing up. If a nuclear physicist were to explain his world view to an aborigine, the latter would tend to find it hard to accept. Similarly, the Eskimo shaman's view of life would hardly be accepted wholeheartedly by a Catholic, nor would the "truths" of a Hindi guru find ready acceptance by a southwest African bushman.

What you "know", in other words, is a mental, definitive image that you were taught – quite apparent from your reference to the "divine". Obviously, the words I express in EoR, which question these core beliefs which you hold, will come across as "rubbish" in the view of your interpretation. (That EoR is somehow "mushy" is a bit of a stretch, however, unless that word means something different in Australia than it does in Pennsylvania. My words are clear, poignant, sincere and direct. No mushiness that I can see.)

The strange part is, though, that if you evaluate my words so negatively, why did you bother reading EoR far enough to find the e-mail address? For every page I write, there are millions of pages of religious, philosophical, spiritual, new age, mystical, etc., to read. You would probably be much more comfortable reading something that fits into your belief system than words which question it.

Of course, you wouldn't grow from simple-minded reinforcement of your existing notions, but you would find them pleasing to your current, restricted view of life...

E82b – What perturbs me is that you are sharing this gush with thousands of lonely, lost people and are confusing them even more. I know this is a leaf in the wind, but there it is.

There are distinct reasons why those people are lonely and lost. If they come to understand what they are, how their mind works, and how their lives unfold, they may well revise the negative status of their lives. It's certainly in their power to do so. If, on the other hand, they (and you) choose to listen to the same, old, worn-out ideas that dominate our culture, they (and you as well) stand little chance of outgrowing their limited lives.

Where does a leaf in the wind end up?

E83 – What is pain? I mean generally speaking, all the different types included.

You understand that the outer realm, the "real" world of events and relationships that make up your experience in life, reflects your inner state *exclusively*. Of all the things that happen in your daily life, some are positive and reflect the fulfillment of your will – what you want to happen – while some are negative. These negate or neutralize your desires, so that the events and relationships you encounter don't reflect your will, but oppose or ignore it. These negative elements may well contain events that require conflict or struggle to overcome.

This negativity is not an external force, like traditional concepts of "evil", bad karma, retribution inflicted by a bad person or punishment by some judging god. It is a reflection of *your own limited self-image*, elements of self-punishment, concepts of an opposing, hostile world, and many other distorted values, beliefs, and conceptualizations you hold within your mindset.

The realization of your mindset into experienced events brings a personal response covering the spectrum from positive to negative of ecstatic, pleasure-imbued good feelings to extreme pain. With the life experience being very rich and intense in your conscious connection to your body and emotional state (actually, that is an interwoven Oneness rather than a "connection" of two separate elements!), the passage of the moment of pleasure or pain can be extremely vivid.

You ask about pain. Pain, whether physical or emotional, is a symptom of negating effects within your mindset. The nature of the illness or accident, the conditions of failure or rejection, all of the complex of interpersonal relationships or body function are brought to bear in the realization of negativity, but they are never the cause. The cause is *always* internal to your mind elements.

Thus, to *eliminate* pain – not overcome it, deal with it, cover it up with synthetic medicines or techniques – but to ***eliminate*** the potential realization of any such negativity into your life (to which pain would be the response), you must sort out the roots of the negation in your mind. Then eliminate them there.

All pain is rooted in mind elements – not imagined, you understand, in the immediate moment, and not psychosomatic per se, but rooted in elements of mind that lead you to negate your creative power and make it work against your will. You always have the power to find the mind elements that lead to pain, and get rid of them.

E84a – If I'm not really confined to my brain, what role does the brain play?

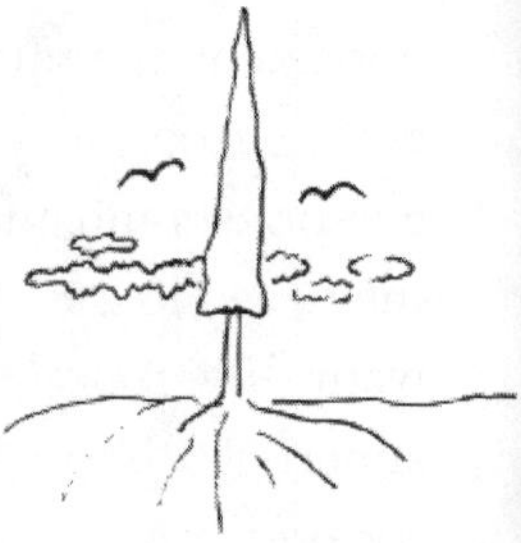

Actually, as queried, you aren't really "confined" to your brain – you are just used to looking at the world from that point of view, out through eyes and other sense organs which are neatly situated in your head. This top-heavy configuration – in terms of senses – contributes to that perspective. With practice, you can accomplish "Out-of-body" experiences, in which your perspective point becomes some other point than your head. I don't see a whole lot of value to that effort, personally, but it is interesting to know it's possible.

Also, in "Near Death" experiences, where an individual dies through heart-stoppage or accident but is revived again, it is often reported by the individual that he/she left the body and hovered above the scene – sometimes giving a detailed recount of the revival process as observed from that angle above the event.

Clearly, though, the intimate encounter of Self with real events is best experienced from a perspective of "inside" the head. Otherwise, living a life would be like watching a movie.

The brain is more of an interface mechanism, a processor of sensory data that gets perceived by the conscious Self through the filter of senses – and also through a substantial filter of beliefs that strongly influence interpretation.

E84b – Thank you, my friend! Do you know when you're going to go in to a new phase of your life, when you're going to start talking publicly? Somehow, I would very much like to meet you.

As to my public presence, you can't get much more public than being on the Internet. One of these days I will become more noticed by the public. For now, I rather cherish my privacy, so I don't encourage too rapid a move into the public eye. Preachers and priests and gurus and such need the public exposure, because they need to live off money they get from their followers. I don't want any followers, won't take any money, and don't need superficial public exposure which often comes in our modern society.

By and large, those who are ready to hear my words encounter them where you see these written. And in this form, they will survive for a long time, while spoken accounts, more vivid to the small, live audience, pass quickly.

(This question was posed early on at the establishment of my website. Since then, and particularly after publication in book form of *The Essence of Reality*, I've traveled well over 100,000 miles to give some 250 talks to various open-minded groups. I don't know that I ever met the person who posed that question, however…)

E85 – I just wondered if you could point out to me the deepest and most hidden assumption most people have (and probably me too, since I don't have a clear awareness of myself yet).

Another quick question: I have asked myself many times if it is possible for me to gather enough strength from within to change all my values "at once". In other words, is it possible to clear out all the negative programming that inhibits my awareness in a second? Just by really, really – I mean *reeeeally* wanting it? I realize it takes a great deal of energy, but I can't see why there should be any limit to what I can do.

In a very real way, each of us is on our way towards seeing the Self. The difference between you and most people is that *you* understand that you are on that path, while most people are blindly running around doing what they are taught to do, oblivious to life's purpose and their own enormous potential.

Without any doubt, the basic assumption to our standard Western view of the world is that this is an objective reality – a material, a physical universe, that exists independently, based somehow on its own generation (Big Bang, matter/antimatter generation or created by a preexisting god) within no explained context. Based on that assumption, it is theorized that our consciousness evolved through an evolutionary process (most popular: natural selection) on this planet to the stage of current human perceptiveness. An alternate concept, based on the same fallacy, but deeply rooted in man's tradition, is that reality is created by some external source (typically a god, a force of event-creation like "fate", or whatever), again existing in an explained context.

These views, of course, are fallacious, the assumptions that underlie them simply false. Consciousness and Reality are two aspects of the same essence – you can't have one without the other. You are the Consciousness that experiences this Reality (as is every individual when considered from their own perspective). In EoR, I illustrate how the mind-held values, which are your nature, blend to flow into the events and relationships which fill your life.

For you to begin to see that, it is vital to see through the illusion that this world was here before you arrived, and exists independent of you. In reality, the aspects of the real world that you encounter daily in events and relationships *are* you. They are a reflection of the values which you entail.

To look at your second question – dealing with all values at once: As you look inwardly to find the mechanisms of mind that you hold, which influence how your life unfolds, you will change them to create better health, better success, better relationships. But each step can involve complex value relationships – and each of these needs to be understood and "reprogrammed". It takes time and sincere, personal introspection. The subconscious is extremely deep and its values complex and interwoven.

Simply sorting out all inner aspects of any particular life problem – as held in various mind elements – is a slow process in itself. Changing these inner negatives does take focus and repetition – the auto-suggestion needed to "rewrite" the subconscious requires repetition and time for adjustment.

Furthermore, as you change intimate, emotionally charged aspects of your Self, energy is released – *emotional energy,* deep feelings that are personally important. This results in a backlash of upheaval in feelings as the subconscious regains its steady state of daily function. This phase, preceding improvement in the life area you are addressing, can be painful, emotionally, as you've exposed your realizations.

So, first of all, the mind and Self are *much too complex* to unravel quickly, let alone instantly. And second, if you *could* address all this at once, the release of so much emotional content would kill you. So, one limit is how quickly you can delve deeply into your mind to identify and change things. The other limit is how much emotional cleansing you handle at one time.

Life, you, and your mind's interface with it are not such a simple structure, nor so unemotional in essence that this is a simple, quick process.

And I would add that all such "quick-fix" solutions – accepting Jesus as your Savior, visualization, achieving peace through meditation alone by simply quieting the mind, bowing to some other god, following a vaunted spiritual leader who will bestow an advanced state on you – *all of these* are phony and illusory. You are, in your core essence, the totality of your mindset.

And that highly complex set of values, beliefs, definitions, expectations, self-image and world view, etc., combines to manifest your ongoing life quality. You cannot qualitatively change the outer without – and except by *first* – revising the inner. And that is done slowly, addressing each issue in life as an indicator of self-defeating negativity – then, once you've thoroughly cleared away limiting mechanisms, conflict and struggle, self-punishment and suggestion, etc., moving on to the next.

When you personally recognize the inner-outer Oneness, you'll realize there is no other possible path, regardless of grand promises and esoteric offerings.

Still some perspectives on the Inner Journey to come. But let's glance into the rearview mirror, taking another look at that long, traditional distortion of general-purpose thinking, religionization in general…

Reconsidering: A Further Look at RELIGION

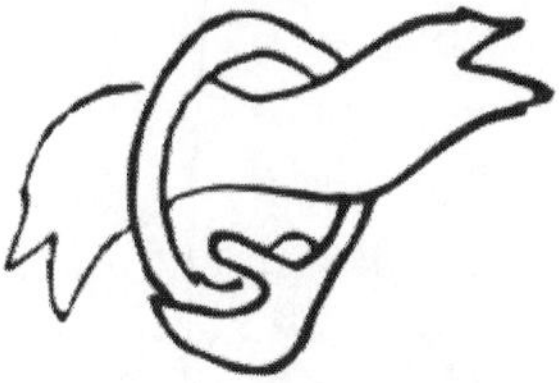

Religion doesn't lend itself well to analysis. Any religion I've ever encountered or examined posits a set of declarations that it claims to be true, often based on ancient accounts, promoted with time-honored authority – and instilled generally by indoctrination of upcoming generations in like thinking by implanting definitions as "truths".

Invariably, though, if you examine these, they prove to be simply mythical in basis, fantasized in detail, uncorroborated in any historical context – and ultimately just *flat out false*. The fallacy, of course, stems from not describing how reality works, but only duping the gullible mind into a deluded state in which the claims seem true. I'm happy to dispense with some of those claims – a task I have some talent at...

Q86 – If God has a plan and is omniscient, then how do we have free will? If God is timeless, then he shouldn't be bound to the temporal laws of the universe and causality and must therefore be able to see all possible temporal states; anything else would violate the semantic definitions of "omnipotence" and "omniscience", unless you want to redefine those terms.

If he did and he were, then we wouldn't. But he doesn't because he isn't and we do – but not how you might think.

People believe in gods, whatever the set, or a single god, whatever the name, because they were taught to do so from childhood. The nature of that god varies widely from religion to religion. It even varies considerably within Christianity from church to church – actually from individual to individual, as no two people hold identical beliefs. Indeed, the nature of "God", the supposed Christian deity with a capital "G", varies radically depending on which section of the Bible you reference.

The Old Testament gods, El and Yahweh, were described (that is, imagined and thus proclaimed) as anything from a personal god (Abraham encountered El in human form) to grand, glorious and remote (Moses' great – albeit incompetent – war god, YHWH). Jesus taught of a loving, forgiving god, where Paul preached of a wrathful, judgmental deity – coming any day now to save the day and/or sort out the sinful. (Except, of course, he never came – an inevitable consequence of not existing in the first place – so the story had to be changed to keep the priesthood employed.)

Somewhere in the evolution of such ideas, God was proclaimed to be all-knowing and all-seeing. Were that actually the case and we lived in his little pet enclosure, then I suspect your conclusion would be right: we could not possibly have Free Will, because all things would be pre-selected and fore-ordained. We would be merely acting out a script, mechanically going through preset motions in life.

But that somehow didn't fit into the sales program of the early religions. So they invented the notion of Free Will to allow, in their archaic manner of thinking, that God had something to judge – other than his own incompetence at creating the system in the first place. That was a rational cop-out that appeared along the way to somehow curb the obvious argument that, if God made us as we are, how can he judge us negatively later on for using the equipment he himself gave us in ways that come natural? Any sins would be on him and his design specs – with fault lying on his own inadequacy.

Of course, there was no Yahweh, no El (the hidden meaning of the traditional French Christmas greeting!) and no God, with (or without) the capital "G". Even as it became clear we occupy a vast universe, billions of light years across – not a small, flat earth with a firmament above it – the notion of a creator god who watches everything that you (and seven billion other people) do persisted.

But the notion of that God judging you for your actions and sending you off to Hell if you don't meet the standards – that thought stems back to Zoroastrianism and their good god, Ahura Mazda – a deity locked in eternal conflict with the proponent of badness, Angra Mainyu. A post-death judgment and relegation for eternity to a good or bad place has nothing to do with what Jesus taught.

Jesus noted that the Kingdom of God was "within" – and existed right now, if you could only see it. He illustrated it in many ways. Much like other visionaries – and, of course, my own point of view – he recognized a certain Oneness to the function of reality. But his superstitious, illiterate peers and generations of their offspring couldn't grasp his allegories and illustrations. And, of course, Paul of Tarsus came along, reintroducing that old Zoroastrian notion of judging good vs. evil and relegating those who fail the test to a nasty place…

So, God, as pictured in evolving Christian myth, became omniscient and forever *looking over your shoulder*. Not coincidently, the deity's nature was not unlike the kings and emperors of ancient times in their treatment of common peasants – or even parents, who commonly treated their offspring as menial objects.

You were deemed, then, to have Free Will, but would be judged later on – at death – as to how you use it. (A bit of a compromise on freedom, don't you agree?)

In actuality, what you ***don't*** have is a god of any sort. What you do, however, have is real Free Will – but it doesn't work in reality like you might think. Yes, you can do whatever you want – within the scope of your wealth, character and prowess. But whatever action you take, whatever you ultimately *decide* to do always fits into the framework of your own nature. And it always manifests results that reflect your own nature.

However, if you really want to affect outcomes, so your life yields more positive events and relationships, you need to delve inward to change your own deeper store. The qualitative outcome of your life stems from your own, inner nature – real-life qualities will revise in response to your inner change.

Thus, you do indeed *have* Free Will. It's standard equipment. But it can only be exercised by seeking and accomplishing change *within*, by adjusting your core nature as detailed in your subconscious – not ever by taking rationalized action.

As to the "if" in your question, it presupposes "God", the Christian fabrication with the capital "G", exists. And that's an obvious, resounding *"**NO**"*. But *you* do. And you have Free Will: you are absolutely free to take whatever action you choose and continue to manifest the same problems in life – or free to delve inward and accomplish real change.

Your only real lever in nudging change is within...

Oh, and one of the more significant changes you can accomplish would be to eliminate the notion that some external deity is hovering over your shoulder waiting to judge you. He isn't because he doesn't exist in the first place – and never did.

Q87 – How can I find God without religion? When I was a child I believed in God. I wasn't religious at all, neither were my family, but still I believed in God. About ten years ago I stopped believing in God. It was a conscious choice that I made after years of internal deliberation. My seemingly unshakable belief in God was extinguished...

How do you find a steering wheel without first coming up with a car? Steering wheels were invented not long after cars. They have no use, no real functionality, without the car.

Gods are like that, too – no value to them beyond the religion they seem to steer. The main difference, though, is that automobiles ***are real***: they will get you somewhere. Gods aren't; they get you nowhere.

Gods were invented way long ago, but only after our remote ancestors began to conceptualize external causes to how things were happening around them. At some point, promoted by a self-serving priesthood which found it could live off people's gullibility without having to actually work, those notions of external forces grew into deity status: sun god to bring warmth, war god to protect your tribe, etc.

Eventually, there were gods for all purposes – love, fertility, luck, you name it. All of these were projections of power to imagined forces – gods up there, on the mountain, above the firmament, making the wind and rain, causing *you* problems. Priesthoods prospered because they claimed to be able to sway the gods – and because people tend to be *really* gullible and fearful, particularly when kept ignorant.

At some point, all the gods got condensed into one – the effective difference being pure arithmetic. Gods are **conceptualizations** – no more than mere ideas residing in the childhood-created belief structures of your mind.

In effect, in life, you attract and manifest the reality you encounter. Issues in your life – health problems, failure, relationship issues – are all attracted by little old *you*. If you want to change those negative patterns, stop imagining that there's a big deity out there, looking after your spiritual well-being, judging you, messing with you, causing things, blessing you or anything else.

If you want to find God, the concocted deity with the capital "G", you'll find Him (with a capital "H") in the superstitious minds of millions of believers. You won't find Him (or her or it) – or any god from any religion – anywhere in reality.

But if you want to understand your own creative role in the manifestation of your life's real qualities, look within. There are specific inner roots underlying all of your real problems in life. You are connected to the flow of events and relationships that constitute your life: you attract them. You create them. The only element in your life that approximates a deity is you – as qualified in your comprehensive mindset.

But the more you look for God, Allah, Krishna or Vishnu, Lakshmi, Yahweh, or any other synthesized deity ***out there***, the farther you get away from understanding life and the conscious Self that manifests it.

Q88 – If I found the true answers to every religion, should I put it on news or stay silent?

Were you to do that, it would look something like this: they are all phony explanations that distort perception and hide life's real flow. Each person manifests his/her meaningful experience based on that individual's personally held mindset.

Gods, fate, the government, bacteria, luck, mothers-in-law and chance are all illusory forces in a reality each of us manifests personally – we attract patterns based on our own personal nature.

Now, equipped with that insight, what should you do? Most mystics who could see at least dimly through life's illusions created by popular (but fallacious) beliefs tried to explain their greater perspectives to others in their society. Many such visionary individuals throughout time, such as Socrates, Yeshua of Nazareth, Galileo, Meister Eckhart and Giordano Bruno, only suffered from the wrath of the closed-minded of their day. For the most part, other people weren't listening. And authorities, whose narrow viewpoints and status within their power structures – that is, religious leaders of their time – took a very dim view of being questioned.

It's very difficult for most people to see past their own limited and limiting beliefs – notions they've absorbed through childhood and share with other common-thinking people of their society. In modern times, religious organizations don't maintain adequate control to inflict damage on questioners – with the possible exception of societal control within cultures dominated by Islam.

But even in the West and in the United States, where freedom of speech is supposedly prized, you may try to your heart's content – or eternal frustration – to "put it on the news". But the media isn't looking for truth and insight. It's looking to stir up controversy in superficial stories to get people to tune in. Blasting viewers' favorite fictional beliefs isn't good for ratings. You'll have a tough time getting any enlightened views on "the news".

You won't get real insight onto PBS or NPR either. They are most strongly oriented to fund-raising from the public. Exposing public notions as archaic and false isn't in their playbook for promoting fund-raising. And their content is mostly provided by big corporations who cater to popular ideas and glitzy presentations, not in-depth content. Plus, their local operatives are anything but visionary people – they will not be open to your version of truth.

Staying silent isn't a great option, either. When you come to see man's plight and its real basis in his own archaic belief system, you want to tell people. You will be motivated to spread the word that religions, far from saving mankind from eternal damnation and science, which only shifts problems from one area of life to another, are neither the solution to man's real issues – but rather are the major elements of the problem!

But how, then? How do you spread the word you've so penetratingly come to grasp? Well, first, you can only present real insights to open-minded people. Others, the great majority of mankind, aren't paying any attention to new perspectives. So, where do you find those capable of listening?

The answer? Over the Internet – where ideas can be presented to people capable of thinking outside "the box" while bypassing main-line media, which only echoes standard notions. Earlier generations didn't allow for widespread distribution of perspectives outside common thinking that refuted cherished fallacy. Now it does.

Personally, I've traveled – at this writing – over 120,000 miles to present perspectives on life to 250+ open-minded audiences. But that only reaches hundreds, maybe thousands of people and only for the scope of the talk.

Websites shared across the world provide the means to reach people without traditional boundaries. YouTube and social media can allow for communication to people capable of thinking.

So the answer to your question is: ***neither***. The first is impossible, the second would render your life – were you to actually achieve a state of enlightenment – meaningless. Were you to join the exclusive, but excruciatingly small club of true visionaries, you would need to develop another means to reach people.

And by the way, it's much easier to gather an audience of people by parroting age-old fallacy – like religion – and structured, but incomplete thinking, as per science. You can much more easily gain listeners by telling them stuff *they already believe in*. The media really goes for that and hordes of follower-types readily latch onto popular fallacy.

Oh, and one further caveat! In addition to your voice, there are hundreds of others out there, each spewing messages guaranteed to be true and without question – big-name self-help experts, talk show hosts, doctors and psychologists, New-Age proponents, Eastern discipline gurus, huge religious movements with glitzy buildings and gobs of money to market and appeal to pre-deluded followers, smooth presenters with advanced degrees and public marketing agents, etc.

Lots of limited voices speak very loudly. Overcoming them

requires a particular knack – which you will have only when you have, indeed, "found the true answer". And that means...

If and when you do, you won't have to ask anybody...

Q89 – What traditions are present in all Religions?

One main tradition (leading to yet another) which is found in virtually ***all*** religions in all times and locations is the universal practice of ***indoctrinating offspring*** and thus, each new, upcoming generation into whatever belief structure is promulgated by the priesthood and its propounded creed.

This is basically unavoidable, as people are bound to rely on their traditions and beliefs in daily practice, including survival, child-rearing, etc. The good part to that is: whatever the culture and time period, it provides a steady, reliable basis for daily life – even if the religious tenets involved are total fantasy and flawed.

The bad part, however, is based on this: *all religions are inherently flawed,* mere conceptualized declarations that lead to distorted perceptions of how life actually works. Holders of the religion don't recognize this because they were so indoctrinated as children – and they continue to interpret reality *through* the distorting lenses of the local religion's artificial declarations. They just keep passing along the religion, whatever it is, as total, unquestionable truth, generation after generation.

And that becomes *really* bad in that it invariably incorporates negative, self-defeating elements into its practice. Projecting of power to gods and the spirit world, for example, adds elements of personal powerlessness to the self-image of each indoctrinated individual – which, in turn, creates tensions and conflict within the society and, ultimately, with its neighbors. Also, of course, that belief-centric, tribal attitude adds conflict at all levels. Belief in one religion inevitably implies that neighboring tribes or countries, harboring different beliefs, are not to be trusted, are evil, are less than human, etc.

Thus, this tradition of indoctrination of younger generations sets up an even worse tradition of religion: ***universal conflict and distrust*** in dealing with other cultural groups that has plagued mankind for ages. Totally convinced that only their own religion is valid and correct, various cultural groups have fussed with, detested and fought against neighboring people for millennia…

Regarding various Western and Eastern religions, ancient pagan rites, shamanistic practices, myth-based religions, etc., these two traditions, one leading subtly but directly to the other, constitute the prime practice that spans all cultures of all times.

Q90 – Do people still believe in the Greek gods?

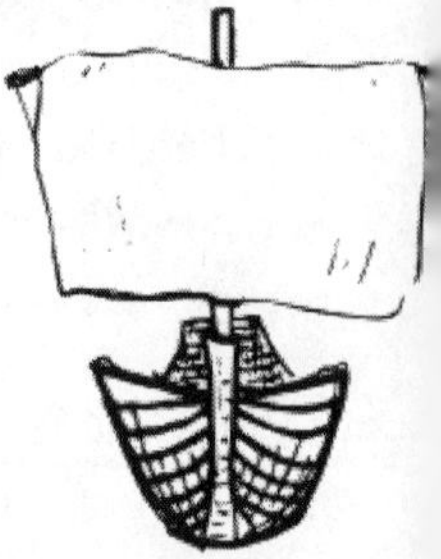

Yes, belief in at least one Greek goddess is quite prevalent in modern society: *Tyche*.

Huh? – you might ask…

Better known by her Roman reference, **Fortuna**, people unconsciously attribute the cause of events to her whimsical interference quite commonly. Every time you use the word *fortunately* or *unfortunately*, you carry on a tradition of many millennia of assigning causality to a force out there, a deity and her whim, that would capriciously or maliciously inflict damage on some "unfortunate" recipient.

In ancient times, as Christianity – with its single imagined deity, named "God" – replaced pagan notions in the populace of Europe, old concepts didn't die away completely. Christianity did try to expand its appeal by adopting various rites and rituals of pagan thinking: Easter, for example, is the spring fertility rite of the old goddess, Ēostre, Christmas the celebration of winter solstice and Roman Saturnalia, etc. But, beyond the adaptation of previous pagan rituals and god-characteristics, many old ideas simply persisted, particularly in the minds of illiterate country folk.

And those forebears of ours passed them along in common cultural notions, generation after generation. Tyche/Fortuna found her way, quite subtly, into common thinking: there is a force out there, making things happen…

Of course, if any user of those words would be asked, he or she would disavow believing in Fortuna. But the subconscious functions – unfortunately, you might say – with a very literal bent. Deeper attributes of mind get woven into one's own experience and even more so into one's interpretation of life's function. Even nonchalant reference to Fortuna tends to reinforce powerlessness in the deeper mind elements of the speaker: something bad just took place, and I can't explain it, so I'll attribute it to a hidden, subtle force called fortune.

That force just happens to be a long, long descendant of the goddess Fortuna – who was thought to inflict just such trying events on people, often capriciously.

Similar to that, by the way, is ***luck***. That word either comes from *Lakshmi*, the Indian goddess – a basic, Eastern cognate to Tyche/Fortuna – or both the word and that deity stem from the same, truly ancient, Indo-European roots.

So, the answer to your question is resoundingly: YES! People still hold within their deeper minds numerous psychological connections to ancient gods and goddesses – without realizing it. They blame Fortuna for events and worship, in a way, as the ancients did, days of the week as under the auspices of ancient gods – Saturday, for example, named after Saturn, comes from the old Greek god Chronus. (The Roman pantheon equated rather precisely to the more ancient Greek one.)

My point: one doesn't have to maintain a literal belief in a deity to subconsciously attribute causation to it. I don't see much of a difference, in effect.

Well, since we touched on Lakshmi, let's continue the segue eastward for a look at ancient traditions that generally contribute to the personal growth of seekers emerging out of Western cultures. While Hinduism and the approach of yogic meditation disciplines seem quite exotic, the deepest roots of Eastern thinking grow out of Indo-European traditions which are actually common to those of Western cultures.

Most of Europe became populated by a culture more advanced than its native hunter-gatherer tribes, spreading outward from the Black Sea area, beginning some six thousand years ago. Cultural groups there to the east, spurred by advanced agriculture, metallurgy, weaponry and resultant population growth, began to expand westwards, eventually becoming the various Slavic, Germanic, Celtic, Greek, Latin and other societies as the original language differentiated due to isolation.

From the same original stock, eastward expansion moved into Persia and the Indian subcontinent. These "Indo-European" peoples, expanding both westward and eastward, brought their myth and early beliefs along with their original language. And that collective proto-religion evolved in time, for the group that settled in what is now northern India, into the Rig Veda and other Vedic lore.

So, the background of Eastern thinking, evinced in Hindu beliefs and yogic traditions, actually stems from the same ethnic/geographic roots of European philosophical attitudes and Greek/Roman/Nordic pantheons – only without the heavy influence of Judeo-Christian notions overlaid on its mythological deities and their antics.

Here, then, are a couple answers to questions looking…

Eastwards: A Fleeting Look at EASTERN Thinking (Or Attempts to Not)

Hindu and Buddhist ideas, rooted in earlier Hindu notions, incorporate a recognition of the Self as a currently incarnated instance of a conscious entity that survives death to reincarnate into other earth-based lifetimes. Both feature recognition of a set of characteristics and propensities carried over from one lifetime to another – karma. And both seek to free the Soul from its cycles of incarnation, ever facing negatives established in prior existences.

Details vary, as Siddhartha Gautama, the Buddha, meaning "enlightened one", revised already ancient notions he encountered 2500 years ago, to more closely reflect reality as he saw it. Here are general questions regarding quieting one's mind and the notion of karma...

Q91 – Why is it so hard to completely quiet one's mind during meditation?

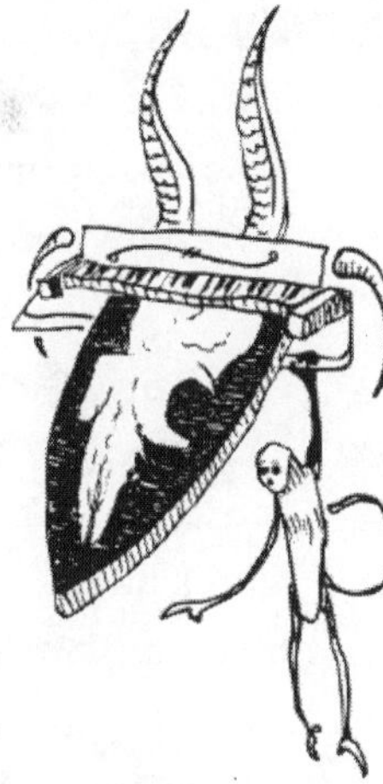

Most elements of your self-image serve conceptually to separate you from the world around you.

Religion, particularly the Western varieties, posit a creator god out there somewhere. This deity, extraordinarily powerful, all-knowing and formative in forging the universe, is necessarily separate from little old you – rendering your nature as temporal, nearly powerless and fundamentally ignorant.

Science and its objective paradigm set you as an entity separate and apart from an expansive collection of objects and people around you. Both recommend a plethora of means to manipulate the world around you – pray and give offerings to the god, hustle and work hard, use force and argument, cheat and bribe if you have to, all to get your way...

In reality, though, you are separate from the universe of material items you encounter. You are innately connected to the flow of events and relationships that constitutes your life: you attract them.

Your health, quality of relationships and degree of success all emanate from you: you manifest your life flow based on your total mindset. This is the case whether or not you are aware of it...

Because you learned while growing up that you had to manipulate the world, your mind is ever busy. Just as it was conditioned to manipulate your mother to get the cookies, you are constantly trying to plan and scheme. You continuously figure how to manipulate your boss, your spouse (perhaps one and the same), your kids and your neighbors – plus actively manage your house, social life, job, hobbies, keep the car running, the dog fed and the washing machine functional. Replete in this self-image and world view is the driving notion that, if you don't keep at it, things in life will break down – because the world is separate from you, has driving forces that either oppose or don't care about you, and it needs to engaged, defied and fought with to work right.

Thus, your mind, fulfilling its imagined rules and beliefs as it engages an illusory opposing world, is constantly trying to make things happen consistent with your desires: gather information, create a plan, execute the plan – over and over and over, as all aspects of life require your attention. So your reasoning mind is constantly busy, mulling over plans, thinking about what you have to do, worrying about snags in your plans and others' interests...

Meditation as a practice, long since introduced from Eastern traditions, can help to quiet the mind, at least temporarily. But, following its programmed rules and interests, the mind cranks up again once meditation is over – resuming its planning and executing, its figuring and manipulating.

To *really* quiet the mind, a much longer process is necessary. You need to become ***fully aware*** of your connection to – that is, your *Oneness with* – the reality you experience around you. And that is accomplished by delving into the subconscious to achieve two things:

1. Eliminate elements that negate aspects of your life that aren't working well (health issues, problematic relationships, failure at achieving your goals). As you do this, you become ever more aware of the inner-outer connection because you see that inner change always induces change in experienced Reality.
2. Dispel beliefs and definitions you hold that project causality to external sources and forces.

When you've managed to jettison religious tenets, scientific shortcomings, notions of luck and fate, thoughts of chance affecting things, etc., you gain awareness of your own role in manifesting/attracting all qualities in your life. At that point – or more accurately, *step by step along the way* – your mind quiets remarkably. It ceases to be overburdened with its need to manipulate and fear of alternate consequences.

That may be a long journey for you – but it's really the only way to fully quiet the mind. And leave it in a vital and peaceful state – ongoing, not just periodic and temporary.

To specifically answer the question posed: it's not only *hard* to quiet the mind through meditation, ***it's impossible***, based on the nature and function of the deeper mind – in its efforts to accomplish desired results while facing a Reality it has learned to see as opposed and uncaring.

Really quieting the mind requires elimination of all the beliefs and definitions you hold as valid "truths". That is a chore that requires specific exploration of deeper psychic stores to eliminate flawed elements and a long-term effort to cull out inner mechanisms that contribute to manifesting health issues, conflictual relationships and failure.

Q92 – When did you stop believing in Karma?

About three incarnations ago…

Just joking on that.

There is a certain validity to karma that is best understood when both the Hindu and Buddhist versions are bypassed. Hindu traditions look at karma as a collection of good and bad deeds one has accumulated through past lives – that there are ramifications pressing on your current life's flow based on negative things you did in previous ones. (That's a general overview, as there are a plethora of different takes, based on sect, etc.)

Gautama's view, as it has come done based on later recording, emphasized that karma needs to be regarded as your *current state of being*, not just an intangible collection of negatives you carry – but don't even recall – from past lifetimes.

The latter view voiced by the Buddha is closer to reality, but not precise or fully accurate.

To understand what's actually happening in life, so that karma's valid gist but inaccurate detail can be recognized, it's necessary to understand how you, yourself, see reality and life. Our typical modern Western mindset generally includes two core paradigms and a bunch of other old myths.

We all absorb some degree of religion growing up – it is built into cultural attitudes and notions. Christianity, in particular, has coexisted with Western culture for centuries. It was widely held throughout Western civilization, virtually without dissent (which, indeed, was ruthlessly stamped out when expressed). Thus, it is thoroughly woven into common thinking: even if you've managed to see through its fallacious declarations and impossible claims, it still inhabits elements of your subconscious as subtle definitions and expectations.

Science, too, in its 400 years of empiricism, has become woven into our world view as unquestionable "truth". It isn't, however. The regard of science only for the outer, material world ignores the most important aspect of being: the conscious Self, the transcendent, engaged consciousness that encounters, indeed, manifests the interwoven flow of events and relationships that constitute life.

Add to religion and science notions of luck and fate – old carryovers from ancient goddesses inflicting negatives on you. And include chance, too, as an illusory factor in life creation – like there's a probability that some good or bad event will spontaneously happen to you, just because of the odds of such an event.

Our standard mindset in the Western culture, then, through those diverse paradigms and beliefs, projects causality for your life outward: to gods and supernatural forces out there (religion, luck, fate) and to real-world sources and forces (bacteria, conditions, wealthy or bad people, bullies, your mother-in-law, etc.).

The difficulty in understanding life is this, oft observed in these answers: whatever your personal set of beliefs and interrelated definitions, whatever ideas you hold as true *will seem to be*.

You interpret encountered reality through your beliefs, judging truth or fallacy based on your current set of beliefs. Thus, no matter what they are, they will seem valid.

That's why a Christian and an atheist, a Muslim and a Shaman, a Communist and a Realist will all evaluate the same situation, but will all arrive at different conclusions as to cause and meaning – and all think that they, personally, each of them, is right and the others deceived…

Here's how life works – it's astoundingly simple: you are a conscious entity engaged in a lifetime, wherein you inhabit a physical form, a body. The flow of events and relationships you encounter *reflect your own nature*: you attract life situations, good and bad, based on your total mindset. The good stuff reflects your intent; the bad manifests out of your fear and your beliefs that indicate separation between Self and other things (including people).

In effect, you are connected to the flow of your life: you attract patterns.

Given the innate inner-outer connection each individual experiences in unfolding life, there are *always* inner roots to outer patterns, the negative ones. If you find them, recognize and itemize the specific inner mechanisms that underlie outer issues, you can change them and eliminate the problematic area – health, relationships, success. (This very process is what my books and YouTube videos cover.)

The degree to which you adhere to religion (projecting causality out to a god) or science (projecting reality out to external forces and sources) is the degree to which you will be blind to the inner-outer connection. Beliefs and definitions you've accumulated and hold now distort awareness of life's interactive, meaningful nature – they never clarify it.

The unfolding of life events is an excruciatingly simple process, however complicated the inner elements that contribute to it. Your current, highly complex, subconscious store of information (both true and false points of rational thinking), hopes, fears, beliefs, intent, emotional connections, drives, talents, propensities, etc. – that all gets realized in a meaningful flow of life that reflects your nature.

The inner manifests the outer, where it is experienced and absorbed as meaningful memory...

OK, now you see how life works. You may not accept that, insofar as it doesn't fit into your current belief structure. But if you can see past your customized set of beliefs, that's what you'd recognize…

Back to karma. Ancient Hindu mystics recognized that consciousness was involved in a continuity, a re-engagement of reality. They could see that bad things happen and reasoned that this was some sort of payback for previous negative actions perpetrated by the Self in previous lifetimes.

Gautama the Buddha's teaching grew out of that same tradition, but he saw the negatives growing out of one's *current state*. His solution was to correct negative actions and thoughts when experienced, and thus revise the flow – working out negative karma (as per his view of it).

Both notions hint at the nature of life, but carry old baggage that distorts the picture. In reality, your subconscious is highly intricate, a vast collection of ideas, memories and emotional connections (and lots more). Negative effects which you experience in life stem from various interrelated mind constructs, such as conflict and punishment. As noted, they can be changed within, thus affecting the outer flow.

That, of course, is the nature of things – *whether or not you recognize it*. (Again, you won't if you accept religion, science and/or some other explanations as true.)

So, doubtless, you've lived many incarnations to get to a state where you're posing questions and exchanging ideas. Your current state, again, for sure is a collage of long experience and personal growth – gained through incarnated existence. So, in a way, your current nature is karma-*like*, a vastly complex state of interwoven meaning and values. And it all stems from what you used to be – your previous nature, gained step-by-step, experience-by-experience, incarnation-by-incarnation along the way.

But it is much, much better (and far more accurate) to simply recognize the aware essence of Self – to see the nature of the mind, with its deeper storage of information/values and unconscious ties to the real universe, than to think of a hidden, obtuse set of bad things you did in previous lifetimes.

So, whether or not you "believe in" karma, your nature, as the full embodiment of your total mindset, contains meaning and self-image elements garnered in previous lifetimes. But that doesn't matter as much as simply recognizing your full inner Self – with the ability to change its content and thus improve your life in the process.

OK, then, to finally answer your initially posed question: I never really "believed in" karma, as I wasn't taught it as an aspect of Western upbringing. I did consider it when I began to explore Eastern thinking. But once I had deleted my wide range of Western and even Eastern ideas, and could see life's flow clearly, I could simply put karma *as a notion* into perspective.

Pretty complicated answer to a simple question. I imagined you would prefer accuracy to brevity.

We'll view karma again from a slightly different angle shortly. Now, attention shifts from the East closer to home. My original view of life, as I've covered to some degree, rests in standard Western ideas – Christianity and science, tempered with Luck, Fate and Chance as driving forces. But those were all jettisoned along my inner journey. That purge has allowed for clarity of observing life that constitutes much of my expression here. So, over time, my views themselves have drawn questions...

Reflective: About MY PERSPECTIVES

Many previous questions drew regard of others' declarations as embodied in philosophical, scientific, esoteric or religious depictions. Over time, though, I have answered various queries directly questioning my own statements or standpoint. Those merit inclusion here, as they likely typify the reaction of many people to my message...

E93a – Your thoughts are interesting – tell me more. I have (in the past) always controlled (ego) everything. Losing this behavior has opened me up to universal understanding. Yet I still have desires that I seek.

The attempt in various Eastern Mystical ventures to eliminate desire is rather self-defeating in effect. The life format in which our consciousness is engaged (yours and mine, currently) entails *change*, in a general mechanism of need and satisfaction. And change is guaranteed, particularly through the course of a lifetime, when phases of youth, pairing, child-rearing, career-developing, middle and aging periods offer considerably different qualities. Regardless of the phase of life and regardless of the situation, though, ***desire*** is part of that flow, often its instigator. Desire isn't an inherently bad part, as implied by the Buddha and other Eastern standpoints. And *attachment* to desire, further deemed to be hazardous in Eastern thinking, is hardly avoidable in life and its inherently changing situations.

But desire can lead to negative experience if the need/desire part *isn't fulfilled,* or if some aspect of the desire part is experienced in excess.

Eliminating desire, a key tenet of the Buddha's Noble Fourfold Path, is an artificial way of defeating the natural flow of this need/fulfillment. Much better it would be to have the longings fulfilled than live in such a vacuum that nothing is desired. It would be like saying, "Red is bad. Let's defeat the eye's color sense and live in a black-and-white world." Maybe you could do that, but life would be much blander.

Similarly, the attempt to dismantle natural desire in any of its avenues robs life of the enormous richness of its interactive nature. But again, that's like going off to a cave in Tibet looking for truth or the self. The self you find there is one who ran away from everything that is life. The truth you find there is a synthetic one somebody else fed you.

I would grant some wisdom to recognizing the excesses of materialistic desires: when you get the items you want, the desire only becomes affixed on additional items – a cycle that simply repeats for the materially oriented...

In general, though, life is a very rich experience – rich in creativity, rich in adventure, rich in potential. What you have today will become boring at some point, and it is a natural attitude of consciousness to desire something different. Consciousness is inherently creative.

But do you have the power, the ability, to actually manifest what you desire in your life? Do your wishes become fulfilled or are your desires negated and/or neutralized? That is the question to be asked. The answer should be apparent, and why that is so is to be found within your mind elements.

E93b – Perhaps you are living on a higher level than me. If so, I would like to move to this higher plane.

Higher planes are departing every hour. Forget the "plane" image, and look toward personal *clarity of perception*. I'm just being who I am, and I'm not trying to achieve any movement upwards or in projection into any other dimension – such a quest only serves to generate a mystical sort of illusion. If you go off looking for astral planes, you'll find them, and they'll be nice and fresh and clean, because you'll have just created them. If you seek a higher level of being, you'll never get there, because you will keep projecting it above and beyond your personal standpoint, regardless of your clarity of perception.

Of course, there is no real limit in projection of consciousness to what sort of reality you can create, but the real lessons in Self-awareness come from seeing *how* you create the elements of the real life you encounter here. And that opens a path of direct awareness for your essential nature, your quality of being.

People go looking for wonderful, mystical realms out there somewhere. This reality, as a clear, meaning-based reflection of the Self, is the plane you need to come to grips with. It's right here, only needing your attention and Clear Awareness.

E93c – Are your beliefs predicated on Eastern modes of thought? Maybe Hinduism? Did you cast off faulty beliefs or did your original beliefs deliver you to your enlightenment?

I've spent many years culling out and eliminating any belief I ever had handed to me – both Western, which I grew up with – and Eastern approaches I encountered when first I went looking. Beliefs never lead to awareness, they just get in the way. The only way to understand clearly how consciousness engages the reality it creates is through direct perception – and that is accomplished by deleting beliefs, not grabbing a more appealing set of them.

Growing up in Western Pennsylvania, I absorbed a combination of religious and scientific thinking, two belief structures often diametrically opposed. As I grew to understand the flaws of both of these philosophical systems, along with seeing ever more clearly how my mind worked in creating affects, both real and illusory, it became clear that beliefs had to be cleaned out, not cultivated.

Underneath all that was a firm commitment to a clear perception – a quality that seems rather rare, but must lie within everyone's mind, however covered over with debris of archaic beliefs. Anyway, I could always see the flaws to standard explanations – both religious and scientific – and, later, to Eastern mystical tenets.

So, to answer your question succinctly: all beliefs are faulty. I personally "delivered" me past a broad assortment of beliefs and definitions previously held, directly to my enlightenment, as you will have to do. Nobody can do this for you.

E93d – I am in the process of upgrading... and so have reorganized my website. When I get it sorted out I would appreciate your evaluation of the results of a search that has been going on for decades. I usually have to reduce to a level of understanding in line with the person I am speaking to. You seem to be (maybe) on a level higher than me...

I have read through your site, as you suggest in the other e-mail you sent. I would compliment your sincerity and style. But I don't want to critique your expression. How I evaluate your place in the scheme of things shouldn't matter so much as your own self-evaluation. Even at that, there is no pedestal at which to arrive, and from which there is no further growth. (Of course, there are an awful lot of "spiritual leaders" who sit on pedestals, thinking they have indeed arrived at the most esteemed level!!)

I certainly don't sit here, surrounded with ethereal clouds and natural incense, calling myself by some otherworldly title. But I do see clearly what and where I am, and I know the pathway on which I got here. I have much to add to EoR, and many years to do it, so check back from time to time.

E94 – I have during this last few months read what you have been writing and something inside me tells me that is how reality works. I have also read Jiddu Krishnamurti, and my question is now: Do you and Krishnamurti tell people the same thing? I mean Krishnamurti did experience clear awareness, but he had a very different way, compared with yours, of describing his point of view of how reality works. I hope you understand my question and will be able to answer it...

If there is an obvious similarity between Krishnamurti's and my perspectives, it is because we both speak about the same thing, *life*, with, as you note, a certain clarity of perceiving it.

I have always appreciated his words and the various collections of his teachings. I did live in San Diego during my 30s (the early 1980s) when Krishnamurti was speaking in Ojai, but I never traveled up there to hear him.

There was/is always a neat, soothing feeling that exudes from his statements, a tranquility that almost conveys peace with it. But his limitation, in my eyes, always was that he spoke of a place where you *should be* without giving any clear indicator of *how to get there*. Perhaps that was due to his roots in a different culture, where, understandably, the orientation and imagery are different.

I stem from an American culture where expectations are more exacting for clarity of depiction – saying things explicitly to describe what you mean. While it often isn't possible regarding consciousness to describe perception in terms entailing great precision, it is at least possible to describe exactly what *isn't* true, thereby pointing out illusions and fallacies. And it is certainly possible to fully illustrate techniques whereby others can delve inward to explore their own subconscious content – thus gaining a full recognition of the inner-outer connection of mind with encountered reality.

With his touching, though vague, references, again Krishnamurti clarified an engaged attitude without providing a means to attain it: he pointedly illustrated a fine house to live in without mapping a route to get there or a means to obtain it.

Krishnamurti had other weaknesses in my eyes. I don't want to sound critical, which I certainly am not. Basically, he issued a great statement about life, which will long be read – and which can only form a positive growth factor in the path of any sincere seeker. Ultimately, however, that great teacher died of cancer and during his later years was engaged in court proceedings against a former associate, contesting ownership of funds, manuscripts, etc. Both of these indicate levels of inner conflict he had no clear-cut means to dispense of.

Thus, as much as I personally benefitted from his message during my younger years and as much as I respect his voice in positively affecting many, many people through his life, I have to observe that he didn't quite recognize the inherent Oneness of things. However intimate his own experience of transcendence in several noted episodes in life, he didn't grasp the nuts and bolts of the inner-outer connection.

Again, that was no criticism of one of the greatest proponents of personal freedom and awareness ever to speak.

The main question from your standpoint, though, is not so much concern over our differing styles of expression, but how might you benefit from the perspectives offered by both of us. Take Krishnamurti's message for whatever benefit it can provide to your outlook. But do, indeed, explore not only my books and readily available videos – but even more important: explore your own psyche, come to relate the inner mechanisms I detail with real aspects of your own life. And grow in awareness from the experience.

This should be helpful to all my readers to more clearly see what's going on – consistent with the good old American style of explicit description!

E95 – I am interested in how your awareness impacts on your life. Obviously, you relate your wisdom because you have it and you wish to be helpful to others who seek answers as you once did. Do you live only in the moment? Or do you use creative visualization to bring about the reality you choose? Are you content to just be? Or are you developing a life path to follow?

Awareness is so interwoven into my life it's hard to say how it impacts anything else! I have a calendar on my wall and a clock here and there, but I recognize their significance and don't worship them. I live in the moment because there's nowhere else to dwell! Of course, we all live in the moment – recognizing that is what's important.

Visualization is a rather illusive effect. Whatever goal you might focus on and achieve will of necessity fit into the whole parameters which constitute your nature. Visualization is thus a great learning step to experience the mind/reality oneness. But you come to a point where such an intense focus on a specific goal is not necessary, since specific events don't really coalesce to yield the whole of experience, but rather the other way around in a fashion. The essence of Self yields the events and relationships of your life – in quality and value. So, you don't need to try to visualize a particular event into existence in order to satisfy a need, if events in general accomplish the fulfillment you really are seeking. Does that make sense?

One major problem with visualization per se is that what you think you want – a material item, a desired relationship, success in an undertaking – often isn't really a goal that will yield happiness. That is, what you think you want and what you really do desire are not the same.

The greatest issue with visualization is much more subtle: getting what you want, then transferring inner conflict and assorted negative mechanisms to other aspects of life. Like you visualize winning the lottery, thinking everything will be wonderful. But then, loaded with money, you find your spouse leaves you because they are changed, your family and friends all want a part of your bundle and now you are loaded with worries about investment, crooks cheating you and many other hazards of newfound wealth.

Am I developing a life path to follow? Who would be leading and who would be following? There is a stage when you feel you need to be captain of the ship, and a time when you think being navigator is the enlightened state, and yet another when you think you ought to be stoking the engine. But then you realize you are the ship – and the ocean, and the cargo, and the destination.

By then, you don't need to engineer and direct life. You fully trust your body to work right and your own now peace-based impulses to lead you in the right directions.

Am I content to just *be*? No, I have goals and interests – things I want to accomplish in life, primarily. And I proceed towards them. But the means to accomplish them is not to hustle, push, try harder or whatever. Success requires the elimination of inner restrictions – negatives, complexities, adherence to conflict and struggle, etc. – that inhibit realization of one's will.

E96 – I wonder how do you look at Karma, past life? Is that real?

The concept of karma from Hinduism has some functional validity to it, but it carries one major, distorting element that makes it appear too daunting, and thus too overwhelming to deal with.

In effect, you are what you are *now* – comprising a collection of interrelated mind-values, complex, deep, and self-aware. Without question, your current status of existence didn't just spring into this state of being this instant or at the point of conceptualization or birth. Since consciousness *always* exists within the environment of a reality that reflects its nature, clearly you "have lived" many life-format existences to become what you are, in terms of value and complexity.

However, these lifetimes shouldn't be squeezed conceptually into the confines of our chronological way of looking at things. Thus regarding "past" lives is an inherent distortion. They are more clearly "other" lives, other focuses, other ventures, other realities, whatever. The next step you take on a path through the forest isn't the only one you have taken or *will* take to get you where you are going. But it is the one you're taking now – others taken, steps that got you to the current point, and steps yet to take are important, but where you are ***now*** is specified by your current step.

Quite similarly – though vastly more complex – your journey of existence isn't fully defined by your current state of being. But it is fully *encompassed* by your current essence. It comprises in a fashion all the stages you passed through to get to be what you are – other lifetimes plus lessons learned and growth attained in this one. It implies what you *will* be, one composite out of considerable possibilities. But your full *nature of being* is comprised of the total, highly complex, state of your deeper psyche *now* – with that being the inner, which combines to manifest the outer.

From an Eastern standpoint, through Hindu traditions, karma is imagined as an accumulation of plusses and minuses from those other "past" lives, bad things you did along with good, gathered as a sort of debt and/or credit on an Akashic accounting sheet. That creates the image of an awesome load of mystic indebtedness that the individual *can't even remember accumulating* – for deeds good and bad, gestures which also aren't even held in memory! Such a ledger of hidden values would be impossible to deal with. Indeed, Hindu notions don't really allow a mechanism to burn off old negative karma.

Buddhism does, though. First, changes proposed by Gautama, over and above Hindu root thinking, view karma (much more accurately than the Hindu model, I would note) as a *current state of being* – what you are now. Just how you got here, what went on in past lives, is much less relevant. And Buddhism suggests (not accurately, say I) how to erase negative karma: follow the Noble Eightfold Path.

Beyond those two models of Eastern thinking, though, reality, that is, the actuality of existence, exists in its essence only in the present moment. All values, all mind-aspects, the totality of what you are, is stored as intertwined values, stored in the vast subconscious – available to you in the concentrated observance of *this* life's aspects. You need only develop the orientation to do so, and some effective self-hypnosis technique (which is nothing more than concentrated focus). There, in the events and relationships that you have encountered in your childhood, in your present life, in any period of your life are the patterns and meaningful effects of your total nature. And in seeing these clearly, you can come to change and clear out undesirable elements.

So, karma, as pictured in Hindu traditions, is a bit of an illusion, a self-defeating one at that, in that it takes these mind elements and projects them out of reach – into some distant, isolated other lifetime. You become, within the flawed Hindu view, a mere puppet, dangling from strings of your own past-life making, hoping only to dispense with them over time and further incarnations. As updated by the Buddha, the focus becomes more current and the model closer to reality, but Gautama's suggested means to work off the negative stuff is ineffective. Correcting actions, thoughts, etc., as suggested in the Noble Eightfold Path is like spurring your horse after the race is over. Based on the real nature of the subconscious and how it works, how it stores information, corrective measures must dive deeper than the Buddha recognized and do so to avoid future negative episodes – not simply react to current ones.

What is real is your own, highly complex inner psyche – a mindset full of stored ideas, definitions, qualitative values, memories based on meaning and consequential hopes, expectations, behavioral traits, etc. Karma is a distorted look at the inner-outer connection – based on some ancient insights much closer to reality than any notions of Western religions or science. But distorted nonetheless.

E97 – You may not "offer proofs", but you are certainly describing and arguing for a paradigm – one which I experience as true. It borders a bit on Buddhism, you'll be unhappy to learn, which is godless, teaches connectedness to everything "real", and requires the individual to take full responsibility for awareness and growth of the self. Any "perspectives" on reincarnation?

A paradigm is a model, a sort of scaled descriptor of the system it endeavors to describe. I don't put forth a paradigm about life, but rather discuss elements of life directly, intending to foster awareness of how reality functions as a whole. The mind tends to latch onto paradigms and hold them as truths, then disregard – overtly or subconsciously – evidence contrary to the paradigm.

Religions put forth paradigms consisting of beings that aren't there and a cosmology that is founded on mythical stories. Science rests on an artificial paradigm of a universe of objects that are made of smaller and smaller particles that interact based on various rules.

I merely observe reality – without a belief structure to interfere, as I have rid myself of artificial tenets over time – and tell you that you and the reality you encounter, the events and relationships that make up your daily life, are two aspects of a Oneness. That singularity rests, in quality, on the values you hold. There is no paradigm in that. That is simply How Life Works. I am discussing *what is*, not putting forth some model to represent it.

Also, by the way, I don't argue for or against anything. What is, simply *is*. My point is to promote awareness of what is – arguments only pertain to synthetic constructs and definitions. I have no vested interest in whether you or anybody else accepts my perspectives (not arguments) at all.

Secondly: of course, I'm quite familiar with Buddhism. If there's a similarity between EoR and Gautama's tenets, it's because we are dealing with the same subject: life. There is a highly perceptive basis to Buddhism building on more ancient Hindu teachings. But, Gautama, while exceptionally insightful in some ways, was also incorrect in others. That, of course, depends on just what Siddhartha Gautama really espoused 2500 years ago – much of what is attributed to him stems from well after his death.

As to reincarnation, certainly, each of us lives through lifetime upon lifetime. Consciousness *always engages a reality*, and the life format is a pretty handy one for encountering one's aspects, growing, being creative, etc. But lifetimes are not chronological and not limited to the bounds of our usual treatment. Also "karma" is a rather distorted view of the values the individual holds. You aren't carrying around past debts and heavy luggage of evil deeds from past lives, but you simply are what you are. When you come to see that, and learn to deal with aspects of self, the heaviness of this karma concept fades.

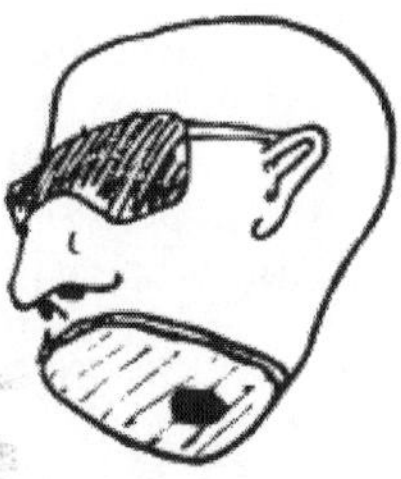

E98a – I stumbled across your site by accident. I had to comment. I think a lot of your ideas are excellent. I especially like the idea of the lowly inheriting the earth as being related to their genuine "inner peace" and purity of the soul. I thought about that before myself. Also, the power of society and control it exerts. I think you should definitely write a book.

(Original answer...) I prefer to publish on the Web. Writing a book entails appealing to some editor with limited perspectives on most anything except putting stuff out there to make money. And that effort is primarily publishing things that have widespread acceptance already. With my EoR site, I write what and as I wish. I don't have to meet anybody's deadline or gain anybody's approval. And I don't have a concern about making money with it – in short, I am free. My words aren't meant to appeal to anybody based on their current tastes, and I have no vested interest whether they do or not.

By the way, the perspectives in EoR are not so much "my ideas", as my clearly expressed view of aspects of life as I see them and it. This is not a creative writing venture espousing my clever philosophical conclusions. It's more of a report as to how life looks when seen without the distortion of any clever philosophical conclusions.

(This question was posed by a reader of my website around the year 2000. In late 2006, John Hunt, owner of this publishing house, John Hunt Publishing, contacted me, offering to publish my writings if I would assemble them into book form. The above two paragraphs voiced my thoughts at that point, six years earlier. But my disinterest in writing a book was bypassed by the unsolicited offer to simply publish my work. Here, I could voice my views without compromise and without trying to appeal to some editor's whims. Since then, with three books in print, I've traveled widely to present my perspectives to groups. I sell books at these talks – but I never compromise my message in order to appeal to some specialist group for the purpose of selling books. Indeed, I don't need book revenue to support me – sales serve only to help offset travel and other expenses.)

E98b – I do... disagree with some ideas. I was wondering if you have read any existentialist philosophers such as Nietzsche. And what is your take on the notion of Nihilism.

Existentialism gets too wrapped up in the intellect and philosophical descriptions to see the whole picture, including the Self that is doing the questioning. I avoid such philosophical movements and schools. Whatever angle you approach life with carries its own assumptions, often very subtle, and inherent pre-composed notions. Until you realize that, you will always either add to the images or debate with them – neither of which gets you anywhere.

Existentialism posits that *existence* precedes *essence* – that one has to *be*, to exist, before one takes on characteristics that seem apparent – one's role in life, one's features and capabilities, etc., which are deemed one's *essence*. Existentialist philosophers – from Kierkegaard through Sartre – seem to get hung up on open regard for the apparent with little or no recognition of the complexities of the psyche in its conscious existence.

Reading the views of various Existentialists leads to great immersion in complex argument and description of an appearance. That particular act, in itself, covers over a clarity of recognition of one's own nature with layer upon layer of fluffy comforters and exotically decorated quilts. If you put so many covers on a bed, you won't even realize there is a bed under all the insulating blankets.

As to Nietzsche, that's another consideration. I have read about his life and explored his writing somewhat; they far exceed the conceptual confines of Existentialism – both in substance and depth. I thoroughly enjoy many of his comments and prize his contribution to man's thinking.

Nihilism is an outgrowth of an objective-oriented view. To disavow meaning in life is absurd – life abounds with meaning. There is meaning in everything you do, in everything you encounter – though you certainly can ignore it or avoid considering it. This is a good example of how an accepted philosophy will blind the holder and limit his/her awareness. The very act of formulating a philosophy of Nihilism entails meaning!!

E98c – I do agree that most people are in search of happiness, more so an inner peace. I don't think you can generalize this. When you make such a statement you are imposing your will, ideas, and assumptions on others.

You might differentiate here between what you are seeking in life and what you *think* you are seeking. I'm not about to tell you either, but most people are looking for fairly mundane things that they learned were important, presuming that the acquisition of these objects or conditions will bring happiness – but all the while they ignore the quality of inner peace, which, if they had it, would lead them to attain most everything else they really wanted.

I have yet, in rather wide travels in my life, to meet anyone who sought to have their wishes denied and their plans negated.

Even if you wanted to have your desires negated (as ascetics seek), that would be yet another aspect of will you were seeking to fulfill. It is not an imposition of *my* will or assumptions to report the perception that people generally want to have their desires fulfilled.

Come to think of it, if you wish to have your wishes negated, you must succeed in fulfilling either your desire or the intent to deny that desire. Whatever happens will fulfill one end of that twist or the other.

E98d – I am not being a wise guy but not everyone is searching for these things, although many are. They are no goals of mine. I expect inner turmoil, society's chains.

If you are looking for, i.e., expecting, inner turmoil, aren't you having your expectation fulfilled when you encounter it? Certainly, some people seem to relish struggle and conflict as a challenge. But that trait is built into their self-perception and self-evaluation, such that the act of overcoming their opponents fulfills the values held inwardly by the individual. However, they can't even do *that* without a certain degree of inner peace.

Is it your goal to struggle endlessly? Again, what will fulfill that goal? A victory over something or somebody? Then what?

Society, by the way, doesn't present or incorporate any chains. Only the individual does, and they are inner.

No surprise that many questions I've received over the years via e-mail through my website have been about me personally. I do mention that anybody who expresses his or her perspectives on life should be willing and open to explain how that viewpoint was reached – and be open to providing personal info that supports any claims to advantageous status based on following that person's suggestions...

Indicative: About ME Personally

So, let's do an about-face here, turning from focus on the world, the reader's own journey inward or my viewpoint – and look at my life. As I've traveled extensively and encountered a great number of people – many deeply aware, sincerely seeking understanding, highly intelligent and quite memorable – life has been quite fascinating. I do think that, at some point, I will assemble my many vivid memories into an autobiography, as there is much to record and preserve for future generations – a glimpse, often behind the scenes, at the late 20th century and its various cultural upheavals.

For now, though, let's just look at some answers I provided readers of EoR online about my personal status. Most of these responses were offered some time ago, around the turn of the millennium, but I'll update and revise the original to reflect things currently, as of my 70th year...

E99 – I still maintain that you cannot help anybody unless they approach you... How does this relate to your explanations on the net? Surely you get endless grief.

I would go along with that initial proposition generally. I never force a discussion in casual company of what life is all about, but I don't hold back if the subject comes up. The Internet is a great filter in this regard – only those who find EoR and delve into it actually "approach me". They are open to new perspectives and can be aided by my words.

No, actually I never get grief from anybody over EoR. People who aren't ready for my perspectives either don't find EoR in the first place, or can't stand to read much of it!

(Added Note: This original answer stands even 15 years later, with tens of thousands of miles traveled, 250 talks given and hundreds more informal discussions, YouTube videos and answers submitted via Quora. I included one negative e-mail above as E82 – the only one I've received. Once, after a talk at a Mensa Annual Gathering in Texas where I voiced perspectives from my third book, *The Illusion of "Truth"*, did a man approach me, rather upset about my critique of the ancient writers of New Testament works. In that case, after a brief discussion, I told him, "Look, you view first century, anonymous writers of the gospels and other works, along with Paul, as spiritual and in tune with a God that you believe exists. I see them as superstitious, primitive in their thinking, unaware of the earth's nature, the environment, how the body works, etc. – with nothing of value to explain to me. Neither of us will convince the other of his standpoint – so let's go have a beer." That ended the discussion – and I had the beer without him. That, I presume, was preferable to us both.

Ten years ago or so, giving other talks to Mensans, I occasionally got pushback in defense of science. Slowly, though, over the years, as I attained ever greater inner peace, I stopped attracting those who only wished to defend their belief systems, not see beyond them.

Once at a talk in Mendocino, a woman aggressively questioned me as to how I could blame breast cancer on the belief structures of millions of women who suffer from or had died from that disease. I calmly said that it was impossible to dive into the deep subconscious structures of other people, but that if you could, you would find conflict and other negatives there. The only real opportunity one has to examine the mind-body connection is in *one's own personal situation*. She wasn't satisfied – of course, her question wasn't a question at all, but a firm statement that she wasn't about to doubt her own beliefs to consider that there was more to life than her mindset allowed.

Beyond those few instances, I never encounter argument or...

Oh, yes, at a Mensa talk in Baltimore, I had a heavy, bearded guy question me something like this: "You know, people that talk about such things as changing life by looking inside the mind, we call them crazy." I answered, "Well, when I saw the world like you do, I had health issues, problematic relationships, failed ventures and lots of other problems. Now, I'm very healthy, have great adventures and rewarding relationships, no weight problems, no conflicts and I succeed at what I undertake. If that's 'crazy', I'll take it over your status of sanity any day!" It got a pretty good laugh.

So, that's about it for "grief", criticisms or negative responses the questioner, some 15 years ago, suspected I must encounter...)

E100a – You say it took much travel, outward as well as inward, to find out what is really going on. I wonder how your trips through North America, Europe and Africa influenced you? Did you really find something out there? Or did you find the only way was to go inward?

There is a distinct cultural indoctrination that undoubtedly goes on in each area, where children are taught (and otherwise pick up through their experience) certain rules and standards as to how things are, how life works. When I traveled around through various countries, it became apparent that other cultures did things much differently, and thought much differently – but it worked just fine for them! Thus, a lot of the background understandings I held were clearly only limited perspectives from my particular place of origin.

It was a great lesson, but gleaned by direct contact with various cultures, not from out the window of a hotel.

Important, too, were the many discussions held with friends and acquaintances from various European countries and other regions of the US and Canada. Attitudes in California and information available out there was much different than standard fare back home in Pennsylvania – or in other regions. Discussions after talks I gave in England, Scotland and Wales involved different viewpoints than encountered elsewhere.

Certainly, the greatest impact on my life was advancement I made by delving inward to revise my subconscious stores of understanding and its inherent operability. But lessons learned by extensive travel were critical, too. I would not have garnered the same breadth of understanding by sitting in a cave in Tibet, meditating or by exclusively reprogramming the subconscious while sitting back home in Tarentum, Pennsylvania.

E100b – How is YOUR life? Are you joyful? Do you laugh a lot? Can you consciously manipulate reality to what you want it to be?

My life has to be one of the most fascinating ever. And I reckon I have the *best* part to go still. Yes, I've spent years cleaning out the negating mental aspects to correct health and success-oriented effects.

Joyful? Yes, but joy isn't always bubbly effervescence. I thoroughly enjoy the accomplishment of what I have done, and enjoy it as well that I can express that openly. Yes, I certainly laugh a lot – in fact, I used to do improv comedy. My sense of humor is my best feature, but I don't "write" funny stuff very often in the EoR material. Talks I give, though, always have twists of meaning and plays on words that have audiences laughing along. My YouTube videos have many little tricks and humorous features built in – some pretty subtle...

To that point, however, I'm not a stand-up comedian. Life always has a place for humor and would be dreadfully bland without it – but in my talks and writing, I address meaningful, often critical perspectives, so I have to keep the focus on more serious aspects of life...

As per your fourth question, I don't have to "consciously manipulate" reality. That's the point. When you are right within yourself, reality unfolds in a desirable fashion.

This is not to imply that everything always goes exactly as I imagine. Existence isn't a game with a goal at the end after which there is no advancement. Don't think you're trying to reach some Nirvana, some Heaven, some end-point state of Perfection (with a capital "P") beyond which no growth is possible or necessary.

The Consciousness which you *are* is an extremely complex blend of values and mental elements, with unlimited creative potential functioning in an unlimited realm with unlimited power. Don't begin to imagine that Clear Awareness is an end to the journey where you win a big prize and spend the rest of eternity in the bliss of orgasmic fulfillment of any desired pleasure. As your awareness awakens, there are always new horizons to aim for, new levels to reach, new growth to accomplish. I am on my path, just as you are moving along yours. My goal has been set very high – just as yours should be. But reaching it only means I'll need to set further goals...

E100c – I was surprised to read that you don't use the word "Truth". Isn't Truth the Essence of Reality? I don't think of Truth as a label applied to an explanation, but rather as something that cannot and has no need to be explained.

One person's truth can be another person's blasphemy. Truth, as perceived by each individual, is rooted in and judged by his/her personal beliefs and orientation. Is there an "absolute" truth? Yes, but it's something that needs to be perceived by each individual, not dictated by me – so I avoid using a label that is overused by everybody who would explain reality – like gurus, preachers, philosophers, etc.

Clear Awareness yields an unfettered understanding to the one who has it. Any explanation of how things work, even by one who sees clearly, will be distorted by the explanation, and truth, *real truth*, is so fragile that it breaks by any distortion. So, I don't do descriptions that I claim to be true, but rather discuss life in such a fashion that the reader might come, through his/her own efforts, to see things clearly – eventually, at his/her own pace, whenever that might occur.

So, there is no need for the label of "truth". My third book, exposing the rampant fallacy of Christianity, uses that whole theme – highlighting in its title, *The Illusion of "Truth"*, claims of eternal veracity which simply aren't.

E100d – My question to you is not who you are, but why you do it. What is your motivation for writing these things and putting them out there for everyone to read?

Now, that's a good question!!! Have you ever met car mechanics who just couldn't be themselves if they weren't covered with grease and fiddling with car parts? Can you picture an artist who just couldn't be anything else in life as he blends colors on a canvas to create visual images and communicate beauty to others. Imagine a musician who can do nothing else particularly effectively but play their instrument or sing. I'm a bit like all of them, but I deal in a sense with the mechanics of mind and the expressive beauty of life. I fix the workings – or rather teach others to fix them themselves. My paintings are video expressions on a computer screen and my musical phrases tones of sound that pierce reality's deceptions!

When I was a kid, my mother took me to a Presbyterian church here in the suburbs of Pittsburgh. I used to sit there, amazed that people would perch in their various pews and nod their heads in agreement to things that were obviously not true. Already, I could clearly see the fallacy to religious dogma, and used to tell adults about that – and they had no argument, except that you had to believe in what they told you!!! Of course, they were horrified that I would actually question their favorite truths.

Well, it took a long path, much travel throughout North America, Europe and into Africa, and very much travel inward, into the values of mind, to see clearly what is going on here. It is just part of my nature to write about that – and to do so without all the trappings and garbage of the guru, philosopher, priest, shaman or other such traditional pseudo-expert role-players.

I can't make you or anybody else realize life's way or touch your inner source of love and creation. But I can cast a broad net to communicate with those who sincerely want to do that, and show them clearly some of the crud and debris that needs to be scraped away, so that they can see life clearly themselves. Being that facilitator is just part of my nature; like the mechanic, artist or musician, I'm just being myself.

Also, of course, it is rather fun to poke holes in some of our culture's most prized, most hallowed fallacies and illusions! It always has annoyed me to hear the varied, loud claims of exclusive "truth" uttered by each and every religion, when I could see with no effort the flaws in their thinking.

E101 – Who are you?

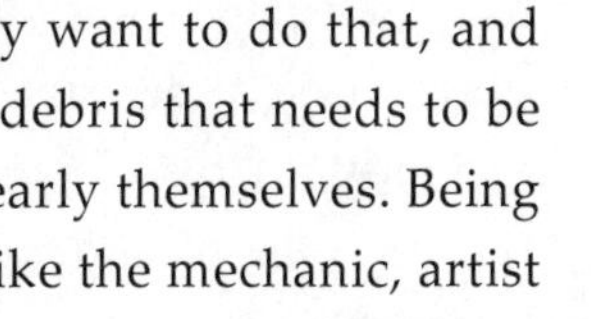

Well, I do, indeed, get many questions – but none are as simple, and yet complex as that one.

Who I am is to be seen more clearly in *"what"* I am. And that is an individual, not unlike others in fundamental nature, but who has come to see through all the artificial cultural, philosophical, traditional mental images of what I am to a clear view of Self and Reality – which indeed are one and the same.

And what I am, as well, is a person who intends to express that view because it is clear that many others in this time seek sincerely after a similar level of understanding, and my accounts can save them many a wrong turn in their path.

Jesus of Nazareth is quoted in the Gospels as referring to himself as "Son of Man". That phrase, *ben-'adam,* is rather appropriate, well beyond its old, original meaning in Aramaic as simply a human or son of Adam. The twist is that, basically, that common phrase of ancient times can be seen to subtly indicate a new generation growing out of the old, a new level of human emerging out of the more primitive form.

This new generation – not exclusive to any ethnic subgroup of mankind – is one, not of genetic revision, not of evolved musculature or overwhelming intellectual prowess, but one of increased perception, with clearer understanding, on an individual basis, of each of his and her own nature and place within existence. This capability to *BE* exists within each of us, but not all will make the journey to realize the Self in their current lifetimes.

Perhaps my simplest answer is to say that "what I am" is nothing more or less than one who can see clearly *what I am.*

E102 – What do you need to cultivate in order to grow awareness?

Self-perception! You need to come to see yourself – to notice your thoughts, where they come from and why. You need to notice how the things that happen in your life make patterns, and how those patterns always relate back to you, yourself.

You need to see inner mechanisms within the psyche through which the mind twists desired images into negating, self-defeating effects, how conditions and situations in your childhood are echoed again and again, recurring with different players and different backdrops, but with the same value effects – in equivalent patterns.

In a manner of speaking, Clear Awareness doesn't really need to be "cultivated" – it grows naturally and easily in ground that is rich from being open-minded and has been softened by prodding into mind elements, has had the weeds of belief removed, and has been watered by the natural rains of love.

E103a – The more I study your EoR the more I feel you are offering Humanity something of great importance and ultimate value.

Of course, I tend to agree with your evaluation! But not everybody is yet at a stage where they are open to my words. That is the great value of the Internet (it's no coincidence that it came along just at the right time), where I can present my perspectives freely. Those who are looking will find my words and videos at pretty much the right time.

But I would also mention that my expression, broken mostly into small, easily digestible pieces, is meant to speak to many future generations. There will never be a religion or following gathering up around my words to distort them and turn them into a farce – a fate which has impacted the messages of many perceptive individuals of the past.

In any case, the importance and value are only to those, apparently like yourself, who are capable of grasping the message and using it to improve their life and thus gain benefit…

E103b – Being a person with CLEAR AWARENESS: HOW DO PEOPLE YOU INTERACT (with) ON A DAILY BASIS, like your own Family – wife, son, people you work with, friends,

etc., accept you being so STRAIGHT? How do they react? Do they – or most of them – even know about your fantastic work? Do you have private group sessions? etc. etc. etc.

Originally from the Pittsburgh area, I traveled quite a bit in my younger years, having lived in Munich for about five years, in San Diego for over seven and in Paris for a year.

I returned to my home area about 30 years ago so my son could grow up in that pleasant environment. Western Pennsylvania is a nice place to live: plenty of forest, some family around, a friendly attitude, good sense of humor and a lot of culture nearby in the city – the Pittsburgh Symphony, Pittsburgh Opera, great museums and other cultural groups, competitive sports teams in the Steelers, Penguins and Pirates… Lots of activities and sense of community…

Of course, in this time frame, most people in Western Pennsylvania are rather deeply mired in old-world beliefs. So, no, in general, only selected people I associate with regularly are aware of The Essence of Reality. That is not necessarily a bad thing. I prefer a rather "normal" life, such as that word can be applied.

With that as a background, how do I relate to people? I let them be themselves. I understand where they are and where they are going, but it's not my job to preach to them, reform them, or convert them!! If the discussion comes up, I speak clearly, but most people around home aren't as attuned to that as the average, open-minded Californian, for example – though some are – so reactions can be mixed. Just as I spend no time banging my head on brick walls with the intent to knock them down, I make no effort to convince firm believers of the fallacy of their beliefs.

(By the way, that seemingly "open-minded Californian" can be just as frozen into a fallacious New-Age philosophy as the local Catholic hereabouts!)

My family and closer friends have their own views of my understanding – impressions which I don't query and they don't say. I've never been, you might guess, swayed or bothered by other people's evaluation of me or my viewpoint. So, I interact with friends and family with a fun attitude, accepting them as they are, presuming them to be the same. Those who weren't, tended to depart on their own.

Group sessions? Years ago, while living in San Diego, I did offer a limited sort of awareness group. But I haven't been doing that lately.

And anyway, who says I am, or in any way appear to be, so "STRAIGHT"!??! I enjoy a lot of things in life, have a great sense of humor and have a lot of fun. I'm not in the least pious, judgmental, adherent to behavioral or restrictive moral standards, or repressive in my demeanor! I'm about as "straight" in that regard as the average Western Pennsylvania country road!

E103c – Do you want SOMEDAY to give up just making a living full-time and doing EoR part-time [and] ACTUALLY switch and do EoR full-time??? HUMANITY NEEDS YOU!!! WHY WAIT???

(Original answer, c. 1999:)

I can certainly picture devoting much more of my life to my writings. I have a great deal of meaningful material sketched out and some always in progress. But I never accept money for any of my works, so the financial setup to allow my full-time devotion to writing will have to come via a different path.

Humanity, as you aptly observe, does need me. But what it doesn't need is yet another Self-Help expert, guru, New-Age preacher or self-promoting mystic. Generally, I have the money to travel at my own expense to speak to groups on a limited, but convenient basis, so I currently offer to speak to groups. No other arrangement allows me to be free. EoR will never be a business, profit or non-profit, never be an organization, and never require something back for what it offers.

I'm not really waiting for anything. I'm growing into the proper, unfettered state I need to be in so that I can satisfy my own standards. Maybe that looks like "waiting" from the outside! In actuality, I am enmeshed in the process of change – as each of us is – and must clear away some remaining inner obstacles before I can comfortably evolve a higher public profile.

(Addendum, 2017:

Very much as anticipated nearly 20 years ago, by about 2008 I was financially independent and able to cease "working" – that is, do things I didn't really want to in order to make money – and devote full attention to EoR and my message. Around then, this publishing house had put out my first book, so I immediately began extensive travel to present my perspectives.

This effort proceeded through my third book in 2014, by which time I had given dozens of talks in three tours of the UK and many across the US and Canada. By the summer of 2015, I had determined to expand my message to videos, making them available to all via YouTube. That spring and summer, then, I developed several skills needed to script and perform ten minute and longer videos, each containing an in-depth look at a specific topic.

This allowed me to not only cover a wide range of topics, but to look much deeper into them than any of my personal presentations could. Indeed, just about every talk I had given – already at least 200 – had had to be a general overview of my basic approach to two things, never a detailed look at any of dozens of topics I wanted to cover.

So, I simplified my writing style, adapting it to writing a script that would be understandable to people whose native language was not English. Then I practiced reading from a prompter so that it didn't *look like* I was reading from a prompter and developed a comfy look and setting. *Then,* I had the non-trivial task of learning to edit video clips and do so creatively. This involved developing a standard intro sequence, including a "hook" to express the topic and standard, brief, sections to explain what was coming – that is, my point of view in a nutshell.

All that took a while, but was accomplished with dedication – and three less-than-satisfactory attempts to start. By autumn of 2015, I had launched my channel and continued from that point to refine my technique and delve ever deeper into subject matter.

Volume 1 of my productions consisted of shorter pieces, nine to twelve minutes in length with overviews on various points. These included two episodes compiling various photos and videos I had taken during my travels, pointing out the synthetic quality of time in *Totally Out of Time* and *Things You Miss*.

Volume 2 delved deeper into specific topics – six parts showing *What's Wrong with Christianity* and two more pointing out the shortcomings of science. Individual episodes looked into *Near Death Experiences* and *Peace in the Middle East,* while others explored *Evolution, Symbols* and *Life's Real Flow* – 18 episodes in all.

Twelve episodes of Volume 3 cover the subconscious and techniques to delve inward to explore it. Volume 4 began release in early 2017, these exploring *The Mystic Experience* and the messages of *The Great Visionaries,* Jesus, Gautama the Buddha and Lao-Tzu. They also compare these unique men to the Great Philosophers and approach the Koran and Muhammad's message as far less visionary.

Volume 5, currently in production, looks at *Words* and *Ideas* – how they create illusory effects in the mind. This will cover 20 episodes by the time I move on to the next volume…

So, from that query and my answer not even 20 years ago, I've done a great deal to reach out to people, offering my insights to those capable of grasping them – and, admittedly, maintaining a high standard of composition to keep those away who simply won't grasp my insights.)

E103d – But are you even interested, at least at this time, to expand worldwide your EoR?

I am certainly open to increased exposure for EoR. I didn't travel this path to keep myself and my perspectives a secret, believe me! But that will evolve through people like you who pass the word along, not so much by my standing up on a box and beating a drum loudly.

Understand: there is a pristine cleanness and clarity to The Essence of Reality that I will never compromise. I am aware of the many movements and various offerings in the California scene, and EoR will not become one of the many. It will remain a personal, sincere expression, because only in that nature can it entail the values I would communicate in its content.

EoR is already "worldwide". Readers have responded from many European countries, Africa, Australia, New Zealand and South America. That can only increase. What EoR won't do is become over-hyped and cheapened in any way.

(That original answer remains absolutely the case nearly two decades later – and will persist throughout my lifetime.)

E103e – What does Clear Awareness tell you about how the Universe came into being? Who or what started all of it? Steven Weinberg's book *The First Three Minutes* looks at it from a scientific point of a scientist. What is your point of view?

Reality comes "into being" in every moment. The apparent flow from past into future of an objective world of particles and forces is illusory in nature.

The Essence of Reality is this: mind image, in terms of value, flows into a perceived, "real" state, where the value content is then evaluated by the perceiver. This is an ongoing, ever changing flow.

You might liken the "reality" side of the consciousness/reality singularity to the tail of a dog. Science looks at the tail as though it were all that exists. It evaluates it in incredible detail, counting hairs, bones and skin cells. But science can never (in this apt little analogy) figure out why the tail wags sometimes or droops or stands high. It's because the "dog", which is the vast realm of mind content in this analogy, is not considered real or valid by the scientific mind – thus the scientist is blind to how reality does indeed work, because he doesn't see the whole picture.

Mr. Weinberg's book (I presume it's the one that details a physicist's model of the initial "time" that supposedly took place after the "Big Bang") and the scientific paradigm of the Big Bang itself are examples of how the mind, once it adheres to a particular structure of beliefs, will find evidence to support the structure. And it will ignore all evidence that contradicts its beloved laws.

I would point out, first, as a bit of background, that I have a degree in Chemical Engineering. I am quite well-read in science, and keep up-to-date in many areas of physics, archeology, astronomy, etc. But, while I recognize science as a handy tool in many useful endeavors, I see its fallacies all too well – that being a consequence of Clear Awareness.

The Big Bang theory is a flawed model. It explains that all the visible universe is expanding as a result of this initial event. But – according to BB theory – this was *not* an "explosion", where matter is expanding outward from a distinct center. It is, rather, pictured in the model as a literal expansion of space itself, where all matter is expanding equally from all other material.

Yet, if the universe were expanding in that fashion, based on the apparent recession of distant galaxies, then ALL space would be expanding. That means that in the course of a couple billion years, if galaxies recede, say, 10%, so would all dimensions – the earth would be 10% farther from the sun, atoms 10% farther from their molecule neighbors, electrons 10% farther in their valence from nuclei, quarks 10% farther from each other, etc.

Of course, there is no evidence of this change, as it is a structural impossibility.

Other oddities plague the BB model. The universe, according to accepted models, is supposed to be about 13.8 billion years old. But images captured by the Hubble Space Telescope of far-distant proto-galaxies indicate that light left them 13.7 billion years ago. If you look in exactly the opposite direction, you will find similar objects that far away. Because the light left both of those light sources at the same time – how did two objects get to be 27.4 light years apart *so soon after the Big Bang?* I've never seen even a mildly satisfactory explanation to this. The universe could hardly have been 27 light years across at a time point only 100 million years after beginning to expand out of an infinitesimally small point.

Yet, that's where those two proto-galaxies must have been, 13.7 billion years ago when light left them headed to where we are now.

There are other conceptual flaws in the Big Bang, but I don't want to drag these comments into a philosophical, cosmological treatise. A clearly reasoned argument against any religious model or philosophical paradigm could likewise be made…

Here, I only want to depict how reality looks when you don't interpret your perception through a preconfigured belief system. You will see clearly that, in the scope of your life (and all of reality is within that scope), events and relationships emerge from your own mind content, inner specs from the complexity of your own propensities. And that includes the entire unbounded background universe in which this format exists.

What or who started all of it? The "what" is your mind content *at this moment*. The who is you. And that simple (not oversimplified, but truly simple) status is identical for every individual consciousness, viewed from his/her perspective.

By the way, this truly isn't just *my* "point of view". It isn't a model offered by some external source that I accept because it fits into my beliefs – an elaboration of an accepted paradigm that I have proceeded to prove with evidence that my mind has filtered to suit the premise.

The inner-outer flow in life is a clear depiction of things, derived from my having spent decades dispelling common definitions and their underlying assumptions. Indeed, we live on a planet orbiting a minor star, two-thirds out from the center in an arm of the Milky Way Galaxy – a collection of over 100 billion stars, gas clouds, black holes and other matter. And that galaxy is surrounded, without doubt, by another 100 billion or more galaxies.

But the Consciousness which is the basis of each individual merges into this physical universe from a transcendent state, shaping its engaged, meaningful environment – the flow of events and relationships that constitute its daily experience – into a life experience. The universe of object, from the microcosm to the macrocosm, forms the staging area of meaningful engagement.

E103f – Scientific experiments have shown that CONSCIOUSNESS, as we normally talk about and consider a worthwhile goal to achieve, is actually an AFTERTHOUGHT... Exactly 100–200 nanoseconds before we become conscious of our doing we are actually DOING and then we think our doing is triggered by our consciousness. What do you suppose triggers our doing before we know?

Scientific experiments always fall into the preordained framework of the scientist's world view. The core scientific assumption on which all of it rests is that an objective world exists out there regardless of any consciousness to perceive it. And – according to the scientific paradigm – our consciousness is a result of complex brain function. Elsewhere here, I debunk that model.

This is a *subjective* universe, not objective. Reality only ever exists in intimate conjunction with consciousness, in any realm. My point is that any such scientific observations concerning consciousness will be tainted with inaccurate presuppositions, relying on faulty assumptions. From my angle, such timing is not vaguely relevant.

I don't wish to hammer away at science's shortcomings, any more than I sometimes hit hard at religion's fallacy, but science is not unlike religion. It has its sacred laws, its effective priesthood, its political, bureaucratic structure. It can create outcasts who doubt its tenets. There's really not much difference – except that science does have considerable value in many pragmatic regards. Religion doesn't…

The exact timing of action, perception of it, response to it by consciousness, etc., most likely varies widely among individuals, proof or no proof. Many a time I had an opponent steal a basketball away from me because his 100 nanoseconds was a lot quicker than my 2.5 second response. That's reality. Of course, in either case, engagement and thought precede action taken.

E104 – How long have you been on this track?

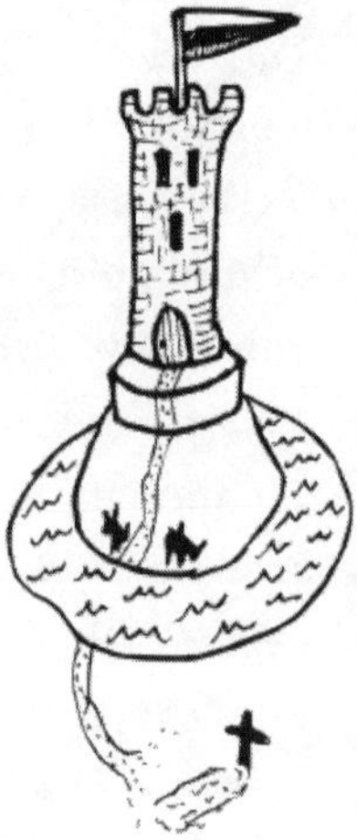

In a manner of speaking, I've been on this "track" my whole life. I can't remember a time I wasn't interested in understanding life, and always, even as a child, could see the inconsistencies and false reasoning to the religious explanations I was taught under the guise of "truth".

I vividly remember the summer of 1953. I was six and spent much of the summer playing with my friends "over in the alley", near our house on the main road through Tarentum,

Pennsylvania. On a couple of occasions, we would just gather in the basement of one friend and talk about life – comparing our thoughts on what our parents had been telling us.

Seeing through my mother's Presbyterian religion was easy – I'd questioned that by age 9, thenabouts (you don't mind me inventing a word now and again, do you?), and rather dove into science as the explanation of all things.

One key point occurred when I had the mystic experience during the year traveling, mostly by hitchhiking, throughout Europe. Not yet 25 at the time, it rattled my scientific view and set me, more determined and with some insight, on a path toward understanding.

I would say, though, that my focus on the inner elements of mind as key to self-perception and progress dates from nearly 40 years ago (I was about 30 then), when I moved from Europe to California and had greater access to other, freer ways of thinking. I soon developed the means and focus to look inward, finding the roots there of my own nature, and developing the ability to see what I am, and change aspects I found undesirable.

For a couple years I gave psychic readings as well. So, for that intense period in my early thirties, I was exploring the workings of my own deeper mind and viewing the same for others, as I could simply pick up on information to pass along to total strangers.

The mind is indeed complex and deep, containing many twists and related values in many, many aspects. It took time, simply, to unravel those elements and clean out the debris of artificial belief and distorted perception. It was only approaching age 50, though, that I began to speak to groups to communicate my insights and establish my website to reach more people.

Growth, change and improvement in realizing my intentions continued, though, as I always attributed any lack of general acceptance of my message, not to the limitations of others' failure to grasp my illustrations, but to my own inner conflict and other restrictions. After all, many a visionary has had to die and have decades or centuries pass by before their message caught the attention of many others. I had intended and still do to avoid that limitation.

Does that give you an idea? I had a very clear awareness of the integrated oneness of Consciousness/Reality probably 35 years ago, but still much negativity within due to cluttering feelings that were based on subtle and negating mechanisms – complexities that were difficult to break through. So, it is hard to answer your question exactly. In a way, I have clearly been on this track for a long time – probably much longer than my memories of this life's experiences even reveal.

E105a – One of the glitches I had a problem with is the number of times you said that "ONLY here will you find what you really seek." That word "only" has been scattered throughout your material and reminds me of exactly what you state religion and science have been telling me since forever. That their information is the ONLY information that will a) save me, b) cure me, c) and/or set me on the right path to enlightenment... Wouldn't it be better if you would say, "Here you MAY find what you seek" or, "This is ONE way of finding peace and ease"? "ONLY" just has a tinge of ego affiliated with it, in my mind, of course. And what is important to me is what's in my mind.

My statement is somewhat more pragmatic than it might seem.

I have been around. I've seen and heard, encountered in books, pamphlet form, and web pages an enormous array of philosophical, religious, pseudo-religious, mystical, New Age, metaphysical, spiritual, scientific, and pseudo-scientific stuff (I kept that list briefer than it really is) concerning how life works.

I use the word "only" simply because I have seen no other source that:

- Doesn't explain life by providing artificial definitions
- Doesn't rely on standard, traditional core assumptions or standard religious or philosophical structures commonly accepted in our culture
- Provides whatever info is to be had with no vested interest (i.e., for free, asking nothing, not wanting followers or supporters or anything)
- Even really knows, by virtue of its offered explanations, what you, the reader, as a sentient, conscious being, is really looking for (beyond dogmatic and/or creamy, gushy phrases or quotes from some overinflated expert mystic/guru/master/priest), and
- Can specify exact inner elements that correspond to precise outer effects – as most contemporary speakers only deal with generalities because they are only aware of such vague connections.

So, until I do encounter another source that meets the above criteria, the phrase "ONLY here will you find what you really seek" is simply the most accurate way I can depict the EoR material.

Of course, neither you nor any reader actually needs The Essence of Reality *nor any other communication* to reach Clear Awareness. At best, my words will only save you considerable time and trouble, since you will come to the same understandings when you see things clearly, with or without my comments – although it might take you some significant number of incarnations to do so!!

It might even be more fun to ignore me and go try meditating on mantras, praying to Jesus, reciting rosaries, bowing to Mecca, or wearing silly beanies on your head. You would come out of it with a greater sense of accomplishment, I suppose, for having seen through all that garbage yourself without me giving you all the relevant clues and finely-depicted answers! (Note: a bit of joking there…)

As to ego, I have a good perspective on who I am and what I have accomplished in this life, even up to now. I have pride in that and am happy to be who I am. I see little value in humility – it only leads you to put yourself down, hold yourself back. I could not possibly have forged through humanity's cherished beliefs, and had the guts to say the things I do about them, without considerable self-esteem.

Christianity fosters humility – the entrenched priesthood wants you to bow down to their expertise and keep giving them your tithes. I suggest you *should* come to think a lot of yourself, because you won't ever achieve anything beyond the level of evaluation you set on yourself.

Still, I don't find myself over-inflated in any fashion. I respect each and every other individual for the values, the qualities and talents that person embodies. Since we are, each of us, unique, I don't see myself as "superior" to others. Judging oneself *against* others is fruitless – I can only be this Self. But I have made great strides to hone this Self into a positive, creative, open package. I'm comfortable with that – quite comfortable. Not egoistic, mind you – but just very comfortable being who I am…

E105b – Do you not believe there is any higher consciousness who created all these bundles of energy? And if you do not, then how did we come about being at all? Did some big amoebae separate itself in billions of consciousnesses? Taking responsibility for myself and my reality is something I have no trouble accepting, but not having any higher consciousness who created me is just a bit unsettling.

There is a higher consciousness that creates you, and You are It.

That is, you are a much "higher" consciousness than you give yourself credit for. The trouble is that our fundamental world view, in many ways, limits the self-perspective to this little physical-based, biologically engineered creature who ***must*** – it would seem – be the product of some other, greater being or greater process. That whole picture is an illusion, one formed by the subtle beliefs you were handed by parents and teachers and such, beliefs rooted in ancient misperceptions.

Your life comes into being in every moment, every new *Now* moment of unfolding events and relationships. When you can clearly see what you carry in your mind elements, and see their innate relationship, their driving, causal nature, to your outer experience, you will begin to realize that the power of creation is a self-evident flow of values. The flow, inner to outer, is a simple conversion, a straightforward, unending surge of essence, of meaning – not an act of external manipulation by some power-wielding deity.

Why might you need this "higher consciousness"? In what context would he (or she) have come into existence? A higher one yet? And what about that one – a higher one above him/her? These are old notions, old myth-based concepts. They will seem to be true if you believe in them.

Shedding that belief, I might add, can be tough, since it might be planted rather deep. But if you wish to see things clearly, shed it you must. And that becomes much easier when you experience how, when you've changed the inner aspects of your subconscious, the outer changes in response...

E106 – I have only just begun to immerse myself in your writings. This is the first page which truly gives an open perspective on life which is not confined by the teachings of a religion. I am merely 17 years old and have recently begun to question the beliefs and teachings of Christianity and all other religions which I was so blindly brought up believing in with

no doubts of following.

I write this to you to let you know that I appreciate and commend your efforts to shed light on the eyes of those who are blinded by the lies and misconceptions of an unchanging religion. Also, what are some of the other engagements you are planning to make an appearance at? I would like to be able to attend one if possible.

When I was 17 I was already questioning such things as well, but didn't have such a source as EoR to draw upon – or, of course, the Internet through which to connect to other open-minded thinkers. It took me many years of travel and introspection to come to this perspective, and I'm happy to be able to share these things with the world, you included.

Most people don't even consider questioning the dogma they've been programmed with in their lives. But there are many, like you and me, who want to see clearly, to understand what's happening here in life, and why.

I only recently mentioned my willingness to speak to groups, and I'm not making a major effort to drum up engagements. EoR is not a commercial venture, and doesn't involve any support groups or organizations, so it might not be too frequent that I get invited to speak – at least at first. But engagements will happen as we move along. Check out EoR to see what's up.

(This answer was ventured years ago, before publication of my books or establishment of my YouTube channel. Since then, I've spoken widely – though I have no idea whether I ever encountered this reader.)

To some extent, it will be up to the readers of EoR to promote my speaking appearance for any particular group. I can picture that student groups will be interested as some of them become aware of The Essence of Reality. Again, that will depend on the networking of people who appreciate my perspectives and spread the word.

E107a – Prior to asking a question or two, I want to thank you for sharing your discoveries and insights with us. I appreciate the fact that you do not spew any dogma or new paradigm for those of us who are self-responsible and are still searching for some insight and understanding.

The world is rather full of geysers spewing dogmatic schemes and detailed structures of cosmologies, all under the guise of "truth". It doesn't need me to add to the steamy output. The only real insight needs to come from the first-person perspective, and all such artificial paradigms only inhibit that insight.

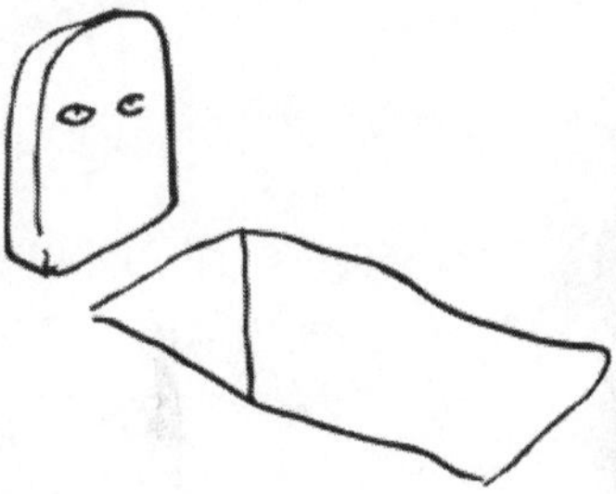

E107b – I have read your perspective "On Death" and I still have questions regarding death. My view on existence is the same as yours – that it is a continuity. And when I look at that continuity, my whole being says and feels that physical aging and death is so unnecessary. My view is that life is immortal and that physical life can be too.

I think that we all meet physical death because we have internalized the rules, the dogma, the traditions, and the culture of all those who have gone before us. And because they have not seen clearly, we do not.

I see no aspect of nature or space that doesn't come into being in a particular form, then pass on. I agree that many aspects of debilitation and decay of aging are tied up in the psycho-induced mechanism of displaying negativity in terms of body function (or malfunction). Much of it is definitely a tradition.

Clearly, much greater health is possible for a lot longer time in the scope of a life.

But several aspects of life come into play here which rather preclude indefinite incarnation as a given person:

1. The periods of life – infancy, childhood, teenage, young adult, adult, middle age and elderly – while they flow almost imperceptibly one into the other, contain characteristics unique to the experience. They provide (or at least *can* provide) an abundantly rich scope of experience to encounter and grow from. Even miserable lives contain rich experience – at the very least, when you are finished with the incarnation.

2. To stop in some period of that flow, hoping somehow to extract indefinite measure from, say, the young adult phase would be a questionable choice. Would you want to spend ten extra years as a twenty-something year-old, for example, looking for a suitable mate and acting semi-mature, with the typical youthful bravado, or twenty, or fifty, or five hundred years like that?

3. How would society look, realistically, if there were a glut forming of *only* 25-year-old looking people, each year always more, competing for the same interests, occupying ever more real estate on this planet, or even others. Your children would catch up to you in apparent age, then theirs would, and theirs, always more and more youthful people. Or you would quit needing babies to replenish numbers, or rapidly need to develop deep space travel to get rid of the enormous overabundance of humans that would result in short order. Or conflict would rapidly escalate over territory, with wars developing over increasingly rare real estate.

4. One day, if you were frozen at a given age indefinitely, even if cultural logistics worked out, all experience would be boring – you would have done everything possible! How many ways could you have sex, or with how many people before it became utterly senseless? How many foods could you eat or mountains could you climb before you lost interest?

My point here is that much of life's value is based on its temporary, fleeting nature, its inherent change into other phases, each with their unique experiences and endeavors.

Death is not an end to consciousness – my primary point in that piece you refer to (on my website) – but a wrapping up of a unique gesture of it. I've had a great life, personally, with a lot more to accomplish. I've developed great health with my personal realization of the mind-body connection, and anticipate many more years beyond my nearly 51 (or now, at age 70, as I'm compiling these notes into book form) – but I certainly would not, in any stretch of even my fertile imagination, want to live on and on and on into the hundreds, even if I could be healthy and stay young.

Regarded in terms of playing cards, I've had wonderful bridge hands. But when they are played out, I look forward to shuffling the cards and playing the next one, even if it's not as "good".

The point here is the *newness*, the freshness of experience. Consciousness yearns, throughout its fabric, for new experience to exact its creativity on. Potentials for creative expression from any given individual are limited – if you don't agree with that, imagine being the same you, just as you are now, for 200 years. Then 200 more… Regardless of the state of the rest of the culture.

I think the cultural tradition you are failing to recognize is the one that associates one's "self" with the physical, biological focus. Given a recognition that I can and will generate another incarnation when I'm done with the lessons I garner through the course of this one, I have little motivation to stretch my current life out indefinitely. Only if I've bought into the undercurrent objective viewpoint that results from a purely scientific view do I necessarily need to avoid death.

E107c – For the past 13 years I have been engaged in helping others extend their youth and middle years. I keep meeting one foe: the expectation and preparation for death. If death is a necessary part of existence, then why do we resist it so? Does death's necessity make the effort of physicians futile?

I think I've let this question affect my enthusiasm for helping and healing. I'm beginning to think that my real job as a physician is to help others see and understand how their thoughts, feelings, and actions present themselves in the events and relationships in their lives.

Primarily we resist it because of point #3 above – if my conscious existence depends on maintaining brain function, then I'd better ought to remain alive if I wish to continue existence. It is that illusion which leads to such monumentally absurd efforts to keep vegetables and worn-out skeletons of human beings alive at all costs.

A physician's role, particularly in this early time of budding awareness into the mind-body oneness, is relegated to helping direct the body back to some level of health, while hopefully the patient will deal with whatever inner factors are leading him/her to display the illness or whatever. In coming times, that role will evolve considerably.

Since the body reflects the mind, the inner realm must be addressed, as that is where problems lie, while the outer effect, whatever illness, whatever injury, is more accurately described as a symptom. The physician of the future will deal with values, assuage pain and physical damage as needed to maintain physical integrity, but help the patient come to grips with the inner source of the outer malfunction.

Looking back, I guess you said that! You are well ahead of the field…

E107d – Also, could you elaborate on one of the paragraphs in your writing on death? That paragraph states, "Death is a phase of your existence that is necessarily out of the scope of your current focus. In this life scenario, that limitation is vital realization of many, many significant value situations." What "value situations" do you mean?

What I mean by that is that death itself figures into many, highly significant situations in life that carry a strong value implication. For example, climbing Mt. Everest would not be the intense challenge it is if it didn't inherently threaten the life of the climber. Auto racing is a thrill to the driver whose life is at stake in every moment.

The soldier, the policeman, the fireman – each of these endeavors is enhanced in value judgment, display of courage and intensification of self-worth in the mind of the individual doing it by virtue of putting his/her life on the line.

In that regard, generally, putting one's life or health at risk for a particular undertaking enhances the perceived value to the individual so doing and intensifies the meaning of the situation.

E108 – If you don't mind, I have one personal question – and that is, how do you experience the world, actually? In my various interviews with "non-dual" people around the world I have had similar responses which accord with my own (although I cannot claim this to be constant). In my case I find that the body-

mind is within me, and this "me" is Awareness. This, as I've said, is not constant, but yet it feels like it's in the background.

To answer your question, I pondered back to how the world used to feel, that is, how my normal, momentary awareness regarded real things happening at an earlier point of my life before I had cleared away many limiting elements. That ought to supply something of a mode of comparison.

In early times of my life, I harbored many fears, feelings of inadequacy, and assorted mental constructs in regarding people, forces and causal sources. At various points, I held some sort of "God" or de facto controller, and pictured situations to have control over me, i.e., some power to make me conform to their rules. This led to a lot of rational thinking to create a response to various situations – to try to manipulate things to accomplish my intent.

So, my view as to how I experienced things then was rather muddled by a lot of mental activity, worry, struggle, etc. And my overall perception was consistent with that view – feeling myself to be an isolated individual that had to deal with powerful external forces: to fight them, to fend them off and defend myself…

But, having come quite some time ago to a realization that I was causal, I began to strip away the illusory, external forces. A long way down the path from that version, then, I no longer harbor fears and mental images that project threats onto some external category. All things I encounter, I approach without fear or apprehension. This allows a fundamental relaxation and a freeness of attitude that was, perhaps, part of my nature all along, but had to be suppressed earlier because of the old mental constructs.

Anyway, now I regard the world openly and freely. I understand "status", for example, in society as a social measure, but am only amused when I see it in practice. I understand the roles people assume as they identify themselves as belonging to a race, fixed in an occupation, as a parent/spouse/adult or whatever. But knowing the impressionable nature of mind, I am not surprised to see them compromise themselves simply because they are "supposed to" be this or that. Should I encounter an individual who, because of the current situation, has authority over me in some regard, I delve into my own mindset to discern the mechanism by which I project that power.

Thoughts do still arise within my mind reflective of, for example, the impression I had just formed, or responsive to an immediate situation – for thoughts are the drawing board of intent and potential. But manipulating thoughts – conclusions of how to handle a current situation or how to deal with an anticipated event – arise ever less frequently as events flow in a desirable fashion. When planned-action-type thoughts do emerge, I see them clearly and trace the thread into mind elements. This cornerstone aspect of the conditioned mind, the rational controller, has been the most recent thread to snip.

Generally, then, beyond the occasional intrusive thought, I spend much of my waking day, not hedged back into the skull-out perspective, trapped in a world of thought and rational calculation, but overriding and fully expanded into the field of sight. Is that descriptive? I see and feel *meaning*, not simply react to collections of objects. I ponder creative potentials; I don't rehash stalled events and try to recalculate efforts that might have changed them (like I used to). I do deal with other people on a level of the current, unfolding event – but again, if I am not satisfied with the nature of the relationship, I don't question that person's attitude or interest, but look to myself to discern my inner bearings in being involved in such a happening.

I could say, I ***am*** clearly what I encounter, and perceive that oneness on an ongoing basis. I encounter a lot of humorous situations and enjoy a lot of things – and I add to both. I encounter annoyances, as well, but deal with them, and as I said, deal with their roots within me.

I don't know if that answer conveys the feeling of freedom and peace that I harbor as a base status! It is hard to be straightforward with such a question, while describing a pervasive attitude that may not be shared by the reader. Basically, I experience the world from the perspective of out from behind my eyes (if you don't mind four prepositions in a row). But I perceive its source and cumulative value as emerging from within me...

E109a – Is it possible to learn more about your life, what you did in the past, how you live today, how old are you, etc.? If you have some bio that could be interesting.

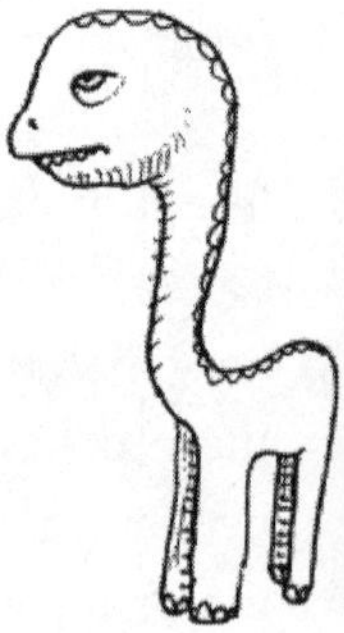

I've done many interesting things in my life – travels and adventures throughout Europe and into North Africa, across North America several times, involvement with fascinating groups in San Diego, and a lot more. But the most vital, important aspects of my life have been the inner explorations, and those can't be well documented in a biography. I suppose one day I'll take the time to write up my various adventures, but for now, the EoR perspectives are more important.

I think also that many people look at and judge exclusively by appearances. Some very beautiful apples are tasteless and pithy, while others of a plainer color and duller skin, even blemished, can be very tasty.

I faced many failures and difficulties along my pathway. These have been necessary for the lessons I've needed, and often resulted as direct displays of changes I made or needed to make within my mindset. But illustrated for their face value, i.e., their biographical content, without understanding the inner aspects, many portions of my life would present an inaccurate picture of their true significance.

Of course, I can take that into account in my writing. So, I can only say that one day I will get around to this task, but now isn't the time.

E109b – I would like to point out your vision to others. Can I translate your material completely, print it out and give it for free to friends? Do you think that some other form of introducing the knowledge to the people would also be appropriate? Should I do whatever I feel I am able to do in this sense as long as I am doing it without charge?

The difficulty with translating my words (which I'm sure you are aware of) lies in the added distortion that must come in the translation. It is difficult enough for me to express some of these concepts accurately in English – taking the expressions yet another step not only disturbs the meaning, but adds the distortion of the translator's step. What my words mean to the translator may not reflect what my words were intended to convey – and even less so in regard to the expressions after translation.

Still, I would not discourage your translating my writing. I would only ask that you emphasize to any Croatian readers the dangers of revised meaning that come with translation. And as you do so, definitely consult with me if a meaning is unclear. Many things I say can have two or more potential interpretations (sometimes purposely!!) and you, as translator, need to understand what is meant.

Beyond that, if no money is intended to be made on the work, I will give my approval. I would ask that you send me a letter in which you state your intention to translate my work, but not sell the translation for a profit. I will then send you written permission to do so to avoid any copyright issues.

It would seem to me to be a lot of work! I speak German rather fluently, but I would hate to have to translate my own work into that language and maintain the meaning!

That ought to give you some impression of what I'm all about on a personal level. And it pretty well wraps up the categorized entries of questions I've fielded over the years. But there have been some few questions on Quora that didn't lend themselves to placement in any specific category. So...

Ummmm... : Concerning THIS and NOT THIS (i.e., THAT)

Let's address some dangling subject matter – my personal take on other sorts of questions. A little diversity never hurts...

Q110 – If I brought a person from 500BC to 2016, what would they think?

Most thoughts about this interesting hypothetical would approach logistical differences. One major factor, though, most critical to regard is the standard thinking process of people of ancient times.

Typically, one would assume the individual, whether illiterate peasant (some 80–90% of humans then) or educated elite, would be able to evaluate the world like we do and draw similar conclusions. But they didn't. Most people back then just didn't think that way – which is key caveat in believing any religion based on ancient thinking.

You would have to take the most sophisticated Greek philosophical adherent to have a reasonably critical thinker, one who could look at modern things – invariably, if anywhere near civilization, very much different than what he or she was used to – and consider them, or converse with people and understand their rational thinking. (Ignoring the obvious language difficulties.)

So, don't worry about noisiness or fancy machinery, automobiles and airplanes, plastics or huge buildings and metal structures, air pollution and such. What the ancient mind would make of those things is not what you would, having been put into the same predicament.

As we grew up in "modern" culture, we absorbed a great deal of background information – far more concerning health, nutrition, geography, world cultures, history, chemistry, politics, etc., than our transplanted ancestor did. But we also became oriented to thinking in line with dominant prevailing notions. People growing up in Western culture rely on several elements of commonly shared thinking, particularly regarding causality – what makes things happen:

1. **Religion:** Generally, Christianity indicates there is a single god out there making things happen. Many learn they have to pray to this deity and keep on his good side to keep life going well. Even those who have outgrown religion still may harbor a sense that there's something out there making things happen.

2. **Science:** The common, overall indication of science is that the world is full of real-world forces and sources that impact one's life – people, conditions, bacteria, etc. To deal with the world, one has to gather information, make a plan and proceed to manipulate people and things as necessary to carry out the plan. If successful, one can happily proceed to the next problem.

3. **Luck:** This common notion suggests that outcomes, no matter how well planned, still may go awry based on some whimsical force.

4. **Fortune:** Tied into the common adverbial usage – fortunately/unfortunately – this widespread notion still, 2000 years after the supposed death of the Roman goddess Fortuna, attributes in the minds of many causation to some independent, metaphysical, capricious force "out there".

5. **Chance:** Based on our overall consideration of potential factors, we often lay odds of this or that happening, thus imagining probability to contribute to events happening.

Based on these very commonly shared elements, modern people (e.g., you) quickly observe a situation, deftly but deeply run the real situation through held beliefs (a customized collage of the above factors) and reach a conclusion as to what's happening and what to do about it.

Our ancestors of 500 BC *did not think like that!* Not at all...

Outside of some early, roughly equivalent thinking in Greece, empiricism hadn't yet been invented – and wouldn't be for another 2100 years. People didn't reach conclusions based on analyzing a situation and taking action accordingly. 2500 years ago, virtually all people thought that their local set of gods – exclusively and unavoidably – made things happen.

Most had specialized gods governing various aspects of life. They would spend considerable effort, in hoping to accomplish something, by trying to discern what the gods had in store for them. And at the same time, they would try things, as they'd been taught, to appease the gods or demons so they would get their desire fulfilled.

People were *highly* superstitious, very fearful, small of stature and lacked critical thinking capabilities. It's not that they were stupid or untalented. There were brilliant artisans, clever farmers, highly adept tradesmen, great generals, etc. But they *just didn't think like we do.*

For one thing, while our culture prizes to a degree being

an individual – being different, being creative – theirs didn't. People did their best to fit in – to not be noticed: all governments (probably outside Greece) were dictatorial and didn't tolerate any free thinking. Priesthoods avidly guarded their domains of mind control – they wouldn't have tolerated *any* questioning. Fitting in, going along with the tribe was normal, expected.

Most adults – fairly young, as people didn't live long back then – had been basically abused by parents and other adults while growing up, so by maturity, they had no self-esteem, no sense of individuality.

They didn't have a religion as we think of it. They had an exclusive thought mode of attributing creative power to the gods which they couldn't question. Gods to them weren't "believed in", their culturally-favored set was real and powerful in their minds, self-evident in the tribal/family scheme of things.

Uneducated in all the subjects we were for many years of school, they had no sense of diversity. They had no recognition of the earth as a planet, no understanding of geography, of climate or weather patterns, no appreciation of cultural differences – other than thinking that all other people were a threat. And that threat might be just over the horizon.

The point is, people were extremely rigidly tied into an archaic mode of thinking very alien to our critical, analytical way of dealing with the world. Much of our background understanding, education and exposure to nature and reality, communication and up-to-the-minute news would be way beyond their grasp.

So, if you could hypothetically grab just about anybody from that ancient time and bring him/her into today's world, that person would be totally lost. Not just because of buildings, noise, cars, planes, smoggy air and such, but because that forlorn primitive would not be able to relate to our way of thinking. They couldn't grasp it.

For an equivalent example, try explaining to a rural African or Arabic tribesman that the Koran is concocted, primitive and false: Allah doesn't exist. See how far you'd get. Try taking a nomad from the plains of Mongolia and explaining that their gods and their rituals are absolutely wrong and ineffectual. How far do you think you would you get?

Now take that difference in thinking times 20 or so.

The ancient person, if you could overcome the language obstacle, the size difference and the total lack (for most) of ever having gone anywhere outside their town or region, would be *totally and fundamentally disoriented* at the prospect of dealing with this modern world.

Q111 – How do I psychologically destroy my enemies?

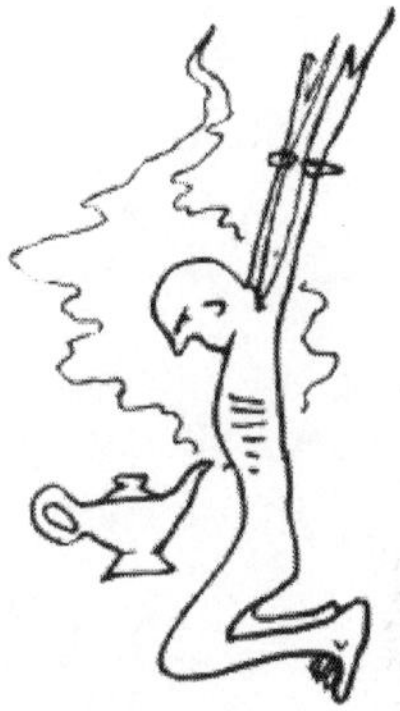

If you try to destroy your enemies as a life goal/ necessity, it will keep you busy for a long time. Indeed, *you'll never run out of them*. In life, you attract events and relationships into your encounter – you are psychologically tied into the reality you encounter, not separate and apart from the real. *Your own* inner conflict and notions of separation – as per religion and science – attract conflictual situations, particularly conflictual relationships.

Thus, if you seek to destroy those you deem as enemies, you are simply engaging life through old, illusory precepts – very common, but inherently flawed, ideas. You figure if you beat the bad guys, you'll win – after all, you've seen that in so many movies and so often in life. What I'm saying is, regardless of your deemed victories, your own inner conflict will simply lead you into additional battles and unending enemies. If you conquer all external ones within your realm, you'll just start fighting your body or conditions or the weather.

Your own inner conflict and skewed understanding will always lead you back to engagement, never to peace.

When you've outgrown the illusion that elements of the real world out there need to be fought against, when you've jettisoned common thinking that separates you from seemingly external forces and sources, when you come to peace and ease ***within*** – only then will you no longer encounter others who oppose you, ones you deem as enemies.

So, whatever strategy might be suggested – well, that might work well for this current "enemy". But it will only last until you've attracted and engaged yet another foe. Your only real enemy is *within,* and that adversary consists of fallacies learned as truths – principal of which is that you are separate and apart from the world you encounter. You'll never beat that enemy, that notion of duality – but you can dispel its many elements to disengage it.

But you'll only be able do that when you've first recognized your own real nature *and* the inner-outer connection that undergirds life.

Q112 – What's wrong with the US health care system?

This fiasco of money exchange among doctors, hospitals, "non-profit" insurance companies (who pay huge bonuses to their management) and pharmaceutical companies is not really "Health Care". It should rightfully be called *The Great US Illness Boondoggle*. It has nothing to do with health, but with illness, the manipulation of the body and making money off it.

If you are healthy, *you have no need of professional care.*

And health, as detailed in my books, website and YouTube videos, **begins within**. The mind and body are connected, not separate and apart as science (in its specialized genre of medical science) assumes with its objective view of reality. Physical issues you encounter always have inner roots. If you delve inward, you can find and eliminate specific inner mechanisms within your mindset that invariably lead to outer manifestation of illness or injury.

Medical science has only the most primitive recognition of this inner-outer connection. And it has no motivation to clarify it – the entire huge business of The Illness Boondoggle *depends on* people getting sick and injured.

I'm 70 years old. I became aware of this body-mind connection in my thirties and began to address one common ailment after the other. I spent years scouring my subconscious for inner elements that led to outer issues. Now, older than I've ever been, I never get sick or injure myself, never need medicine or vitamins. My body works just fine with no intervention. *That's how it's supposed to work.* Your mind-body knows how to work right if you let it. But you are feeding it negatives with inner stress, a propensity for conflict in many ways, and lots of other downers – including the basic, commonly reinforced conviction that it doesn't know how to work right and needs to be forced back into proper functionality.

Readers who want to free themselves from the huge, expensive mess that is dubbed "Health Care" should seriously regard my words – including techniques illustrated in my books and online communication. I'm not spouting philosophy, but explaining an innate aspect of life – the inviolable inner-outer connection. I provide tools for delving inward (self-hypnosis, ideomotor responses, dream analysis, meditation) and explain what to look for in terms of inner mechanisms – and how to change.

The best thing you can do with the grand boondoggle that is

medical science is outgrow it. When your body works well on its own, you don't need any of it.

Remember: the mind and body are absolutely and unavoidably connected. If you overcome one illness but don't eliminate the inner conflict, struggle, suggestion, punishment, etc., that actually caused it, you'll simply recreate another physical manifestation of the same inner mess. And you'll be thoroughly caught up in the fiasco of medical science implementation of the huge, phenomenally expensive US Illness Boondoggle industry.

Q113 – Can you tell me something about myself just by reading this sentence?

Yes, I certainly can: your next question will be, "What is it?"

Q114 – How much more effective is an average modern-day firearm than a WWII firearm?

Actually, in terms of the effect meant for the weapon *to accomplish* – not simply killing people, but achieving particular goals laid out by politicians, despots or the clash of world cultures – any firearm is no more effective than bows and arrows or, at an earlier time, clubs. Yes, they kill more effectively. But killing ignorant schleps on the other side of a conflict is a really, really poor way to solve problems; it is not the ultimate purpose of using the weapon.

Especially when the guys doing the killing are ***not*** the ones who initiated or perpetrated the core problems being fought over.

Most weapons are engineered and built for soldiers to go kill people they've never met and know little about – except for what is provided by their "training", which manages to redefine those other humans as "targets" or "enemies", in effect, as the *bad guys*. In reality, those other humans on the other side are taught the same thing – neither realizing that he (or she) is only following the dictates of commanders and, above them in authority, rulers and governments caught up in traditions, distorted values and often bluster.

Untold numbers of wars have been fought over religion, political interests and the intent to dominate neighbors, less frequently over territory, resources or simple traditional rivalry. The governmental or religious leaders, kings, popes or dictators who generate the need to engage in conflict are *never, ever* the guys who actually have to fight it.

In general, conflict is a really poor way to settle disputes in any case – wars being the epitome of conflict. Again, the guys fighting it aren't the guys who got it going in the first place.

So, technically, a firearm today might be much more sophisticated, considerably more damaging and far more lethal than earlier versions of weapons designed to inflict damage on other human beings. But in accomplishing *anything*, any modicum of improvement in the collective lives of mankind, a modern-day firearm is no more effective than a large rock secured to the end of a stick.

And far less effective than open-minded discussion of real issues that concern people's lives.

Q115 – How should a spiritual person respond to negativity?

There are various ways you can encounter negativity. Let's consider Person A, Person B and you.

If A and B are engaged in some sort of conflict, it's not your problem. I have empathy for others' pain, but each of us experiences a meaningful reality that reflects our own nature: A, B and you all attract events and relationships according to each of your inner states.

If A and B are fighting in some fashion, physical, emotional or otherwise, they are both fulfilling each other's level of inner conflict. That not only isn't *your* problem, but you can't provide a solution unless they are open to greater awareness of the inner-outer connection in life – because you can't change the inner turmoil each holds within their mindset.

Now, if A is engaging you – that is, negating by action or status your personal intent – that **is** your problem. In those terms, your problem is not A, *per se* – your problem is *your own inner conflict*. Same thing if your body is producing negative, i.e., painful malfunction. Same thing if you encounter natural disasters or failure in business projects, ants infesting your basement or noisy neighbors.

If you face negating events and/or relationships in the flow of your life, they are always, always, *always* reflecting your own inner values in some combination: inner conflict and struggle, punishment, suggestion and flawed common notions you hold as true.

In the case of direct confrontation with negative situations, deal with them as best you can in the moment – take aspirin for pain, deal with threats or failure in any way you know how. But...

But then later, in quiet, delve inward to find the inner roots to that outer, undesirable situation. You are connected to life events in exactly how they impact you – there are always causal, inner elements within your mindset that lead you to engage problematic situations...

So, facing external, conflict-ridden situations not involving you, no response is needed or effective. Sure, help people or kids or whatever as far as you can and to the degree they need your help. But you can't correct that situation at its basis – within the mindset of the individual. The Middle East is loaded with conflict-based religions, for example – not a single thing you or anybody can do will settle that region until the people dump their archaic religions where believing in fantasized deities invariably leads to personal powerlessness and conflict.

That's not going to happen within your lifetime. Don't let it bother you.

But for negativity you face in life personally – health problems, relationship issues, success/failure – deal with them as best you know how in the immediate encounter. Then take the time to delve inward (techniques illustrated in my YouTube videos, Volume 3 pieces, my website and books) and clear out your own, inner store of conflict, self-punishment, low self-esteem, doubt, flawed beliefs, etc.

And keep doing so until your life is peaceful – until you attract fulfilling relationships, display great health and succeed at what you do.

That inner cleansing is your *only effective response* to encountered negativity. Certainly, it might take a while to clean the inner sludge – but until you do, you'll continue to encounter conflict, not fulfillment of your intent.

Q116 – Does your subconscious have its own motives? What would they be?

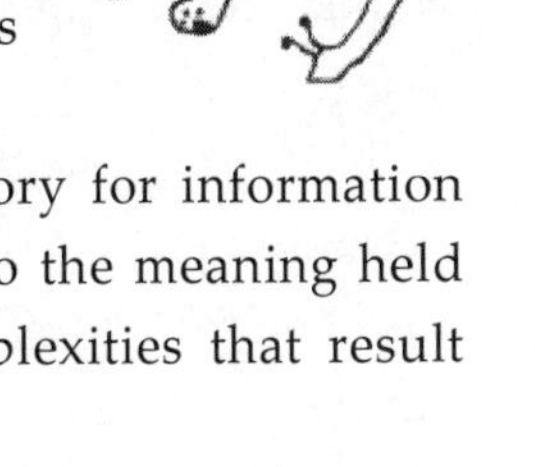

The way your question is asked contains a potential for misunderstanding that requires differentiation from the outset.

The subconscious is the storage repository for information of various types and, in combination due to the meaning held within them, values and interrelated complexities that result from the nature of the information it stores.

This inner Self, per se, has no motive, hidden, subtle or obvious. It is not an alternate Self with opposing intentions, desires or something to gain by fooling the conscious Self.

The subconscious, considered by itself (which is something of a distortion to begin with, as it is part of the whole of the functioning conscious mind, having no distinct boundary and fully integrated such that it couldn't exist *apart from* the ego-Self), is dispassionate and uncaring. It's kind of like Spock on *Star Trek* to the ego-Self of emotion and full, living engagement, Captain Kirk – more so like Data on the later *TNG* series: information only, no judgmental preference or bias – *in and of itself*.

A simple answer cannot give you a full appreciation of the depth of information and values you hold within, nor a full recognition of the critical importance of grasping the nature of your own cognitive nature.

So, no, the subconscious does not have its own alter-ego; it isn't a second Self, doesn't care, doesn't emote and doesn't second guess your choices. It just feeds information you request (with some reservation based on your own complicated value system). And, of course, it stores the complex belief system *you hold* and by which you evaluate the reality you encounter.

Thus, the subconscious is neutral in and of itself.

However, because motivation and skewed ideas as to how reality functions can be stored in the mindset, layered within the belief system, it can easily appear that you have inner, hidden motives that are separate from your will. In actuality, the motives are merely part of the informational accumulation within stored data – not part of an isolated subliminal functionality, but rather explicit within aggregated, often emotionally charged, material that constitutes your memory/value storage.

If that sounds complex, well, it is – but only based on the exceptional complexity of mind content, *not based on any sort of hard-coded, subliminal operative process*. The subconscious itself is simple and straightforward in function.

Again, phrased otherwise, the subconscious is unbiased and without motive ***itself***. But the complex, often contradictory and negative content it holds – consisting of information you've absorbed throughout your lifetime (coupled with propensities you brought with you into an incarnation) – may contain overlapping and interwoven motivation. I may well hold self-defeating and inherently conflictual convictions – including totally false information, invalid assumptions and fantasy-based conjecture, all held as true.

And those inner motivations – along with false beliefs and unfounded definitions – can be discerned and gotten rid of. Motivation, along with its counterpart, *punishment*, is a highly negative mechanism to hold – and doubtless, practically everybody holds multiple, interwoven elements of motivation…

When you were a child, very often in our culture, you were rewarded by parents for doing what they wanted you to do – not necessarily what came naturally to your impulses. This process, along with punishment inflicted for doing things they didn't "allow", loaded your subconscious with conflict and struggle – often multiple layers deep and interconnected.

The point here is, your subconscious is vast and complex, interwoven and connected, with its complexity tied not only into rational understanding, but into emotional responses and meaning tied to life elements. My books and YouTube videos provide more depth to the explanation, but more valuable and useful are techniques I illustrate for others to delve into their own subconscious, explore it, get to understand how their own deeper Self works and relates to decision-making and conscious engagement of life. Grasping how one's own mind works is vital to clearer awareness of life meaning – and personal engagement of the inner levels is key to that – and key to improving life in all ways…

So, again, and to answer your question directly, the subconscious has no motives within its innate functionality. In effect, it only supplies information (values, facts, relationships, data points, truth judgments, emotional triggers and much more) to the conscious mind for its daily function.

But that information easily could and very likely would contain interactive and interrelated elements that contain motives for meaningful life gestures.

Thus, it may *appear* that the subconscious has its own, separate interest and motive, but, functionally, it doesn't. Only you as a total Self, a fully integrated *Conscious Self,* hold the engaging force of dealing directly with life – and that exists as a comprehensive compilation of inner meaning, drives, mechanisms and motivations.

So, while the subconscious has no motives, the complexity of information it holds and delivers to the conscious Self may well have motivation woven into it.

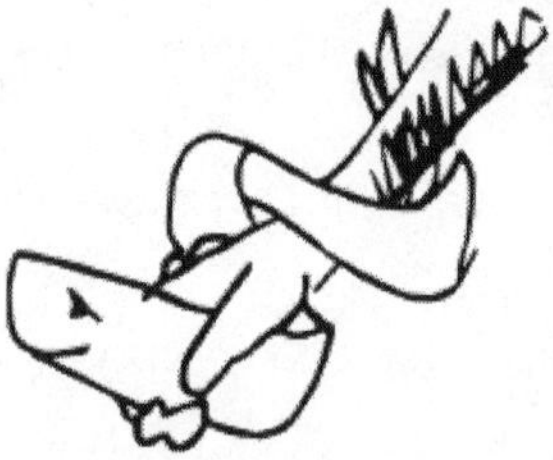

Q117 – Do enlightened people get angry at those who cause suffering?

No. When you recognize the interrelated Oneness of things, your perception of *causality* changes.

Each of us engages a cohesive, integrated Reality that reflects our own comprehensive nature. Each of us manifests into that flow of Reality a complex of values that emanate from his/her own mindset.

Thus, *you* create, directly and exclusively, the quality of events and relationships you encounter. You will see that clearly if you look at the flow of your life – you attract and thus *create* patterns. People come and go, situations evolve, reconcile and repeat, qualitatively.

The difficulty in seeing this is all of the beliefs and definitions you've absorbed that project causality to things *out there*: gods, bacteria, conditions, the government, bad guys, bad luck, your mother-in-law, etc. In reality – in *this reality* that you encounter every day, you attract those apparent sources and forces. Life isn't inflicted on you by luck, fate, chance or bad people.

So, no, those who perceive the Oneness of all things don't get angry about anything. Because they (i.e., *we*) recognize that misery and suffering are resultant situations of inner conflict and notions of separation on the part of the beset individual – not imposed from the outside.

Any who might question this account of the Oneness – we *do* like to find evil sources to blame things on – need to look at their own belief structures to explore the ideas there that formulate their world view. What I'm describing isn't some idealized, new-age, smiley-faced view of things. It's how life works. The problem isn't my glossy view, but inherent flaws in the religious/ scientific mindset common to modern man.

Both religion and science project causality to illusory sources – and those paradigms permeate modern thinking, along with carryover mythical notions like luck and fate.

Anger itself comes from perceived separation and blame of negative situations on an illusory source. Get rid of the illusion and you'll see that *each afflicted person*, through inner conflict, struggle and other negative elements of mind, *attracts the suffering*.

So, the main point is about "causality". It doesn't come from evil sources out there, but from within. When you see that, anger in response to third-party situations simply dissipates. And your life works a lot better when you've eliminated the inner conflict yourself…

Q118 – Are there any still religious people who think or even entertain the possibility that they have been brainwashed? Or would they just leave their religion upon such a realization?

Among our human counterparts, there seems to be a certain type of mentality that just accepts ideas it absorbed – typically as a naïve child – without question. This type judges the nature of the world encountered *based on* a fixed set of beliefs and accepted definitions – and never would or *even could* question the beliefs themselves.

The alternate, the seeking, open-minded mentality, looks at reality rationally and with curiosity – if it sees that the world works differently than explanations it's been offered, it questions the idea, not its perception, its real experience.

True believers in Christianity would never consider the great body of rational evidence that belies their convictions. Nor can they, by virtue (or vice?) of their nature of thinking, question the foundation conjecture that underlies their faith.

Given that gullible, fixed base mentality of rigid thinking for a large portion of mankind, it should be of no surprise that trying to convince a sucker that he/she has been duped is next to impossible. That person can never see beyond their "truths", their experts and their held definitions to consider reasoned argument…

No, actually it isn't next to it, ***it is*** impossible. If that person were capable of evaluating his/her beliefs vs. how reality works, the flow of events and relationships that constitute daily life, he or she would have already jettisoned the archaic, primitive claims that constitute Christianity.

Christian declarations simply don't match up at all with reality.

So, the answer is *"NO"*. Anybody capable of critical, rational thinking who had Christianity imposed on them during the formative years of childhood has already rejected belief in or acceptance of:

- An external, meddling deity,
- A silly superman Christ who has all the answers to everything,
- A Trinity that consists of three nonexistent fantasies,
- The need for martyrdom in a realm supposedly controlled

by an all-knowing, all-powerful deity,
- A second coming when there really wasn't a first,
- Any sort of useful explanation coming out of first century superstition, oral traditions rife with evil spirits and primitive cosmology, and no historical validity,
- Senseless rituals (repetitions, baptism, communion, confession, etc.) that accomplish nothing,
- A self-serving, dull-witted clergy that lives off the gullibility of its "flock",
- Bible-thumping con men who pose as spiritual advisors...
- Etc. – I could go on.

It's always been difficult to explain to that or any sucker that *he's been had*. The same lack of mental acumen and objective evaluation capability that led to buying into false ideas in the first place inhibit any later change of thinking – plus, the hardheaded resistance to *admitting* being duped by stupid ideas *in the first place* further limits greater recognition of the fallacy of religion.

So, no, those open to critical thinking already left the fold. Those who aren't, probably won't. Well, maybe somewhere at this very moment somebody is wising up and dumping archaic conjecture as a world view. But it only happens once for any truly open-minded individual, so don't go looking for volunteers among the two billion faithful. Most of them will take their closed minds into the next incarnation intact.

Q119 – White supremacists claim that if it weren't for white people the world would still be living in the Stone Age. They also claim that white people brought enlightenment and the modern world we know of today. Is this true?

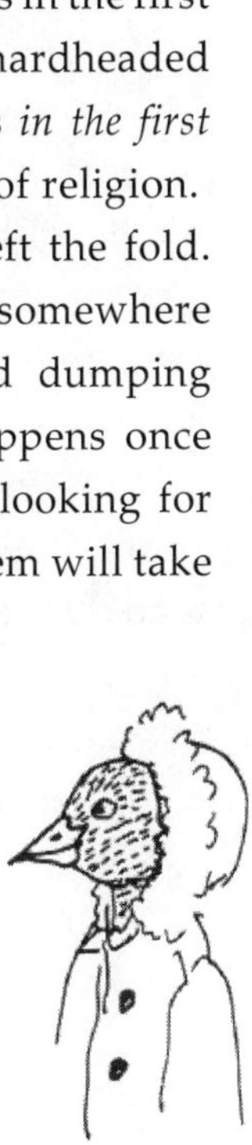

No, that premise is not true at all! The problem is, they draw lines in the wrong places – artificially designating a grouping in which *they put themselves* to be the drivers of the advancement of civilization.

Here is where the line needs to be drawn separating those who have moved man forward from those who have always held man back in more primitive lifestyles: between liberal-thinkers and conservatives. All of mankind's advancements in technology, awareness, peaceful relations and social improvement were made by people *capable of thinking outside the conceptual box* formed by old notions.

This is not to imply that all liberals come up with great ideas. New ideas, outside conventional thinking and mores, are not necessarily better ones. But only liberal thinkers do come up with ***new*** ideas, outside the scope of current ways and means, some of which prove to be better – and ultimately change man's way of life. These are generally implemented over time *only against the resistance of conservatives*, who invariably oppose change.

Skin color, race, cultural basis and geographical location have little to do with the imaginative characteristics needed for inventive, liberal consideration – for thinking outside conventions.

Actually, *no*, those visual qualities have ***nothing*** to do with creative thinking. Nothing at all.

I don't think white supremacists by any grotesque stretch of the imagination can be considered liberal. If a grouping of mankind is to be isolated and designated to have spurred enlightenment and advancement, that group would be *liberal thinkers* and it would not include any subset of rigid, reactionary people such as the aforementioned mentioned in your question.

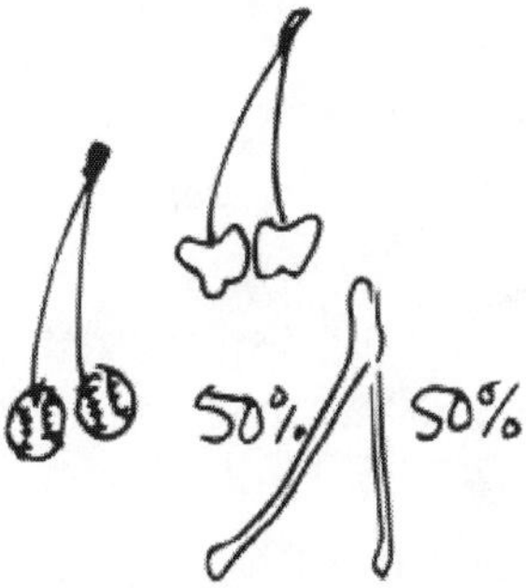

Q120 – Why do people seem to absolutely refuse to speak plain English, instead choosing to have several pretentious "college-style" words peppered into every sentence, making it nearly impossible for any layperson to understand living in the Stone Age?

I do that all the time, not only on Quora here, but in my books, on my website and on my YouTube channel. And I do it on purpose – well, for two purposes, actually. Neither is based on a pretentious air.

Most of the questions I answer here – or elsewhere for that matter – pertain to Consciousness, to philosophical viewpoints and to subtle aspects of life. Many of these require complex conceptualization to simply illustrate – thus, I have to draw from the rich vocabulary of the English language to just properly shape my point. Dumbing down an explanation in many instances shifts a fairly accurate depiction of reality into the realm of the false. Many aspects of life are indeed intricate and require equivalent description to carry over the real meaning.

Long and uncommon words, in this instance, aren't a sign of pretense, just a reflection of the shaded nature of life and need to specify points accurately to convey meaning.

Second, from my angle, I *purposely* use my entire vocabulary to discourage people who aren't going to comprehend my answer anyway, to actually "get it", from reading my words in the first place. My answers depict an innate Oneness between Consciousness and actual, experienced Reality. Most people (not necessarily a majority of Quora readers, but most of the general population) are tied into their pre-programmed thinking – religion, science, notions of luck and chance. They imagine a god doing things; they attribute causality to external forces and sources. Comparatively, the more curious among us, those more inclined to seek real understanding, are quite happy to read richer accounts with more extensive, indeed, richer vocabulary. They are pleased to learn new words and be exposed to new ideas.

Ones who want simplified answers, particularly answers that fit into their current belief structure, then, generally, aren't intellectually curious enough to grasp the often deep and shaded explanation I'll be giving. Others may lack the attention span to concentrate on complex explanations. I'm quite happy to ward off both of those groups with an extensive vocabulary and complex grammatical structure – *because they'll only misinterpret my meaning anyway.* Those fixed in their beliefs will only try to defend their limited point of view, rather than expand it.

So, yes – GUILTY here! I refuse to speak plain English, first, because simple words and grammatical structures won't cover the intricacies of my explanation to get my point across. And second, unmitigated complexity repels people who aren't going to get my point anyway.

Have I missed anything? Questions, no doubt, will continue. I still frequent Quora.com to see what sort of queries pop up there. I enjoy reading others' many answers and do think, based on upvotes, that readers there enjoy mine. At talks I give, even more questions find their way into discussions. For the most part, though, questions I encounter at talks reflect those documented here.

For those readers who have gained benefit from this collection and my other books, videos, talks and website, I'm pleased to have helped you. I will carry on, answering other queries from my unique sort of angle on things.

My purpose was and remains: to show others, those equipped with open minds, how life looks and how well it works – how creative and adventurous it can be, free and joyful – when you recognize the timeless, unfettered nature of your own being.

It's all about awareness: personally recognizing, in all facets of life, the innate Oneness of you, your unique Self, with the meaningful flow of events and relationships you encounter daily. Such a clarity of perception requires an immersion in the complex subconscious far Deeper Than…

BOOKS

O-BOOKS

SPIRITUALITY

O is a symbol of the world, of oneness and unity; this eye represents knowledge and insight. We publish titles on general spirituality and living a spiritual life. We aim to inform and help you on your own journey in this life.

If you have enjoyed this book, why not tell other readers by posting a review on your preferred book site?

Recent bestsellers from O-Books are:

Heart of Tantric Sex

Diana Richardson

Revealing Eastern secrets of deep love and intimacy to Western couples.

Paperback: 978-1-90381-637-0 ebook: 978-1-84694-637-0

Crystal Prescriptions

The A-Z guide to over 1,200 symptoms and their healing crystals

Judy Hall

The first in the popular series of six books, this handy little guide is packed as tight as a pill-bottle with crystal remedies for ailments.

Paperback: 978-1-90504-740-6 ebook: 978-1-84694-629-5

Take Me To Truth

Undoing the Ego

Nouk Sanchez, Tomas Vieira

The best-selling step-by-step book on shedding the Ego, using the teachings of *A Course In Miracles*.

Paperback: 978-1-84694-050-7 ebook: 978-1-84694-654-7

The 7 Myths about Love...Actually!

The journey from your HEAD to the HEART of your SOUL

Mike George

Smashes all the myths about LOVE.

Paperback: 978-1-84694-288-4 ebook: 978-1-84694-682-0

The Holy Spirit's Interpretation of the New Testament

A course in Understanding and Acceptance

Regina Dawn Akers

Following on from the strength of *A Course In Miracles*, NTI teaches us how to experience the love and oneness of God.

Paperback: 978-1-84694-085-9 ebook: 978-1-78099-083-5

The Message of A Course In Miracles

A translation of the text in plain language

Elizabeth A. Cronkhite

A translation of *A Course in Miracles* into plain, everyday language for anyone seeking inner peace. The companion volume, *Practicing A Course In Miracles*, offers practical lessons and mentoring.

Paperback: 978-1-84694-319-5 ebook: 978-1-84694-642-4

Rising in Love

My Wild and Crazy Ride to Here and Now, with Amma, the Hugging Saint

Ram Das Batchelder

Rising in Love conveys an author's extraordinary journey of spiritual awakening with the Guru, Amma.

Paperback: 978-1-78279-687-9 ebook: 978-1-78279-686-2

Thinker's Guide to God

Peter Vardy

An introduction to key issues in the philosophy of religion.

Paperback: 978-1-90381-622-6

Your Simple Path

Find happiness in every step

Ian Tucker

A guide to helping us reconnect with what is really important in our lives.

Paperback: 978-1-78279-349-6 ebook: 978-1-78279-348-9

365 Days of Wisdom

Daily Messages To Inspire You Through The Year

Dadi Janki

Daily messages which cool the mind, warm the heart and guide you along your journey.

Paperback: 978-1-84694-863-3 ebook: 978-1-84694-864-0

Body of Wisdom

Women's Spiritual Power and How it Serves

Hilary Hart

Bringing together the dreams and experiences of women across the world with today's most visionary spiritual teachers.

Paperback: 978-1-78099-696-7 ebook: 978-1-78099-695-0

Dying to Be Free

From Enforced Secrecy to Near Death to True Transformation

Hannah Robinson

After an unexpected accident and near-death experience, Hannah Robinson found herself radically transforming her life, while a remarkable new insight altered her relationship with her father, a practising Catholic priest.

Paperback: 978-1-78535-254-6 ebook: 978-1-78535-255-3

The Ecology of the Soul

A Manual of Peace, Power and Personal Growth for Real People in the Real World

Aidan Walker

Balance your own inner Ecology of the Soul to regain your natural state of peace, power and wellbeing.

Paperback: 978-1-78279-850-7 ebook: 978-1-78279-849-1

Not I, Not other than I

The Life and Teachings of Russel Williams

Steve Taylor, Russel Williams

The miraculous life and inspiring teachings of one of the World's greatest living Sages.

Paperback: 978-1-78279-729-6 ebook: 978-1-78279-728-9

On the Other Side of Love

A Woman's Unconventional Journey Towards Wisdom

Muriel Maufroy

When life has lost all meaning, what do you do?

Paperback: 978-1-78535-281-2 ebook: 978-1-78535-282-9

Practicing A Course In Miracles

A Translation of the Workbook in Plain Language and With Mentoring Notes

Elizabeth A. Cronkhite

The practical second and third volumes of The Plain-Language *A Course In Miracles*.

Paperback: 978-1-84694-403-1 ebook: 978-1-78099-072-9

Quantum Bliss

The Quantum Mechanics of Happiness, Abundance, and Health

George S. Mentz

Quantum Bliss is the breakthrough summary of success and spirituality secrets that customers have been waiting for.

Paperback: 978-1-78535-203-4 ebook: 978-1-78535-204-1

The Upside Down Mountain

Mags MacKean

A must-read for anyone weary of chasing success and happiness – one woman's inspirational journey swapping the uphill slog for the downhill slope.

Paperback: 978-1-78535-171-6 ebook: 978-1-78535-172-3

Your Personal Tuning Fork

The Endocrine System

Deborah Bates

Discover your body's health secret, the endocrine system, and 'twang' your way to sustainable health!

Paperback: 978-1-84694-503-8 ebook: 978-1-78099-697-4